CROSSING BOUNDARIES

MINE MIGRANCY IN A
DEMOCRATIC SOUTH AFRICA

IDASA'S PUBLIC INFORMATION CENTRE IS AN
INFORMATION-GATHERING AND POLICY-EVALUATION
SERVICE THAT AIMS TO ENHANCE TRANSPARENCY,
ACCOUNTABILITY AND EFFECTIVITY IN GOVERNMENT.
THIS BOOK WAS PRODUCED BY ONE OF ITS PROJECTS,
MIGRANCY IN SOUTHERN AFRICA.

An edited collection of papers presented at an international conference on
"Transforming Mine Migrancy in the 1990s" held in Cape Town, June 1994.

THE EDITORS

Jonathan Crush is professor of geography at Queen's University, Canada.

Wilmot James is executive director of the Institute for Democracy in South
Africa and honorary professor of sociology at the University of Cape Town.

ACKNOWLEDGEMENTS

The conference, and much of the research, was supported by the International
Development Research Centre (Canada).

Jonathan Crush also wishes to thank the SSHRC of Canada for its generous
support.

Photographs by Ernest Cole from House of Bondage, 1967. New York: Random
House

CROSSING BOUNDARIES

MINE MIGRANCY IN A DEMOCRATIC SOUTH AFRICA

EDITED BY JONATHAN CRUSH & WILMOT JAMES

ASSISTED BY MOIRA LEVY, JANET LEVY & GAIL JENNINGS

IDASA/IDRC 1995

Published by the Institute for Democracy in South Africa,
Albion Spring, 183 Main Rd, Rondebosch, Cape Town 7700

and the International Development Research Centre (Canada),
P O Box 8500, Ottawa, Ontario KIG 3H9

copyright IDASA/IDRC 1995

ISBN 1-874864-12-8 (IDASA)
ISBN 0-88936-764-7 (IDRC)

First published 1995

Cover and text design by Manik Design, Cape Town
Typeset in Palatino

Printed and bound by Creda Press, Epping, Cape Town

CONTENTS

OPENING ADDRESS

MR MARCEL GOLDING
Member of Parliament,
Cape Town, South Africa

Research into migrant labour and the mining industry, and the sharing of its findings and conclusions, is fundamental if we are to develop effective and beneficial policies for South Africa and the region. It will also ensure that we keep track of this very important section of South Africa's working class – and the way in which it has improved its own living and working conditions.

The democratisation process in South Africa has provoked a range of questions and challenges for various sectors, and in the mining industry migrant labour will be a critical issue. The industry is a major employer of labour, providing an income for between 10 and 12 percent of all workers. It is also a major source of foreign exchange – about 66 percent of total exports – and state income. Many areas in southern Africa depend on the remittances of migrant workers, and many industries depend on the fortunes of the mining industry.

The challenge for employers, unions, employees and government is to ensure that the democratisation of the mining industry guarantees its sustainability, and that the transition to democracy in this country is managed in such a way that the future of those who depend on the mining industry is secure.

In a state of the nation address, President Nelson Mandela said that the South African Government of National Unity intends to take what it calls a "people-centred approach" toward policy making. In other words, it will develop policies that will restructure the lives and material well-being of South Africans.

The South African mining industry is a difficult place to introduce change. Although in the last 10 to 15 years substantial changes have taken place, not all the forces influencing change were domestic and not all the results have been positive (such as the substantial retrenchments in the industry). Some of the most important factors causing change can be identified.

Firstly, there has been a fundamental structural change world-wide in the gold-mining industry and in the role of gold as a store of value. Investments which give better returns than gold have been developed, although the demand for gold has increased and there is a shortage on the supply side.

The second major factor is the cyclical process of commodity demand. The world recession has dramatically affected South Africa, and the demand for various commodities such as coal, chrome, copper and antimony has fluctuated. These fluctuations have impacted directly on the South African mining industry.

Government policy on mining, in the form of the Minerals Act, the proposals emerging from the Marais Commission on Marginal Mines, and the tax laws, have also affected the industry. Unionisation, particularly the establishment of the National Union of Mineworkers (NUM), has probably been the greatest domestic factor to influence the mining industry. Through organisation, migrant workers have changed their lives and their working conditions.

The first phase in this organisation process began with the establishment of the NUM in 1982 and lasted until about 1990. During this phase workers' rights of representation were established and collective bargaining structures were set up. The union focused on how to secure access to premises, how to build a culture of solidarity amongst workers and how to improve employment security for workers. For almost eight years much of the debate and struggle of the union centred on developing a body of jurisprudence that could protect workers against unfair and unilateral dismissals.

A brief glance at South African trade union history will indicate that some of the key employment security cases were initiated by the NUM. A groundbreaking case was that of the NUM versus Marievale gold mine in 1985. Striking workers were dismissed and the union went to court to try to secure their return. The Industrial Court handed down a judgment that gave protection from eviction from company housing to African miners engaged in a lawful strike.

This case set the basis for procedural and substantive fairness in South Africa's jurisprudence around labour rights and formed the platform on which the NUM built a whole range of subsequent case laws to protect workers.

The NUM versus Kloof gold mine was also a case about procedural and substantive fairness, and the NUM versus West Driefontein gold mine centred on health and safety. These cases form part of a body of law that the trade union movement has developed over many years to prevent the unilateral conduct of employers.

The mining industry remains peculiar, however, in the way in which employers continue to use proprietary rights to limit organisation on the mine. Mine managements' use of private property to regulate the conduct of trade unions remains one of the greatest challenges today. The new South African Constitution secures and guarantees private property and, at the same time, guarantees a range of rights. This is likely to raise an interesting debate – how is it possible to balance the right to organise with the right to private property? Can the right to freedom of speech be exercised on an employer's property? Significant constitutional battles are sure to be waged over these issues.

During this first phase of unionisation, institutional relationships developed to try and regulate employer/employee practices into a set of rights with an associated set of obligations. With the provision of certain workers' rights came reciprocal obligations. And although this situation has not changed much, what governed the practice of employer/employee relations then was the persuasive power of force.

The second phase of union organisation started in the 1990s when many mine workers were retrenched. The international recession, the decline in the gold price, the cyclical demand for commodities, profit squeezes and the low grade of ore being mined signalled a crisis in the industry.

Between 1990 and 1993 the NUM tried to protect workers who were losing their jobs and at the same time tried to re-organise the workplace in a way that would be of mutual benefit to all the stakeholders.

However, the high level of illiteracy within the migrant work-force and the inexperience in decision-making made reorganisation difficult. The lack of an effective culture of transparency also hindered reorganisation attempts.

In an attempt to improve the skills of workers the NUM devised the slogan "one worker, one calculator". The aim was to enable workers to check managements' arguments that they faced a profit squeeze. The workers would be able to calculate, for example, whether the figures were correct. But the problems of productivity and workplace reorganisation are complex, and can only be solved when a skills base has been developed in the industry.

Linked to reorganising the industry is the concept of the social wage and what this really means. Employers have a legitimate crisis, but at the same time the trade union and workers have real concerns. While the employers may be experiencing profit problems, particularly in marginal mines with declining ore grades, workers are legitimately claiming that their wages are low and that their social conditions are appalling.

Government has to find a way to guarantee standards across the industry but at the same time deal with peculiarities and differentials between individual mines. Through the profit-sharing scheme the mining industry has begun to deal with some of these complex problems.

In the last two years the union itself has been trying to adapt in structure and practice to deal with the challenges facing the industry today. The mining industry is becoming more complex and policies have to be developed that acknowledge that complexity.

It is my hope that this conference will be able to give some constructive guidance to unions, government and employers in dealing with the complexities of migrant labour and the industry.

There is an old proverb that says if you want to discover new oceans you must be willing to lose sight of the shore. As we move through the transition, if we want to discover something new that will benefit our society, we are going to have to have the courage to do precisely that. ◆

INTRODUCTION

PROFESSOR JONATHAN CRUSH
Department of Geography,
Queen's University,
Kingston, Ontario,
Canada

PROFESSOR WILMOT JAMES
Executive Director,
Institute for Democracy in South Africa,
Cape Town, South Africa

The title of this book, *Crossing Boundaries*, highlights the fundamentally bounded character of mining and migrancy in South Africa. Throughout his working life the mine migrant confronts a series of boundaries that he must choose to either observe, cross or ignore. For foreign miners the most obvious boundaries are the international borders between South Africa and the surrounding states. Migrants have always seen this border crossing as a kind of rite of passage and interpreted it in highly symbolic terms (Coplan, 1994).

Though illegal migrants are now crossing these boundaries in large numbers, mine migrants may still cross legally, provided that they have valid contracts and passports in hand. Though many have spent all of their working lives in South Africa, their boundary crossing is always temporary, never permanent. They remain in South Africa as temporary residents without their families and without the rights and privileges accorded to normal immigrants. For retrenched or repatriated foreign miners, the borders now represent a more formidable barrier. Their dilemma is whether to wait for the remote chance of a legal crossing or to join the border jumpers and cross into South Africa to look for other work or to wait at the mine gate.

Under apartheid, the homeland boundaries demarcated the territories where South African migrants were supposed to leave their families when they went out to work and to which they were supposed to return on the expiry of their work contracts. The collapse of influx controls in the 1980s and the reincorporation of the homelands in the 1990s erased these boundaries and provided people with new freedom of movement. The old apartheid boundary restrictions are therefore gone but other boundaries remain largely intact. To cross the boundary on to mine property, for example, is still to enter a cloistered, restricted and tightly regulated world (James, 1992).

Hostel walls and fences represent another set of boundaries to cross. These boundaries exclude outsiders and insulate insiders. It is easier to get in than out if you are a miner; the reverse is true if you are a wife or dependent. Within the hostel and mine there is a network of visible and invisible boundaries that control the miners' working day and leisure time. Mine migrants do what they can – as individuals, groups or through their union – to contest the boundaries of the mine. Mine security spend their time patrolling and enforcing them. These boundaries are now also increasingly policed by "electronic eyes" (computerised surveillance). Passage from one part of the mine to another, and between the surface and underground, is controlled by computerised tracking systems (Crush, 1992).

The continuing presence of restrictive boundaries in the mining industry alerts us to one of the toughest choices South Africa has to make over the next few years. Freedom of movement and the absence of boundaries are valued commodities in a democratic society. Mine migrancy and all the problems associated with it – such as hostels, the separation of families and rural poverty – are a legacy of segregation and apartheid, and have an uncomfortable place in a democratic society. If regional mine migrancy stays, the new democratic government will effectively endorse one of the most inequitable labour systems yet seen in the industrial world. If it goes, the Mandela government will be fuelling such regional hardship that South Africa's borders will be flattened in the rush of impoverished ex-miners and their families. Before the 1990s most experts agreed that transformation of the mine labour system would not come without a fundamental change in the state that helped erect and police the boundaries. In April 1994, when South Africans voted in their first non-racial election, the country as a whole crossed its most important political boundary ever. The state – the one that would commit itself to the lowering rather than raising of boundaries – is now in place.

Crossing Boundaries tries to cultivate an understanding of the complexity and depth of the problem of removing and restructuring the visible and invisible boundaries of mine migrancy and the hardships they represent. It seeks also to indicate the limits, possibilities and consequences of keeping the boundaries intact. The book consists mainly of edited papers first presented at a conference on "Transforming Mine Migrancy in the 1990s" that took place at the University of Cape Town in June 1994. The conference was the culmination of a three-year programme of co-operative research between the University of Cape Town and Queen's University (Canada) known as the Migrant Labour Project and funded by the International Development Research Centre (IDRC) of Canada, the co-publishers of this book. The first phase of the Migrant Labour Project (1990-1992) assessed the prospects for transformation in the mining industry through an analysis of state and company policy on accommodation issues, the views of both the National Union of Mineworkers (NUM) and ordinary miners on housing, and an evaluation of concrete alternatives to contemporary forms of imposed housing delivery and urban planning. The results were published in a number of academic journals and in a special issue of the Canadian journal *Labour, Capital and Society*[1].

The second phase of the project (1992-1994) assessed the economic performance of the gold-mining industry, aspects of the health consequences of labour stabilisation and, in particular, was concerned with the possible rural impact of changes to the migrant labour system. We wanted to develop a much clearer sense of what contemporary migrancy meant for the people who lived and survived in the so-called "sending areas" – such as Mozambique, Lesotho or the homelands of the Eastern Cape – and to assess the consequences of any move towards the permanent urbanisation of mine labour.

Families and communities in the rural areas (both outside and within South Africa) depend on migrant remittances and deferred pay. Some of these communities have already been cut off from access to mine employment for reasons of political expediency (Malawi), civil strife (Mozambique), economic rationalisation (northern Botswana and parts of the Transkei and Lesotho) or corporate labour recruiting strategy (the Ciskei). The retrenchments following the 1987 miners' strike and particularly those associated with down-scaling in the early 1990s had their most severe impact on the rural families and communities most dependent on mine wages.

The conference in Cape Town brought together many of these larger research issues in a discussion that raised the possible policy implications of our findings. With that in mind, the conference went beyond the individual and research concerns of those originally involved in the project by inviting other researchers active in the field as well as people representing or forming part of the broader "stakeholder" community – the ANC, the NUM, The Employment Bureau of Africa (Teba), the Chamber of Mines (COM) and the mining companies. Though

---

1. *See Crush, J and W James. 1991. "Depopulating the compounds: migrant labour and mine housing in South Africa," in World Development, Vol 19: 301-16; Crush, J. 1991. "The chains of migrancy and the Southern African Labour Commission," in C Dixon and M Heffernan, (eds,) Colonialism and Development in the Contemporary World. London: Mansell; James, W. 1992. "The erosion of paternalism in South African gold mines," in Industrial Relations Journal of South Africa, Vol 12: 1-16; Crush, J. 1992. "The compound in post-apartheid South Africa," in Geographical Review, Vol 82: 388-400; Crush, J, W James and All Jeeves. 1992. "Transformation on the South African gold mines," in a special issue of Labour, Capital and Society, Vol 25, No 1: 7-17.*

the COM was represented, no one from the world of corporate management chose to attend. In contrast, the new government was well represented. The proceedings were opened by Marcel Golding, former assistant general secretary of the NUM and currently a member of parliament and chair of the parliamentary standing committee on mineral and energy affairs. Labour Minister Tito Mboweni also attended part of the workshop.

The first session of the workshop attempted to evaluate the future prospects for the transformation of the mine migrant system against the backdrop of its historical development[2]. The first paper in this collection, jointly written by Alan Jeeves and Jonathan Crush, traces the entrenched character of migrancy and shows that although the system came under periodic challenge, these were never serious enough to compromise the system as a whole. The pressures to move away from migrancy came from different directions but they were always successfully resisted by those who had a vested interest in the status quo. Jeeves and Crush conclude, somewhat pessimistically, that the obstacles to change are still enormous and that a quick transition away from migrancy is unlikely. The best short-term option is to find ways to democratise a notoriously undemocratic system. In the second paper, Crush traces the recent history of mine migrancy and argues that the classic system of long-distance oscillating migration has been eroded in significant ways over the last 20 years by deep-seated structural processes. His paper focuses primarily on what became one of the major points of discussion at the workshop – the place of foreign miners in a post-apartheid South Africa.

The second part of the workshop dealt primarily with the thorny question of mine hostels, the bane of the mining industry. They are still sites of intense conflict and violence, and of social problems associated with men living in single-sex, isolated and alienated environments (Moodie, with Ndatshe, 1994). The papers by Catharine Payze, Anthony Minnaar, Kent McNamara and Catherine Laburn-Peart are all based on recent research on hostel life and indicate a full range of social problems tied to single-sex existence. Such problems are, in many respects, indefensible in a democratic South Africa. They also indicate how slow and partial the progress towards normal housing for black miners has been in the gold-mining industry. Many migrant workers reflect, in their preferences, the cumulative impact of migrancy itself by opting for hostel accommodation as the cheapest, easiest and, in some ways, safest place to stay in their absence from home and family.

The upshot of this is that the mining houses, as well as the NUM, have had to think creatively about alternative forms of accommodation. Both have formulated alternative sets of proposals which have often come into conflict. In her paper, Sue Moorhead outlines the NUM's new housing strategy including the general principles informing the union's thinking and its emphasis on local solutions and participatory decision making. In discussion, COM representative Ahmed Jooma noted that management was also rethinking its options in the

2. See also Jeeves, AH. 1985. _Migrant Labour in South Africa's Mining Economy_. Kingston and Montreal: McGill-Queen's Press; Crush, J, A H Jeeves and D Yudelman, 1991. _South Africa's Labour Empire: A History of Black Migrancy to the Gold Mines_. Boulder and Cape Town: Westview Press and David Philip.

light of the Reconstruction and Development Programme and that the chamber had recently embarked on an industry-wide survey of housing policy and options.

The final paper in this section moves off mine property into the neighbouring townships and settlements. The paper, by Dunbar Moodie and Vivienne Ndatshe, is based on interviews with partners and wives of migrant miners who have themselves migrated to the cities. They confirm the dire conditions under which many of these women are forced to live, but also their resilience and creativity in the face of boundaries erected against their full participation in mine communities. Indeed, the overall sense from these papers is that hostels are unlikely to be dismantled in the near future – but with creative thinking and political pressure to lower the boundaries of control there is considerable scope for humanising a dehumanising environment.

The third set of papers links closely with the second by exploring the health implications of continued reliance on migrancy in the mining industry. This is a major issue in its own right and one on which a number of major epidemiological and social scientific projects currently under way in various parts of the country are based. Given the IDRC's interests, health and safety issues have not featured largely in the Migrant Labour Project per se[3]. But the issues are too pressing and important to ignore altogether and the project did commission work in four important areas: work stress, hypertension, tuberculosis (TB) and HIV/Aids. At the workshop, Matsheliso Molapo as well as Randall Packard and David Coetzee presented papers on hypertension and TB. A third paper on work stress by Julian Barling and Kevin Kelloway was tabled and a fourth, on the politics of Aids, is included elsewhere in this volume (see below).

Molapo, who lived as a participant observer at Western Deep Levels for an extended period, provides a poignant picture of the everyday tensions and stresses on the mine. Through verbatim transcripts, workers speak with characteristic honesty about the trauma of underground work and the hardships of hostel life. These are certainly not new problems or perceptions, but in a volume of distanced, policy-oriented papers the miners' words provide a salutary reminder about the issue of whose voice should receive most attention from the new policy makers. The paper by Packard and Coetzee builds on earlier influential work by Packard on the political economy of TB in the mining industry (Packard, 1989). This is a report on work in progress which confirms Packard's earlier arguments that the upsurge of TB on the mines cannot be understood in epidemiological terms alone. The collaboration of Packard, a labour historian, and Coetzee, a medical doctor and epidemiologist, is suggestive of the possibilities for creative analysis and problem solving when the social and medical sciences interact.

The next set of papers deals with developments in the rural source areas of

3. *The National Centre for Occupational Health and the Sociology of Work Programme at the University of the Witwatersrand have done important work in this area: see Leger, J. 1992. Talking Rocks: An Investigation of the Pit Sense of Rockfall Accidents amongst Underground Gold Miners. PhD dissertation, University of Witwatersrand; and Arkles, R. 1993. The Social Consequences of Industrial Accidents. Disabled Mineworkers in Lesotho. MA dissertation, University of Witwatersrand.*

migrant workers. One area that has already been hard hit by the expulsion of its workers from South African mines is Malawi. Wiseman Chirwa documents the disturbing events of the mid-1980s when Malawian miners were expelled from the mines on the pretext that they were Aids carriers. Chirwa points out that Malawian miners were a minor threat given regional patterns of disease transmission. They were, in effect, the victims of a set of new boundaries that victimised the sufferer and non-sufferer alike. James Cobbe, David Coplan and Thoahlane Thoahlane, as well as Judith Head, all demonstrate that in Lesotho and Mozambique dependency on mine migrancy to South Africa is as deeply entrenched as ever. Any summary expulsion of workers from these countries along the lines of the Malawian model would have catastrophic consequences for the entire region, South Africa included.

A pall was inevitably cast over the conference's discussions by the current crisis in the mining industry. Over the last decade the drying up of job opportunities for the sons of miners has created severe hardship among households in the rural areas. More recently, the effects have been compounded by mass retrenchments, though none of the foreign supply areas has been as hard hit as rural areas within South Africa itself. Down-scaling and retrenchments are clearly having a devastating impact on the rural communities that depend on migrant income. This desperate situation is undoubtedly exacerbated by the legacy of apartheid-era migrancy which has left the rural poor with precious little to fall back on during depressed economic times. As a number of the conference participants with recent rural fieldwork experience pointed out, the rural areas are swarming with unemployed miners who find it hard to conceive of a life without mine work. Coplan and Thoahlane reveal from their interviews with miners that a retrenchment "industry" has grown up which cheats many ex-miners out of the compensation due to them.

The fifth session dealt with some of the economic causes of the current crisis and the responses at the centre. The crisis is often portrayed as purely economic in character, the inevitable by-product of an unco-operative gold market. This is not the first time in South Africa's history that gold mining has been in crisis. Usually the causes of crisis relate not simply to the exchange value of an ounce of gold but, as Nicoli Nattrass suggests, the complex set of processes and relations by which that ounce is produced. In the past the mines have always represented crisis in the worst light to justify the down-scaling and restructuring that often takes place in tough times. The hardest hit mines, as always, have been the marginal, low-grade producers. Until the 1980s the mining companies persuaded government that the interests of the industry as a whole were coincident with the needs of the marginal producers. The new government will need to decide, very rapidly indeed, whether it can afford to resurrect that policy and arrest the current precipitous decline in mine employment.

The papers by Gay Seidman, Kate Philip and Motlatsi Thabane focus on the institutional responses of management and the NUM to retrenchments. Seidman graphically portrays the serious consequences for mining towns of down-scaling – raising once again the age-old spectre that haunts every mining community.

Philip and Thabane clearly show the overwhelming task that confronted the NUM when workers turned to the union for assistance to cope with retrenchments and down-scaling. Before the NUM arrived on the scene, dismissed or retrenched workers were left to cope alone. The NUM has taken a very progressive policy position in an attempt to ameliorate the hardships but the enormity of the challenge emerges clearly in the discussion of the NUM's struggling rural job creation programmes. There is a strong argument that the NUM should not have to shoulder this burden alone and that government and the mining companies should assist far more than they have in the past.

At the end of the conference three questions remained:

◆ What future does gold mining have as a generator of wealth and employment in a democratic South Africa?

◆ How best can the new government facilitate the normalisation of an abnormal labour system?

◆ In the context of high domestic unemployment (and mass retrenchments of South African miners), why should foreign workers still be employed in such numbers?

These questions resurfaced continually in the presentations, commentaries and floor discussions. In this volume we have included the commentaries although, for lack of space, not the discussions.

In the final session, "Towards a New Policy", there was general agreement on a number of policy-related principles. First, there was a strong sense that positive change, though slow and halting, had already begun to erode the more pernicious social, racial and physical boundaries of the mining industry. Symptomatic of the extent of change, perhaps, is Roger Rowett's discussion of the changing role of Teba in the 1990s. Teba's traditional (and for many years only) function – labour recruiting – is of rapidly declining importance. Recruiting is being replaced by a portfolio of service activities which would have been unthinkable to earlier generations of recruiters.

Second, there was agreement that there is certainly no room for complacency. Mining and mine migrancy still retain some of their more objectionable apartheid-era features, as interviews with workers make only too clear. Any change that would give workers greater freedoms, wider choices and more participation need to be fostered and, where there is resistance, legislated. The participants agreed that despite the rough economic times, the political possibilities for hastening transformation are now more prevalent than ever before. The questions implicit in much of the discussion were whether and how to seize that opportunity. The operative principle in the development of policy instruments and interventions should be "normalisation". For too long miners have been treated as if they simply do not matter. Miners are essential to the current and future economic health of the country. Any policy measures that ignore this central fact will rebound to everybody's detriment.

Finally, as is emphasised in the papers by Robert Davies and Judith Head, and Crush and James, policy around the question of the future of foreign migrants on the mines of South Africa cannot be divorced from broader regional considerations and responsibilities[4]. The expulsion of foreign miners would be catastrophic for the mines and for the supplier states. What is required are creative, long-term solutions, including normalisation of the exceptional status of foreign miners. In addition, the question of mine migrancy should not be divorced from broader questions of regional migration. A sudden decline in mine employment will only intensify the magnitude of illegal migration to the country. Solutions must be sought and planned with regional partners. The workshop and this volume are intended to keep these issues on the table at a time when there is a tendency either to close our eyes to the problem or to respond with bellicose and even xenophobic rhetoric. We can no longer delay making wider strategic decisions about immigration and development in the southern African region as a whole, not just for South Africa alone. These decisions involve mine migrancy, but they also involve clandestine and brain drain (skilled) migration in the region. Beyond this book, then, are wider areas on which research is urgently needed to provide the information through which comprehensive regional policies can be built. We end therefore with an urgent plea for further policy-oriented research on issues which are of enormous significance for the entire southern African region. ◆

REFERENCES

Coplan, D. 1994. In the Time of Cannibals: The Word Music of South Africa's Basotho Migrants. Chicago: University of Chicago Press.

Crush, J. 1992. "Power and surveillance on the South African gold mines," in Journal of Southern African Studies, Vol 18: 825-44.

James, W. 1992. Our Precious Metal: African Labour in South Africa's Gold Industry 1970-1990. Cape Town and London: David Philip and James Currey.

Moodie TD with V Ndatshe. 1994. Going for Gold: Men, Mines and Migration. Berkeley: University of California Press.

Packard, R. 1989. White Plague, Black Labour: TB and the Political Economy of Health and Disease in South Africa. Berkeley and Pietermaritzburg: University of California Press and University of Natal Press.

---

4. *A third paper tabled at the workshop reached similar conclusions; see F De Vletter. "The implications of changing migration patterns in southern Africa." Paris: OECD.*

HISTORY OF MINE MIGRANCY

THE FAILURE OF STABILISATION EXPERIMENTS ON SOUTH AFRICAN GOLD MINES

PROFESSOR ALAN H JEEVES
Department of History,
Queen's University,
Kingston, Ontario,
Canada

PROFESSOR JONATHAN CRUSH
Department of Geography,
Queen's University,
Kingston, Ontario,
Canada

The herding of South African black mineworkers into communal single-sex barracks away from their families has a long history. It developed alongside the migrant labour system itself and was fully functioning by the 1890s. Nevertheless, in the first decades of the century, and later during recurring moments of crisis, the gold-mining industry experimented with other ways of employing and housing its workers.

While migratory labour emerged as the dominant pattern, the mines tried many alternatives. They developed labour farms some distance from the mines themselves, where workers received land where they could live with their families and stock in return for varying periods of work on the mines. This was sort of halfway between classic migrancy and fully stabilised labour in family housing. In addition, before 1910 family housing for permanent (as permanent as any employment was on such dangerous and unhealthy mines) black workers was more common on the mines than it is today (Moroney, 1982).

Mining executives and managers tended to experiment during crises when profitability was at risk or when the black labour supply faltered – or both. Their jobs depended on maximising profits; the economics of mining required the continuous operation of expensive ore-reduction works, which demanded, in turn, reliable supplies of labour. By establishing labour farms or creating villages on or near the mines, managers could strengthen their control and provide incentives for miners to accept longer-term employment in rigorous underground work.

CRISIS, STABILISATION AND THE TIN TOWNS, 1902-1914

Before the 1970s, the gold-mining industry experienced three occasions when severe difficulties raised basic questions about the migrant labour system. The first occurred in the decade following the Anglo-Boer War. When production resumed, an unorganised, spontaneous and widespread worker stay-at-home (the mines had cut the already low pre-war wages) forced the industry to seek official support for recruitment outside southern Africa. Following intergovernmental negotiations, importation of workers from northern China began. Between 1904 and 1911 about 60 000 Chinese workers arrived in the country.

Access to densely populated northern China and the prospect of developing the southern African supply on a sub-continental basis seemed to promise a long-term solution to shortages. The search for stable labour supplies was reinforced when the industry's recruiting system managed to maintain its monopoly of recruited labour from southern Mozambique (Jeeves, 1985: 46-58; Richardson, 1982).

The appearance of restored stability was, however, illusory. From the beginning, opposition in Britain to Chinese "slavery" was strong. Opposition to the mining industry and to Chinese labour was also a powerful rallying cry in the 1907 Transvaal election. When Louis Botha and Jan Smuts won the election one of their first decisions was to phase out Chinese labour.

After many years of poor recruiting results, mine managers were convinced that there were simply not enough black workers available at the industry's low wages and they prepared to curtail operations. Some of them thought that the new government would be hopelessly inept, if not actively hostile, and unable to manage the requirements of an increasingly sophisticated and complex mining economy. The political upheaval after the war produced ferment within the mining industry too, and aggravated long-simmering disputes and rivalries. This led to the complete collapse of the co-operative recruiting arrangements under the Witwatersrand Native Labour Association within South Africa, although they survived precariously in Mozambique (Jeeves, 1985: 46-58). To make matters worse, the mines also had to contend with a newly militant white labour-force and a government apparently sympathetic to it.

A former mine manager, FHP Creswell, came to prominence in the campaign against Chinese immigration in 1903-4. He later broadened his programme to encompass the idea that the mines should move toward a whites-only labour policy. Once in office, the new government appointed a commission to report on the feasibility of Creswell's theories. Creswell himself became a member of the commission and turned its hearings and report into platforms for his ideas. His theories had revolutionary (or counter-revolutionary) implications both for the mining industry and the social order in the Transvaal.

The political events of 1906-7 threw mining labour policy into complete disarray. The decision to phase out Chinese labour and the apparent popularity of Creswell suggested that the mines might soon lose the labour recruited from outside South Africa as well. The importation of workers from the tropical areas of southern Africa, permitted on a small scale since 1904, was also at risk because of the resulting high rates of mortality (mainly from pneumonia) among recruits without previous experience of the harsh conditions on the mines (Baker, 1989). Within South Africa the recruiting system remained in turmoil because of internal mining industry conflicts and competition which the politics of the period had exacerbated.

The years following the war seemed to demonstrate that sufficient numbers of black mineworkers were simply not available within South Africa. Some mine managers pressed ahead with the experiments to make their labour supplies more reliable. Through the provision of family housing some African workers were attracted into permanent mine work. The mines used various incentives to attract and retain valuable skilled and experienced workers. They permitted African "locations" (or "tin towns") to develop on mining properties or adjacent land, and rudimentary black housing sprang up across the Witwatersrand. In order to retain the growing numbers of stabilised workers, managers provided or permitted them to settle with their families in accommodation on or near the mines.

In 1913 about 5 000 men (and 12 000 people in all) lived in married quarters on the mines (Moroney, 1982: 264-6). Many more lived in tin towns and slumyards away from the mines. In the same year, a survey of tin towns found around 12 000 individuals and a further 2 742 families resident. The proportion of stabilised labour on individual mines ranged from 1,5 to 15 percent (Moroney, 1982: 266).

Typically much less regulated than the compounds, the tin towns conferred a valued element of social freedom, both for residents and compound workers who visited the locations, particularly at weekends.

Although the municipal and other governments condemned the tin towns and opposed unregulated housing of black families near white areas, they lacked the bureaucratic capacity and police power to prevent it, at least initially. There were therefore few effective barriers to black families seeking permanent urban residence during the earliest phase of South Africa's industrialisation.

This relative freedom did not last very long. After Union in 1910, the Native Affairs Department and the Native Labour Bureau began to monitor the growth of the urban African population and to discourage the spread of uncontrolled locations, particularly on or near the mines. In 1911 the Native Labour Regulation Act made mine locations the responsibility of mine management. Many of them were demolished in the years that followed. In 1923 the first Union-wide legislation on Africans in the urban areas became law. The Natives (Urban Areas) Act empowered, but did not require, municipalities to regulate urban conditions for Africans, and was a harbinger of more intrusive regulatory measures imposed in 1930, 1937 and 1945 (Greenberg, 1987: 13-18). By the early 1930s, less than 1 500 workers were housed in the tin towns of the Witwatersrand. Those towns that survived were in an atrocious condition.

Mines outside the Johannesburg urban area or with access to land away from white residential areas were most likely to persist with stabilised labour experiments. On the coal mines of Natal and the Eastern Transvaal, for example, a much larger proportion of the labour-force was stabilised than on the gold mines. Other mines used the labour farm alternative. While some of the rural mines created fully proletarianised labour-forces and provided family housing at the mines, those that offered land at a distance produced the pattern of inflexible migrancy which is emerging as a prominent feature of the mining industry in the 1990s.

A white miners' strike in 1907 had the unintended result of showing how much of the semi-skilled and even skilled underground work was actually being done by black miners (earning a fraction of the wages of whites) who were able to keep production going with minimal supervision from non-striking managers and scabs. A successful attack on the colour bar would also have produced a shift away from migrant labour. Short-term migrancy inhibited skills development by black workers.

The crises of 1906-7, therefore, produced forces which might have led the mining industry to move toward a permanently proletarianised, largely black labour-force. There were a number of executives and mine managers who argued for just this approach.

Why did nothing of the sort materialise? Perhaps the major reason is that it would have required a major confrontation with the government and an all-out battle both with white labour and Creswell's white populism, and the mining industry recoiled from the risks.

Thus the crisis passed with the mines' labour system largely unchanged. When the government called out British troops against the strikers in 1907 the miners returned to work, and Smuts stopped flirting with Creswell's white-labour theories. A new government Native Labour Bureau, coupled with the mines own recruiting efforts, and assisted by severe economic recession in the labour supply areas, were spectacularly successful in mobilising labour.

These arrangements and the political compromise which they involved were expressed in two important acts of the first Union parliament: the Mines and Works Act and the Native Labour Regulation Act (both passed in 1911). The first confirmed that the colour bar would continue to protect white employment on the mines, and the second entrenched the migrant labour system by extending government regulation and control of the recruitment and treatment of black miners. Black miners would remain temporary, unskilled workers. Significantly, the economics of mining did not directly dictate this outcome. It was more the result of a political bargain laboriously constructed in 1906-7. The possibility of making more permanent, productive and efficient use of a black labour-force, working as career miners and living with their families, faded from the industry's agenda. This was an early victim not of profitability concerns but of the politics of white supremacy.

THE POLITICS OF MIGRANCY

The 1910s and 1920s were difficult decades for the mining industry. The departure of the last of the Chinese workers in 1911 was followed two years later by a ban on the employment of workers from Nyasaland. Wages rose sharply during World War One, mainly because of inflation and the gains won by the white unions, while production was somewhat constrained by shortfalls in imported mining supplies and recurring unskilled labour shortages. The gold mines continued to press for renewed access to the labour of northern Mozambique and Nyasaland. Rather than compete for labour in South Africa through wage increases and improved working conditions, the mining industry preferred to recruit in areas where competition was less and the workers had little alternative employment. Yet the state remained hostile to large-scale labour importation from new source areas.

Following the war, the state developed other reasons to oppose expanded use of foreign labour. When Smuts took over as prime minister in 1919, he began to plan for the post-war future of the subcontinent. Initially his attention focused on Southern Rhodesia and southern Mozambique, but Rhodesian settlers rejected incorporation into the Union. In Mozambique, Smuts aimed to secure control over the colony's transportation system and perhaps even sovereignty over its southern half. However, negotiations in the early 1920s to renew the Transvaal-Mozambique Agreement of 1909, which governed the labour, trade and railway linkages between them, exposed stubborn Portuguese resistance to Smuts' ideas (Jeeves, 1986: 73-92; Katzenellenbogen, 1982: 120-143). Smuts hoped that by restricting the employment of Mozambicans and sharply reducing the flow of mine earnings to Mozambique, the Portuguese would be brought to heel. Coercion was the main motive for the new Union-preference labour policy for the mines announced in July 1922 but the government soon found itself raising the limit significantly, as the demand for labour on the mines and in commercial agriculture grew rapidly.

Hertzog's Pact government, which came into power in 1924, was even more eager than Smuts to reduce dependence on Mozambique. Creswell, Hertzog's coalition partner, had campaigned against the importation of foreign unskilled workers for more than 20 years. By restricting the mines' access to foreign black labour he wanted to force the industry to use a higher proportion of white labour.

Hertzog was as unwilling as Creswell to see the Union "suck into itself an increasing agglomeration of African natives and other low-grade types from beyond its borders". The mining industry's efforts to persuade the government to permit at least an experiment with renewed tropical labour importation met hostile, or at best equivocal, responses.

In 1925 the Pact government formally accepted a quota system to constrain the importation of Mozambican labour. Despite this, the numbers continued to rise above official limits as general economic and mining expansion fed the demand for cheap labour. Growing competition between the two major low-wage employers, the mines and farms, and the complaints from both sectors about the development of chronic shortages, forced the government to reconsider its principled opposition to foreign labour.

In the Mozambique Convention (1928), the Portuguese insisted that the numbers of mineworkers who could be recruited annually from Mozambique be reduced by about 20 percent. However, the Mozambican authorities were no more able than the Union government to maintain the restriction for very long.

Had either Smuts or Hertzog succeeded in reducing the mines' dependence on foreign labour, the result would have had profound implications for the migrant labour system. Replacing the 80-100 000 mineworkers from Mozambique with South African workers would have forced the mining industry to draw in more adult males from the supply areas, raise wages and compete more intensively with white farmers and other employers. This would have meant lower medical standards in the recruits and more aggressive, less scrupulous recruiting.

To recoup the higher costs, the industry would have needed to address even more forcefully the issue of the colour bar and the ratio of white to black on the mines. Defeated in the 1922 strike, white miners remained particularly vulnerable to the consequences of a Union-preference policy in black employment. They were the certain losers in any policy to use African labour more efficiently and intensively. Placing Africans in more skilled jobs would have required a shift toward more stable patterns and longer employment periods for the miners who remained migrant. A certain consequence of enforced reliance on local supplies of labour would have been a more stable labour system with black workers living on or near the mines with their families.

During the depression (1929-33), the preconditions for stabilisation began to evolve. Partly because of the limits of recruitment imposed by the Portuguese in Mozambique, but mainly because of poverty and distress in South Africa's rural areas, local recruiting for the mines surged. By 1933 the mines were employing 240 000 black workers, of whom barely 50 000 came from Mozambique. But for the depression, such large increases in recruiting would have required wage incentives to draw labour from other sectors.

Labour shortages and the resulting wage increases would have led in turn to the development of a more skilled, less transient labour-force. A big loser in any such shift in labour policy would have been the farming industry. Commercial farmers, particularly the cane and cotton planters of Natal and Zululand, had become significant competitors of the mines in the supply areas of the Transkei and Basutoland. Even at the low wage levels of the early 1920s, most of them could not pay mine wages and had to rely on the younger, older and less fit workers.

In order to shelter their labour supply, the 1911 Native Labour Regulation Act had closed many of the principal white farming areas to recruitment for the mines and other industries. Such restrictions could not have survived the introduction of a ban on the use of foreign mine labour. Tenants were already leaving on their own for the mines and towns in large numbers. Any loss of protection against outside recruitment would certainly have accelerated the outflow.

DEPRESSION AND RECOVERY, 1929-39

When the mines did increase their local labour-force between 1929 and 1932, the fall of farm prices and widespread distress in the white rural areas during the depression, meant that the demand for recruited black labour in commercial agriculture had temporarily collapsed. Following the devaluation of the South African pound in December 1932, gold output and profits immediately surged. With the sudden revival of profitability and the resulting development of new mining areas, the growth of mining employment had a dramatic quickening effect throughout the economy. But employment of South African workers on the mines continued to increase from 135 000 in 1933 to 160 000 in 1939.

While farmers continued to complain bitterly about labour shortages, the political intensity of their complaints was less severe than it would have been had the agricultural sector recovered as quickly as mining. Because black unemployment levels remained high, the mines continued to increase their intake from the reserves without appreciably increasing wages. The recovery of Mozambique recruiting also eased their supply problem. By 1934, the Portuguese had reversed their campaign to limit mine recruiting and negotiated revisions to the Convention that required minimum quotas from Mozambique. Finally in 1933, the state permitted the mines to open experimental recruiting in the northern territories. The mines had some assurance that their future needs could be met from non-South African sources.

When a crisis in the local supply did overtake the industry between 1946 and 1953, it led to an immediate surge in tropical recruiting and the opening of new source areas (Tanganyika in particular). All of this meant that there was no need for the industry to reconsider the fundamentals of its labour policies during the 1930s, certainly its most prosperous decade since the 1890s.

No government in the 1920s or for many decades thereafter could bring itself to challenge the labour strategy which had been laboriously constructed by the first Union government. Embodied in the basic legislation of the segregationist state, the system sought to divide existing supplies of black labour and existing employment opportunities for whites among the main competing interest groups in white society. Sometimes styled the "alliance of gold and maize" (mining and farming), the strategy was also much broader, encompassing the interests of white workers, and white mine labour in particular (Morrell, 1988: 619-35). The Mines and Works Act of 1911 confirmed industrial segregation in the mining industry and secured for white miners the protection which their skill levels no longer provided against an increasingly experienced and capable black labour-force. The Native Labour Regulation Act was essentially companion legislation. By committing the authority of the state to the migrant labour system and imposing severe controls on black workers, it transferred the cost of the colour bar from the mining companies to their black workers.

These laws embodied the complex historic political compromise hammered out in the early years of Union which governed South African labour policy into the 1970s. The state sought both to subordinate black labour to the service of white employees and to mediate the increasingly intense differences among competing economic interest groups in white society. Since fundamental change in any single element of the equation would threaten the whole, later governments shrank from the major changes in mine labour policy suggested by Smuts' geopolitical ambition and Creswell's ideological commitment.

OPPENHEIMER AND THE ORANGE FREE STATE 'EXPERIMENT'

The conservative policies adopted to deal with persistent black labour shortages in the decade after 1945 followed from the gold-mining industry's established reliance on migrant labour. The most influential mining group remained the long-dominant producer, Rand Mines Limited and its London parent, the Central Mining and Investment Corporation. Individual companies belonging to this long-established group, particularly Crown Mines and the East Rand Proprietary Mines, had experienced recurrent problems of profitability. For these mines and others like them, replacing the compounds with family housing units in large new residential townships made no economic sense. Even had they been able to find the money, both of these centrally located mines lacked the space necessary to house their workers' families.

Equally, mechanisation to reduce the need for unskilled black labour was not an option for most of these properties. The older, still dominant, mining houses were therefore those least likely to contemplate radical alternatives to migrancy. Their supremacy was only challenged when the newer firm, the Anglo American

Corporation (AAC), became dominant on the opening of the Orange Free State goldfields at the end of the 1940s.

It was AAC that proposed a potentially radical change for the new mines. The group's chairman, Ernest Oppenheimer, suggested that up to 10 percent of the regular black labour-force on the new Orange Free State mines be stabilised. For the newer, better-equipped and lower-cost mines of his group, a departure from established and entrenched labour policies could be contemplated with much less financial risk. Furthermore, the new mines would be providing this family housing from the start. They did not face the problem of the older mines, which in order to do this would have had to scrap some or all of their existing migrant compounds at considerable expense just when they were ending their productive lives.

In response to its critics, the Chamber of Mines (COM) meanwhile mounted a vigorous public defence of the migrant labour system in front of successive government commissions of inquiry. Often they were pushed on the question of stabilised labour; just as frequently they rejected it on the grounds that the workers themselves did not want it. The workers themselves were never actually consulted about their preferences. The proponents of migrancy also retreated into a litany of the costs of stabilisation. The COM argued that to house married South African workers with their families would raise the development costs of the average new mine by £1,35 million and the recurrent costs by £100 000 per annum. Admitting that without migrant labour, South Africa's low-grade reefs could never have been exploited, the Chamber concluded "that the gold-mining industry stands firm in its belief that migratory labour continue".

In 1952, James Gemmill and several colleagues from the COM said about 12 percent of the black labour-force could eventually be stabilised. Gemmill's own commitment to migrancy was apparent when he referred to this percentage as "an extreme target figure". In fact, only AAC was contemplating this target. The other mining houses argued that they were unlikely to put more than 3 percent at the outside in married quarters. Most stressed the prohibitive costs involved in family housing for the whole work-force. Running costs would also be much higher than for the compounds.

So the migrant system remained deeply entrenched, and Oppenheimer's proposal for an expanded component of stabilised labour yielded little result. At several of the new Orange Free State mines AAC undertook a limited experiment to set up small family villages. The corporation built seven villages of between 50 and 150 housing units each for its mines in the Orange Free State. By 1953, however, a mere 740 workers were housed in the villages. Family housing was earmarked for a select group of skilled and supervisory workers. The houses were rented to workers and if the employee left the mine or died, his family was evicted.

During 1953, the Native Affairs Department of the new National Party government tried unsuccessfully to persuade the mines to settle those permanent black employees in neighbouring townships rather than in mine villages. In the early 1950s the state's Natural Resources Development Council (NRDC) drew up a regional development plan for the Orange Free State. A Subsidiary Planning Committee of the council investigated the matter of black married housing on the Orange Free State mines. The committee was hamstrung by the presence of a Department of Native Affairs official who reported directly to HF Verwoerd.

The department flatly refused to countenance any plan that did not place a limit of 3 percent on the proportion of African workers in family accommodation. The department's primary objection to extensive stabilisation was that the future of retired miners and their families remained uncertain. Verwoerd was blunter when he publicly chastised Oppenheimer's plan "to have a large number of native villages spread over the Free State". (*Rand Daily Mail*, 3 February 1953). The Subsidiary Planning Committee of the NRDC approved the 3 percent restriction, passing it back to the various government departments, and so on to the mining groups. Ironically what came to be known as the "unwritten law" of 3 percent was the figure that the COM's strategists had originally fixed upon in presenting their case for more married quarters. In a subsequent meeting with a truculent Verwoerd, Chamber executives hastened to assure him of the modesty of their plans for stabilisation and that the migrant labour system would continue to be the basis of the industry's labour policy.

In 1954, the total number of black mineworkers in married mine accommodation on the Rand and in the Orange Free State was still less than 3 000. By then the mining companies had all but abandoned earlier moves to contest the "unwritten law". In the decades that followed, there was little sustained protest from management or the Chamber, both of whom found the regulation a useful defence against critics of migrant labour. Between 1950 and 1975, no gold mine even came close to the 3 percent figure. The primary reason for this was the growing predominance of non-South African workers in the mine labour-force in the 1950s and 1960s. Even the most skilled foreign workers were prohibited from taking up residence in married quarters. Those who claimed Union domicile or had married locally were also barred.

In the 1960s, the gold mines became critically dependent on foreign labour when numerous black South Africans left the mines to work elsewhere. By the early 1970s, almost 80 percent of mineworkers were migrants from Malawi, Mozambique, Angola, Botswana, Lesotho and Swaziland. On some mines, the proportion of foreign workers rose above 90 percent (Crush et al, 1991: 102-3). These workers became particularly dominant in supervisory and skilled job categories on the mines. The South African government and those of the neighbouring states shared a common interest in ensuring that these workers remained migrants. The mines now had even less incentive or need to build family housing for their black workers. The AAC built only 200 married housing units for black workers between 1960 and 1970, and the proportion of workers in married housing in the industry as a whole actually fell from 1,28 percent to 0,87 percent.

A survey of 40 gold mines conducted in March 1974 provided startling evidence of the consequences of the industry's disinterest in alternatives to migrancy. At that time, only 0,7 percent of black mineworkers were living in married quarters on mines and in townships. Only five mines had ever applied for an exemption to the 3 percent rule and only 15 projected a need for additional married housing before 1980. It was not until 1974, when the government refused a request by Harmony mine to increase its stabilised component above 1,25 percent, that the Chamber began to seriously reconsider the impediment of the "unwritten law". Even then, rather than making a unified case for relaxation, the member companies could agree only to approach the government on an ad hoc basis for individual concessions (Crush et al, 1991: 167-73).

CONCLUSION

During the period 1886-1974, the gold mines periodically experienced economic, political and labour crises. None of those crises led to a fundamental shift in policy or to serious consideration of the abandonment of short-term migrancy as the fundamental way of mobilising and using black labour. What began as a transitional phenomenon, not uncommon in industrialising society, became entrenched as a central feature of South African society and the regional economy. The entrenchment of the system should not be seen as the inevitable product of economic necessity in the mining industry. It was rather the result of the particular conjuncture of economic forces and political programmes which together produced systematic segregation and later apartheid.

Since the mid-1970s, notwithstanding an unprecedented abundance of migrant labour, some mining groups have shown renewed interest in creating a stratum of skilled, stabilised black production workers. In the 1980s, with the growth of the National Union of Mineworkers, the stabilisation of migrant miners became much more than a technical requirement of the changing skill profile of the mine work-force. Housing delivery and home ownership were increasingly tied to an industrial relations strategy to depopulate the compounds, segment the work-force and co-opt skilled workers (Crush et al, 1991: 173-5 and 208-9; Crush and James, 1991: 301-16).

Despite the repeal of apartheid legislation, there are still many impediments to a significant move away from migrancy. They include management's continuing preference for migrant workers, cost in a time of fiscal stringency, the fear of creating ghost towns, the high proportion of foreigners in skilled categories and the advent of "inflexible migrancy" which affords the companies much of the benefit and little of the cost of full stabilisation. Even the most optimistic estimates do not foresee more than 10 percent of the black work-force in family quarters by the year 2000. What is certain is that the future shape of the mines' labour system – like its formation in the years between 1886 and 1920 – will be affected far more decisively by the preference and strategies of the workers themselves both formally (through their union) and informally (through the development of a variety of new household strategies). ◆

An extended version of this paper, including full citations, first appeared in Labour, Capital and Society, Vol 25, No 1, 1992. The editors wish to thank the publishers, the Centre for Developing-Area Studies, McGill University, Montreal, Quebec, Canada for granting permission to publish this revised version.

REFERENCES

Baker, J. 1989. The Silent Crisis: Black Labour, Disease and the Economics and Politics of Health on the South African Gold Mines, 1902-30. PhD dissertation, Queen's University.

Chanock, M. 1977. Unconsummated Union 1900-1945: Britain, Rhodesia and South Africa. Manchester: Manchester University Press.

Crush, J, AH Jeeves and D Yudelman. 1991. South Africa's Labour Empire: A History of Black Migrancy to the Gold Mines. Boulder and Cape Town: Westview Press and David Philip.

Crush, J and W James. 1991. "Depopulating the compounds: migrant labour and mine housing in South Africa," in World Development, Vol 19: 301-16.

Greenberg, S. 1987. Legitimating the Illegitimate: State, Markets and Resistance in South Africa. Berkeley: University of California Press.

Jeeves, AH. 1985. Migrant Labour in South Africa's Mining Economy: The Struggle for the Gold Mines' Labour Supply 1890-1920. Kingston and Montreal: McGill-Queen's Press.

Jeeves, AH. 1986. "Migrant labour and South African expansion, 1920-50," in South African Historical Journal, Vol 18: 73-92.

Katzenellenbogen, S. 1982. South Africa and Southern Mozambique: Labour Railways and Trade in the Making of a Relationship. Manchester: Manchester University Press.

Moroney, S. 1982. "Mine married quarters: the differential stabilisation of the Witwatersrand workforce, 1900-1920," in S Marks and R Rathbone, (eds,) Industrialisation and Social Change in South Africa. London: Longman.

Morrell, R. 1988. "The disintegration of the maize and gold alliance in South Africa in the 1920s," in International Journal of African Historical Studies, Vol 21: 619-35.

Packard, RM. 1989. White Plague, Black Labour: Tuberculosis and the Political Economy of Health and Disease in South Africa. Berkeley: University of California Press.

Richardson, P. 1982. Chinese Mine Labour in the Transvaal. London: MacMillan.

Mine Migrancy in the Contemporary Era

Professor Jonathan Crush
Department of Geography,
Queen's University,
Kingston, Ontario,
Canada

The migrant labour system on South African mines is one of the major legacies of the apartheid era and a principal development problem for a post-apartheid, democratic government. The entrenched character of migrancy makes it particularly difficult to envisage concrete alternatives to the present system. To foster change without destroying the wealth and employment-creating capacity of the mining sector is a challenge for all of the major actors in the new dispensation. Any genuine transformation will have a widespread impact upon miners, their families, their home communities and the economies of the neighbouring states.

Since major changes would also affect the economics of mineral production and supply, the impact will be felt internationally as well. Confronting the complex legacy of migrant labour and creating a viable alternative create urgent policy issues which are part and parcel of the struggle for a new social order in South Africa (Crush et al, 1992: 7-17).

The debate about migrant labour is almost as old as the system itself. In the late 19th and early 20th centuries, the future of mine labour aroused great controversy in South Africa and Europe. Within South Africa, the 1914 Buckle Commission, the 1932 Holloway Commission and the 1948 Fagan Commission debated the question of mine migrancy at great length. So too did successive apartheid commissions – including Froneman in 1961, Du Randt in 1975, Riekert in 1979 and Wiehahn in 1980. Agencies such as the International Labour Organisation (ILO) have had a recurrent interest in the migrant labour system. In the 1980s, the former frontline states tried to formulate a common policy on migrancy under the auspices of the Southern African Labour Commission (De Vletter, 1990; Crush, 1991). More recently, a major conference in Lesotho continued the debate (Santho and Sejanamane, 1990).

Before the 1980s and the rise of the National Union of Mineworkers (NUM), many of those who debated the future of migrancy shared one thing in common: a disregard for the voice of the workers themselves. Everyone claimed the right to speak on their behalf. This is one aspect of the past from which we need to make a clean break. Every effort must be made to try to find out what migrancy means for the migrant and his dependents, what they think about its abolition and how they are responding to its erosion. [Many migrant men and women are already reconfiguring the migrant labour system in important new ways (James, 1992; Moodie and Ndatshe, 1992).]

The past history of migrancy suggests that transformation by decree has always been difficult, if not impossible. Political interventions in the system have often run up against entrenched powers and brute economic realities. Like much else in contemporary South Africa, the political context for transforming the migrant labour system has now changed dramatically. So too, one hopes, has the will to change the system in ways that will give workers' interests high priority. However, the economic parameters are now more intractable. In the past, crisis prompted change and simultaneously set limits on its direction and extent. The history of migrancy shows us that the recommendations of our predecessors (whether for or against migrancy) were rarely implemented or implementable in the way they planned. Policy intervention in the migrant labour system has rarely achieved its intended effects and has often had dramatic unintended consequences.

Perhaps a little more optimistically, the migrant labour system is not, and has never been, a static entity impervious to challenge and change. A new phase of transformation began in the early 1970s (Crush et al, 1991; James, 1992). At one level, today's mine labour system shows great continuity with the past, but nothing about the recruitment and use of mine labour is as certain as it once seemed. Many of the changes would have been unthinkable 20 years ago. Many of the changes still to come may be unthinkable now.

It is the question of change and stasis in the migrant labour system in the contemporary era that this chapter addresses. It draws four general conclusions about shifts in the character of migrancy to the gold mines since 1970. First, the migrant labour system has shown extraordinary resilience over the last 25 years, despite unprecedented pressures for change from within and outside the industry. Over 90 percent of the industry's African employees are still migrants, living for most of the time in the single-sex hostels and visiting their primary place of residence only periodically. Policies to introduce more married accommodation and home-ownership schemes, particularly since 1986, targeted only a small elite group of workers (less than 3 percent of the work-force in the case of Anglo American workers) (Crush and James, 1991). Until and unless there are affordable and desirable alternatives, most miners will be forced to continue to endure the hardships of hostel life.

Second, the spatial patterning of migrancy has become a great deal more complex over the course of the last decade. Formerly, it was hard to distinguish between the migrant behaviour of a foreign and a South African miner. Both were recruited through The Employment Bureau of Africa (Teba) offices in the rural areas, both were forced to leave their families behind and sign legally enforceable contracts and both had to return home at the end of their contracts. Influx controls and pass laws (in the case of South Africans) and the Aliens Control Act (in the case of foreigners) meant that neither could seek other forms of employment in the urban areas. The only significant difference was that foreign migrants tended to have to travel further and cross international boundaries in their journey to the mines.

Many of the domestic legal props of this system (such as influx controls and the 3 percent rule restricting the number of miners allowed to settle at the mines) were removed in the 1980s for reasons that have more to do with broader political and social changes than specific developments in the mining sector. The immediate result for mining was that the geography of migrancy became a lot more complicated, particularly among South African migrants. In the early 1980s, the mines began to aggressively hire workers from areas closer to the major goldfields. This meant that many, but by no means all, workers could get home more often than the once a year allowed under the old system. Some mines tried, not all that successfully, to hire urbanised workers from neighbouring townships. More often, migrants hired from rural areas have been using living-out allowances either to move out of the hostels altogether or to establish a residence nearby in a township or informal settlement.

In 1993, for example, some 9 000 Anglo American workers (6 percent of the work-force) exercised this option (Table 1). Some landless miners have abandoned the rural areas altogether. Others maintain an urban and a rural home and shuttle between the two. In other cases, spouses and partners have themselves moved closer to the goldfields, on either a temporary or permanent basis (Moodie and Ndatshe, 1992).

Foreign miners, in contrast, have been more limited in their options. None have been allowed to legally emigrate to South Africa (though some have done so clandestinely). All are still subject to the controls and constraints of the past – they cannot legally bring their families with them; they cannot own property near the mines; they must return home for leave at the end of their contracts; they have to remit a high proportion of their wages to their home countries and so on. Many try to evade these restrictions, but everything is done under the threat of arrest and prosecution. Thus, while the migrant labour system is diversifying and even slowly eroding within South Africa, something like the classic pattern of migrancy still prevails among the industry's many foreign migrants.

Third, and partly as a result, the mines have continued to employ foreign

TABLE 1 : ACCOMMODATION FOR BLACK MINERS AT ANGLO AMERICAN MINES, 1987- 1993

	1987		1993	
	NO	%	NO	%
HOSTEL	175 918	97,5	133 337	89,1
MARRIED HOUSING	2 630	1,5	3 127	2,1
HOME-OWNERS	28	0,0	4 279	2,9
LIVING-OUT	1 870	1,0	8 895	5,9
TOTALS	180 446	100,0	149 638	100,0

miners in large numbers since 1970. At one point in the 1970s it looked as if they would try and replace all foreigners with South Africans, but it soon became apparent that they intended nothing of the sort. Although foreign labour is now essentially discretionary rather than necessary, the mines have had various reasons for maintaining their foreign labour component. This is probably good news for foreign miners and their home governments. For South African miners, who have born the brunt of lay-offs and retrenchments, there are fewer grounds for optimism.

Fourth and finally, there have been significant changes in the temporal character of migrancy over the last two decades. Labour surplus and computerisation have forced major shifts in every migrant's behaviour. The freedoms, limited as they were, of the classic migrant labour system have now gone. Once a worker did have some control over where he worked, for how long and how often. Now he has none. In a sense, migrant behaviour has become normalised. Migrants, like all other industrial employees, now work continuously with fixed annual leave at the same company and job, or they are replaced by someone who will. The question is this: what are the costs and implications of normalising only one part of an historically abnormal labour system? And if the whole system of mine labour is to be normalised, what is our model of normalisation to be and how feasible will it be to implement?

INTERNALISATION/EXTERNALISATION

What role, if any, should foreign workers have in the mining industry of the future? There are entrenched interests in the mining industry and region that still feel that the continued employment of non-South Africans is both desirable and necessary. New policies directed at any other outcome are therefore likely to be contested.

During the last 25 years of foreign labour on the mines, the Chamber of Mines (COM) and its member companies continued to enjoy a great deal of autonomy over where they would draw their migrant labour from. As a result, they were able to resist efforts to get them to employ more South Africans by arguing about the importance of foreign workers to the very survival of the industry. The period of mass retrenchments and lay-offs after 1986 actually entrenched rather than reduced the relative position of foreign miners vis-a-vis their South African counterparts.

Only 20 years ago almost 80 percent of the gold mines' migrant work-force came from outside South Africa. In a dramatic few years in the mid-1970s, the proportion of foreign miners on the gold mines plummeted to 40 percent (Figure 1, pg 32). This change was primarily a reflection of two things: Malawian president Hastings Banda's recall of 120 000 Malawian miners from South Africa in 1974, and a drop in the Mozambican complement from 97 000 to 35 000 in the three years after Frelimo took power. These workers were primarily replaced by South Africans, but migrants from Lesotho, Swaziland, Botswana and Zimbabwe also helped make up the shortfall. The reasons for this reconfiguration of the mine labour system have been considered at length elsewhere and need not detain us here (Crush et al, 1991; James, 1992). What is more important is the interpretation given to these changes by academics, policy makers and bureaucrats.

The term "internalisation" was coined by the ILO to describe a strategy by which the South African mining industry and government (the two were rarely distinguished) were supposedly replacing all foreign miners with South Africans. Various commentators predicted that this would lead to a greatly reduced foreign presence on the mines by the end of the 1980s – less than 20 percent in some predictions.

However, the bare statistics give scant support to the argument that the mining industry was shedding foreign workers in the 1980s. Figure 1 clearly shows that the proportion of foreign labour on the mines actually stabilised around 1980 and, if anything, gradually increased during the 1980s. Obviously the overall labour mix is a complex composite of decisions taken at the mine level in many cases and at head office in others (Crush et al, 1991; James, 1992). Some mining houses and mines did reduce their heavy reliance on foreign labour in the 1980s, particularly mines in the Gencor group who explicitly declared their intention to move in this direction in the early 1980s (Table 2). Overall this was more than counterbalanced by the others who held their foreign labour complements steady or actually increased them over the same period.

TABLE 2 : FOREIGN LABOUR EMPLOYED BY MINING GROUP, 1974-1992

| | PROPORTION OF WORK-FORCE (%) | | | |
	1974	1980	1986	1992
AAC	72	41	40	47
GENCOR	77	35	28	36
GOLD FIELDS	85	51	49	53
RAND MINES	80	52	59	57
JCI	88	43	41	45
ANGLOVAAL	83	39	52	52

The apartheid state was always internally divided on the question of foreign labour. Some state departments (particularly those concerned with domestic manpower and unemployment) strongly favoured internalisation, while others (particularly foreign affairs and mining) argued for foreign labour on the grounds of political leverage with the supplier states and negative economic impacts. This stand off within the state traditionally allowed the mining industry, through Teba, to continue to pursue its own foreign hiring policy uninterrupted. There were numerous occasions in the 1960s, 1970s and 1980s when the COM successfully resisted the state's efforts to expel foreign miners.

By the early 1980s the mining companies were in a very strong position to pursue a full policy of internalisation if they had wished to. The historical argument that South Africans would not work on the mines for the wages the industry could afford to pay ceased to have much credibility by the late 1970s. There was now a massive and highly visible army of unemployed South Africans willing to accept mine work. The mining industry could probably have replaced all unskilled and semi-skilled foreign labour with South Africans over the course of the 1980s with only minimal disruption to production and profit. Certainly it would now be even easier, with retrenched South African miners waiting for jobs in large numbers.

What of the demand from the supplier states for mine jobs in the 1980s? Despite a rhetorical commitment to withdrawing their labour from South Africa, only one frontline state (Zimbabwe) actually did so. The body charged with co-ordinating this withdrawal – the Southern African Labour Commission – was utterly ineffectual (De Vletter, 1990). One reason was that most of the supplier governments spent the 1980s making secret deals to try and get South Africa to take more of their citizens and devising ways to make sure that migrant wages were spent at home and not in South Africa (Crush et al, 1991). Compulsory deferred pay schemes, though deeply unpopular with miners, ensured that the bulk of the earnings were remitted by the mines to banks in the home country. There was not then, and there certainly is not now, any sentiment amongst supplier governments for the ending of migrancy to South Africa (James, 1989; Santho and Sejanamane, 1990; Coplan, 1993).

By the 1980s, therefore, the presence of foreign labour had become essentially discretionary rather than (as in the past) necessary. Why then did foreign workers continue to be employed in such numbers?

The mines' public explanation, not devoid of truth, was that foreign workers comprised a reservoir of skills, experience and work-discipline which the mining industry could not do without. In addition, they argued, the phenomenon of "career mining" (see below) had greatly reduced their room for manoeuvre. Certainly, as Fion de Vletter (1990) has shown, foreign miners were disproportionately represented in higher, more-skilled job categories and were more experienced and generally more educated than their South African counterparts (Figure 2, pg 32). When state intervention in the labour market meshed with their own interests, however, the argument about vital skills and experience seemed to go by the board. Thus, when the South African government demanded that all Malawian miners be tested for HIV and Aids before being allowed into South Africa (and the Malawian government refused to allow pre-testing), the mines were only too willing to go along with the state's expulsion of all 18 000 Malawians, whether they were HIV-positive or not (Jochelson et al, 1991). The speed with which the Malawians – for all their skills, experience, discipline and lack of militancy – were replaced only confirms the suspicion that if the will or the motive had been there, it would not have been too difficult to treat workers from Swaziland, Botswana, Mozambique and even Lesotho in exactly the same way.

Another common argument advanced by mine management was the old racial myth that particular ethnic groups were somehow psychologically better suited to certain kinds of tasks; a view successfully demolished by Jeff Guy and Motlatsi Thabane (1988) amongst others. On the other hand, many managers continued to play the micro-politics of ethnic divide-and-rule (Golding, 1985; Moodie, 1992). The mining companies were less willing to admit in public that they thought foreign workers would be more submissive because they were more vulnerable to dismissal (a factor of increasing weight in the face of NUM's unionisation drive of the 1980s) (Crush, 1989).

Another motive for a foreign labour presence was management's desire to cultivate multiple sources of labour and avoid over-reliance on any one source, a strategy Wilmot James (1992) has called "heterogenous sourcing". These powerful arguments help to explain the mining industry's opposition to Botha's threats to expel the Mozambicans, but their response was also conditioned by a more fundamental principle. The COM maintained that the mines should have the right, as always, to choose labour from wherever they wanted, including non-South African sources. This is an argument that reverberates into the present.

DOWN-SCALING

The last few years of down-scaling and lay-offs have affected the presence of foreign labour on the mines. Further research is still needed on the policies of the various mines and mining houses toward lay-offs, but the statistical evidence is most suggestive. In the last six years the gold-mining industry has lost nearly 180 000 jobs to down-scaling and retrenchments (Seidman, 1993).

Jean Leger and Martin Nicol (1992) recently estimated that under current conditions (including a static gold price) the mines could lose another 150 000 jobs by the mid-1990s. The inevitable result is that there is greater competition for fewer jobs and many unemployed South African miners are aggrieved that foreigners remain on the mines in large numbers. The spatial pattern of lay-offs provides an important clue to the mining industry's continuing commitment to the foreign worker during the early 1990s.

Table 3 suggests that almost all source areas have been hit by mine retrenchments since the peak employment year of 1986. However, it is clear from Table 4 that domestic, not foreign, source areas have been most affected by lay-offs. Many traditional mining source areas within South Africa – such as the Transkei and Ciskei – have been particularly devastated with lay-offs approaching 50 percent of the work-force. In contrast, the decline in major foreign suppliers such as Lesotho and Mozambique is only of the order of 20-25 percent. In the case of Mozambique there was a temporary increase after the Nkomati Accord in 1984. Retrenchments have simply reduced the Mozambican complement back to pre-Nkomati levels.

In the case of one foreign supplier, Swaziland, the number of miners actually increased over the period when the industry as a whole lost 150 000 jobs. In 1992, the proportion of foreign workers in the mine work-force rose to almost 50 percent. Four of the six major mining houses (Anglo American, Gencor, Gold Fields and JCI) had a greater proportion of foreign miners in their work-force in 1992 than they had had in 1986 (Table 2).

The statistical evidence on lay-offs at mine level is even more striking. During the period 1986 to 1992, every single mine except one (Kloof) laid off workers, but very few laid off more foreigners than South Africans (Table 5). On Anglo American mines, four South Africans were laid off for every one foreign worker (Table 6). On Gencor and JCI mines, the ratio was three to one. It is true that Rand Mines and Anglovaal laid off more foreigners than South Africans, but then Rand Mines had a disproportionate number of foreign workers to begin with. Only Gold Fields had anything approaching parity in lay-offs though even here the net effect of lay-offs was an increase in the foreign complement from 51 to 53 percent of the work-force.

What are the implications of these trends for migrancy to the gold mines in the 1990s? One must obviously be wary of reading too much into these statistics. Without further corroborating evidence it would be premature to argue that mine managements have deliberately discriminated against South Africans. Given the

TABLE 3 : EMPLOYMENT ON SOUTH AFRICAN GOLD MINES, 1986-1992

| | AVERAGE NUMBER EMPLOYED | | | | | | |
	1986	1987	1988	1989	1990	1991	1992
SOUTH AFRICAN							
TRANSKEI	133 965	128 513	120 008	108 957	98 924	86 790	77 282
CISKEI	13 116	12 249	11 593	10 569	9 925	7 713	6 331
BOPHUTHATSWANA	15 172	15 197	13 861	12 038	10 862	9 470	7 764
OTHER AREAS	103 897	117 553	119 806	113 992	105 251	90 227	79 693
TOTAL SA	266 150	273 402	265 268	245 556	224 262	194 200	171 070
FOREIGN							
LESOTHO	103 742	105 506	100 951	100 529	98 200	88 281	83 877
MOZAMBIQUE	56 237	45 917	44 084	42 807	43 172	41 596	42 467
BOTSWANA	19 106	17 939	17 061	16 051	14 918	13 388	11 159
SWAZILAND	14 239	15 743	16 171	16 730	16 387	15 623	15 120
MALAWI	17 923	17 620	13 090	2 212	29	5	0
TOTAL FOREIGN	211 247	202 725	191 357	187 329	172 706	160 253	153 371
TOTAL	**477 397**	**476 127**	**456 625**	**432 885**	**396 968**	**354 453**	**324 441**

tendency of lay-offs to target the lower job grades first (where South Africans are disproportionately represented) it would be necessary to examine the patterns of lay-offs within job grades at particular mines to see if this apparent pattern of favouring foreign workers still holds.

Even then there would be some anomalies that need explanation. It is hard to see the rise in Swazi workers on Anglo American and Gencor mines, in particular, as anything other than a deliberate strategy. Clearly there is a need for further investigation, and the establishment of some form of monitoring of mine sourcing policy as well as mechanisms of accountability for decisions that might work against the interests of South African workers and their communities.

Irrespective of the motives and mechanics behind lay-off policies, the effect has been to discriminate against South Africans and favour foreign miners. Are workers aware of this? The evidence on other issues (such as promotions) suggests that tensions are heightened when workers from one area are favoured at the expense of those from another. Does this also apply to lay-offs and retrench-

TABLE 4 : EMPLOYMENT DECLINE ON GOLD MINES, 1986-1922							
	1986	1987	1988	1989	1990	1991	1992
SOUTH AFRICAN							
TRANSKEI	100	96	90	81	74	65	58
CISKEI	100	93	88	81	70	59	48
BOPHUTHATSWANA	100	99	91	79	72	62	51
OTHER AREAS	100	113	115	110	101	87	77
TOTAL SA	100	103	99	92	84	73	64
FOREIGN							
LESOTHO	100	102	97	97	95	85	81
MOZAMBIQUE	100	82	78	76	77	74	75
BOTSWANA	100	94	89	84	78	70	58
SWAZILAND	100	111	114	117	115	110	107
MALAWI	100	98	73	12	0	0	0
TOTAL FOREIGN	100	96	91	89	82	76	73
TOTAL	100	99	96	91	83	74	68

ments? Is the pattern of lay-offs related to union strength and composition on the mine? Have South African workers (and their Basotho counterparts among foreign miners) been targeted because of their greater commitment to and involvement in the NUM? What does a discriminatory firing policy (whether deliberate or inadvertent) mean for union solidarity and action?

As a result of these trends, South Africans and South African rural areas have been hardest hit by retrenchments, although it could be argued that with fewer alternative employment opportunities at home, the impact of lay-offs are more severe in the foreign areas. However, high rates of domestic unemployment certainly mitigate against this argument. South African miners may justly ask why, in an era of down-sizing and lay-offs, they have had to bear more of the cost than their foreign counterparts.

In the past, differences of opinion between different departments in the old apartheid bureaucracy allowed mine management to pursue its own policy on foreign labour virtually unhindered. The same differences of opinion may well reassert themselves in the post-apartheid era, some arguing that domestic unemployment is the key issue, others that relations with South Africa's neighbours are more important. There is clearly a need for a unified, coherent government policy on the future of foreign migrants in the mining industry. Without it, ad hocery is likely to prevail, raising tensions, reducing accountability and working to no-one's advantage.

Finally, and this is what makes the policy question so pertinent, the evidence presented here certainly does not suggest that the mining companies have been planning to abandon the foreign miner if they can possibly help it. Is this something that the new government wants to leave up to the mining companies to decide? Clearly, the reasons why the mines employ foreign miners (real and claimed) are persuasive enough to managers to ensure that foreign labour will remain and might even continue to grow in relative importance. While neighbouring governments would probably find the status quo quite palatable, it is less clear that it would be unequivocally to the advantage of foreign miners. While they might have work, they would still be long-distance, old-fashioned contract migrants, treated as single men, forced to live in the compounds, unable to own property and susceptible to all the hardships of the old system.

There are therefore three issues at stake here – what level of foreign presence in South Africa is desirable? What mechanisms should be put in place for making the desirable feasible? And, if foreign migrants are to remain, should they continue to be as badly treated as they were under apartheid or is there a case for a more generous and humane approach to the rights and freedoms of the foreign migrant in South Africa?

This question takes us to another major transition of the 1970s and 1980s – the phenomenon called "career mining" or "stabilisation" by mine management; "pseudo-stabilisation", "commuter migrancy" or "inflexible migrancy" by the critics.

INFLEXIBLE MIGRANCY

Migrant labour to the South African gold mines is a particularly enduring and entrenched way of life for many rural communities in the region. Whole areas depend on migrant remittances for their survival and many rituals and cultural practices have migrancy at their centre (Murray, 1981; First, 1983; Shanafelt, 1989; Harries, 1994). In the 1980s, with massive regional unemployment, a mine job became a prized possession. The result was the emergence of the "career miner" who had to work continuously on a particular mine or forfeit his job. This has exacted a heavy toll on miners' health (Packard, 1990; Leger, 1992; Crush, 1992a) and shut out a whole generation of new work-seekers who could once have counted on a mine job, if nothing else. Mine migrants have become a relatively privileged absentee rural elite in the midst of abject poverty. As Basotho miners point out, there is only one thing worse than having a mine job in South Africa and that is not having one (Coplan, 1993).

The advent of inflexible migrancy in the 1980s marked a significant change in the old pattern when a migrant tended to work intermittently and for various periods of time, often interspersing periods of mine employment with other jobs. By the 1980s this kind of discretionary behaviour was no longer possible. Miners were increasingly employed on fixed annual contracts with fixed periods of leave. By the late 1980s the vast majority of miners employed were on standardised 52-week agreements with four to six weeks' annual leave. Workers began to return regularly and repeatedly to the same mine and very often the same work gang. Return rates on most mines had reached over 90 percent by the end of the decade. In a labour market characterised by high unemployment and few alternative employment opportunities, most miners conformed, however reluctantly, to the new employment regime.

For the mining companies the advantages of an inflexible migrant regime are probably obvious. What is inflexible from the worker's standpoint is quite the opposite for the employer. Without having to permanently stabilise the workforce in family housing, the mines could achieve many of the benefits of stabilisation. In the 1980s they were able to lower the cost of recruiting and training new workers, impose new standards of work organisation and discipline, eliminate the drainage of skills and experience from the mines and engage in far more detailed manpower planning than has ever been possible before.

Workers were now forced to spend a greater and greater proportion of their working lives away from home living in the hostels. Already this has taken its toll in increased stresses on family life. Career mining is also at least partially responsible for the alarming upsurge in occupational disease on the mines documented by Jean Leger (1992) and Randall Packard (1990). Perhaps paradoxically, miners forced to live semi-permanently on the mines with little choice or respite became far more dissatisfied with conditions on those mines. This is one reason, amongst many others, why the NUM found the mine hostels such fertile recruiting ground in the 1980s (James, 1992). Management was also forced to make early concessions by introducing the 11-shift fortnight, allowing workers living

TABLE 5 : LAY-OFFS BY MINE, 1986-1992

	1986	1992	JOB LOSS	FOREIGN	SA	BREAKDOWN FOR %	SA %
AAC							
ELANDSRAND	8143	7843	-300	+173	-473	0	100
VAAL REEFS	47690	37936	-9754	-1758	-7996	18	82
WESTERN DEEP	25035	20127	-4908	-1686	-3222	34	66
FS GEDULD	28847	22588	-6259	-988	-5261	16	84
FS SAAIPLAAS	10888	10068	-820	+422	-1242	0	100
PRES BRAND	19858	13622	-6236	-1533	-4703	25	75
PRES STEYN	20940	14628	-6312	-940	-5372	15	85
W. HOLDINGS	21037	13553	-7484	-1966	-5518	26	74
SUB-TOTALS	**182438**	**140365**	**-42073**	**-8286**	**-33787**	**20**	**80**
GENCOR							
GROOTVLEI	6349	1710	-4639	-818	-3821	18	82
WEST RAND CONS	5503	197	-5306	-1267	-4039	24	76
WINKELHAAK	10330	8527	-1803	+559	-2362	0	100
KINROSS	8975	6941	-2034	-626	-1408	31	69
MARIEVALE	1202	159	-1043	-347	-696	33	67
STILFONTEIN	11955	341	-11614	-3999	-7615	34	66
UNISEL	4022	2954	-1068	-250	-818	23	77
BEATRIX	7316	5549	-1767	-1073	-694	61	39
BUFFELSFONTEIN	14646	6856	-7790	-1477	-6313	19	81
ST HELENA	10824	7144	-3680	-733	-2947	20	80
SUB-TOTALS	**81122**	**40378**	**-40744**	**-10031**	**-30713**	**25**	**75**
GOLDFIELDS							
LUIPAARDSVLEI	440	38	-402	-75	-327	19	81
VENTERSPOST	3096	2778	-318	-160	-158	50	50
DEELKRAAL	6602	6258	-344	-197	-147	57	43
DOORNFONTEIN	10486	5263	-5233	-1552	-3681	30	70
LIBANON	8121	6041	-2080	-1053	-1027	51	49
W. DRIEFONTEIN	16096	13935	-2161	-1022	-1139	47	53
E. DRIEFONTEIN	13636	11155	-2481	-2143	-338	86	14
KLOOF	16431	18785	+2354	+1453	+901	62	38
SUB-TOTALS	**74908**	**64253**	**-10665**	**-4749**	**-5916**	**45**	**55**
RAND MINES							
ERPM	20497	5318	-15179	-10867	-4312	72	28
DURBAN DEEP	11092	4333	-6759	-3016	-3743	45	55
HARMONY	30872	13008	-17864	-10678	-7186	59	41
BLYVOOR'ZICHT	11290	5852	-5438	-2978	-2460	54	46
SUB-TOTALS	**73751**	**28511**	**-45240**	**-27539**	**-17701**	**61**	**39**
JCI							
HJ JOEL		1731	+1731	+854	+877		
RANDFONTEIN	14921	11543	-3378	-650	-2728	19	81
WESTERN AREAS	11424	7320	-4104	-1775	-2329	43	57
SUB-TOTALS	**26345**	**20594**	**-5751**	**-1571**	**-4180**	**27**	**73**
ANGLOVAAL							
HARTEBEES.	17300	16033	-1267	-1506	+239	100	0
LORAINE	8716	3994	-4722	-2417	-2305	51	49
SUB-TOTALS	**26016**	**20027**	**-5989**	**-3923**	**-2066**	**65**	**35**

TABLE 6 : LAY-OFFS BY MINING HOUSE, 1986 -1992

| | NO EMPLOYED | | NO OF LAY-OFFS | | | PROPORTIONAL JOB LOSSES | |
	1986	1992	TOTAL	FOREIGN	SA	FOREIGN %	SA %
AAC	182438	140365	-42073	-8286	-33787	20	80
GENCOR	81122	40378	-40744	-10031	-30713	25	75
GOLD FIELDS	74908	64253	-10665	-4749	-5916	45	55
RAND MINES	73751	28511	-45240	-27539	-17701	61	39
JCI	26345	20594	-5751	-1571	-4180	27	73
ANGLOVAAL	26016	20027	-5989	-3923	-2066	65	35
TOTAL	464580	314128	150452	-56099	-94353	37	63

close enough to home to return for occasional weekends. Basotho miners were rechristened "weekenders" for taking advantage of this concession. Then, in turn, managers began to employ workers closer to the mines they worked on – trying to turn them into at least weekly or monthly commuters.

Defenders of the policy of inflexible migrancy within the mining industry argue that all that has happened is that South African miners have simply become like any other industrial worker. Though we may not like it, all of us have to work continuously if we want to hold on to our jobs. All of us know that we run the risk of being fired if we don't come back to work after our vacation. Isn't this merely the normalisation of the miner's work behaviour? Doesn't the policy simply make him like everyone else?

The question which this defence raises, of course, is whether it is possible to have normalisation in an abnormal system. Clearly, inflexible migrancy has been a boon for the mining companies, but for workers it has, if anything, simply exacerbated the well-documented hardships long associated with the migrant labour system. This is the ironic cost of normalising only one part of a coercive labour system.

Two subsidiary questions therefore need to be posed. First, within the context of a migrant labour system, what has the advent of career mining actually meant for workers and their dependents? Have the effects been primarily positive or negative? Second, can migrancy be normalised or is this just another way of saying that it ought to be abolished altogether? What is normalisation in the context of an entrenched and historically coercive labour system? Should normalisation involve the dismantling of the hostels and the stabilisation of all workers in family housing in mining communities? Or are our goals to be more modest?

COMPUTERISATION

The final innovative feature of migrancy in the contemporary era is computerisation. I have examined this issue in greater depth elsewhere (Crush, 1992b). The role of information technology in the organisation of South African labour markets under apartheid has actually attracted surprisingly little attention. Within the mining industry, Bill Freund (1991) has pointed to the widespread use of computers for exploration and the monitoring of seismic activity in deep-level gold production. Indeed, argues Freund, the mines are probably South Africa's (and Africa's) major user of these new technologies. They are also the major user of computer technology for purposes of labour control and surveillance.

The COM, through Teba, has always been a fastidious gate and record-keeper. Teba recently estimated that it had the work and employment histories of some 10,5 million workers on file, dating back to the early 20th century. These records covered kilometres of shelf space, but the powers of cross-matching were very limited and no recruiter had instant access to a potential employee's full work history.

In the 1980s, these manual systems were increasingly computerised, greatly enhancing the efficacy and usefulness of the data collected. The Manpower Data Centre (MDC) at the Teba depot is linked to the recruiting network, and plans to link up with all regional offices. The MDC in Johannesburg contains a central database storing full personal details of workers as well as their employment histories and work records. Each worker was assigned a single industry number and a standard identity card. These Teba cards carried a photograph of the card-holder, his industry number and a thumbprint. Teba has almost instant access to a worker's record through a laser disc scanning process incorporating bar coding and computerised photo imaging.

These cards have now been integrated into computerised mine-security systems and workplace monitoring. In the late 1980s they also began to be used for on-mine banking purposes.

How did workers respond to the new electronic eye?

Surveillance and control was hardly something novel to most workers. Computerisation eliminated many of the frustrations and delays in the recruiting process which characterised earlier manual systems. Now, with bar-coded ID cards, the whole process was more impersonal and considerably more efficient. In a tight labour market with mine jobs at a premium, workers have been forced to accept the ID system as a pre-condition of entry. An industry number and ID card seems a small price to pay for a job on the mines.

The evidence from outside South Africa shows that computerisation has two faces – tightening mechanisms of control and regulation while simultaneously providing apparent benefits to the card-holder. Recent interviews with miners conducted in the Transkei clearly reveal that they are more impressed with the advantages than the disadvantages of the system.

What does computerisation mean for migrancy? The evidence suggests that the new technologies of control are meshing with and reinforcing the old. Computerisation, at least in the short term, appears to make the operation of a migrant labour system more efficient and effective, ironing out imperfections and shutting down spaces formerly available to miners to work the system to their own advantage. Computerisation in the context of an abnormal labour system is not a transforming technology. If anything, it provides the operators even less incentive to consider alternatives to migrancy.

In other countries, as David Lyon (1994) points out, the objects of electronic surveillance are rarely aware of the multiplying uses of computers to control and compile information about every aspect of their lives. The ethical issues of confidentiality and privacy have prompted a serious examination of the legal framework governing decisions about what is not acceptable in the information age. Such a debate is urgently needed in South Africa too, both inside the mining industry and outside it.

CONCLUSION

Since 1990, there has been renewed debate about the future of migrancy to the gold mines. Should it be abolished – and, if so, how and at what cost to the source regions? If migrancy continues, should it be "internalised", since 150 000 less jobs for foreigners means 150 000 more for unemployed South Africans? Should migrants be subject to the same draconian controls of the past and, if not, how best can these abuses be stopped? Should the hostels be dismantled and, if so, what should they be replaced with and who will pay for the alternatives? How these highly politicised questions are resolved has very real implications for the miners and their dependents as well as their home communities.

Planning for the future should not ignore the past. The long history of the migrant labour system has some important general lessons to teach about the constraints on transformation and normalisation. Analysis of the recent history of the migrant labour system is probably even more pertinent, since it helps identify important underlying processes shaping the system of migrancy to the mines and imposing limits on the nature and direction of transformation and change. I have briefly reviewed the outcomes of a number of such processes – internalisation/externalisation, down-scaling, career mining and computerisation. My conclusion is a simple one – that all have tended to change the form but not the content of the system of migrancy to the gold mines. Left unchecked, or uncontested, they will probably have the same effect in the future. ◆

REFERENCES

Coplan, D. 1993. "Damned if we know: public policy, labour law, and the future of the migrant labour system," paper presented to the Conference on Labour Law, Durban.

Crush, J. 1989. "Migrancy and militance: the case of the National Union of Mineworkers of South Africa," in African Affairs, Vol 88: 5-24.

Crush, J. 1991. "The chains of migrancy and the Southern African Labour Commission," in C Dixon and M Heffernan, (eds,) Colonialism and Development in the Contemporary World, London: Mansell: 46-71.

Crush, J. 1992a. "Inflexible migrancy: new forms of migrant labour on the South African gold mines," in Labour, Capital and Society, Vol 25, No 1: 46-71.

Crush, J. 1992b. "Power and surveillance on the South African gold mines," in Journal of Southern African Studies, Vol 18: 825-44.

Crush, J and W James. 1991. "Depopulating the compounds: migrant labour and mine housing in South Africa," in World Development, Vol 19: 301-16.

Crush, J, W James and AH Jeeves. 1992. "Transformation on the South African gold mines," in Labour, Capital and Society, Vol 25, No 1: 7-17.

Crush, J, AH Jeeves and D Yudelman. 1991. South Africa's Labour Empire: A History of Black Migrancy to the Gold Mines. Boulder and Cape Town: Westview Press and David Philip.

De Vletter, F. 1990. "Future prospects for foreign migrants in a democratic South Africa," in S Santho and M Sejanamane, (eds,) After Apartheid. Harare: SAPES Trust: 28-51.

First, R. 1983. Black Gold: The Mozambican Miner, Proletarian and Peasant. New York: St Martin's Press.

Freund, B. 1991. "South African gold mining in transformation," in S Gelb, (ed,) South Africa's Economic Crisis. London: Zed Books: 110-28.

Golding, M. 1985. "Mass dismissals on the mines," in South African Labour Bulletin, Vol 10, No 7: 97-118.

Guy, J and M Thabane. 1988. "Technology, ethnicity and ideology: Basotho miners and shaft sinking on the South African gold mines," in Journal of Southern African Studies, Vol 14: 257-78.

Harries, P. 1994. Work, Culture and Identity: Migrant Labourers in Mozambique and South Africa. New York: Heinemann.

James, W. 1989. "The future of migrant labour: prospects and possibilities," in Industrial Relations Journal of South Africa, Vol 9.

James, W. 1991. "Class conflict, mine hostels and the reproduction of a labour force in the 1980s," in R Cohen et al, (eds,) Repression and Resistance. London: Hans Zell.

James, W. 1992. Our Precious Metal: African Labour in South Africa's Gold Industry, 1970-1990. Cape Town: David Philip.

Jochelson, K, M Mothibeli and J Leger. 1991. "Human Immunodeficiency Virus and migrant labour in South Africa," in International Journal of Health Services, Vol 21.

Laburn-Peart, C. 1992. "Transforming mine housing in South Africa, in Labour, Capital and Society, Vol 25, No 1: 104-15.

Leger, J. 1987. "Mozambican miners reprieve," in South African Labour Bulletin, Vol 12, No 2: 29-32.

Leger, J. 1992. "Occupational diseases in South African mines – a neglected epidemic?" in South African Medical Journal, Vol 81: 197-201.

Leger, J and M Nicol. 1992. "Gold mining in South Africa: priorities for restructuring," in Transformation, Vol 20: 17-35.

Lyon, D. 1994. The Electronic Eye: The Rise of Surveillance Society. Minneapolis: University of Minnesota Press.

Moodie, TD. 1992. "Ethnic violence on the South African gold mines," in Journal of Southern African Studies, Vol 18: 584-613.

Moodie, TD with V Ndatshe. 1992. "Town women and country wives: migrant labour, family politics and housing preferences at Vaal Reefs Mine," in Labour, Capital and Society, Vol 25, No 1: 116-32.

Murray, C. 1981. Families Divided: The Impact of Migrant Labour in Lesotho. Cambridge: Cambridge University Press.

Packard, R. 1990. White Plague, Black Labour: Tuberculosis and the Political Economy of Health and Disease in South Africa. Berkeley: University of California Press.

Santho, S and M Sejanamane, (eds,) 1990. Southern Africa After Apartheid. Harare: SAPES Trust.

Seidman, G. 1993. "Shafted: the social impact of down-scaling on the Free State goldfields," in South African Sociological Review, Vol 5, No 2: 14-34.

Shanafelt, R. 1989. Talking Peace, Living Conflict: The Mental and the Material on the Borders of Apartheid. PhD dissertation, University of Florida.

Wilson, F. 1972. Labour in the South African Gold Mines 1911-1969. Cambridge: Cambridge University Press.

FIGURE 1: PROPORTION OF FOREIGN LABOUR, 1960 – 1993

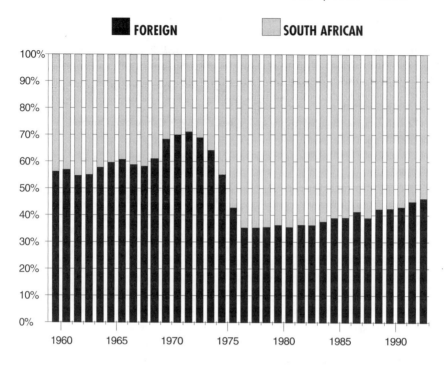

FIGURE 2: SOUTH AFRICAN AND FOREIGN LABOUR SKILL LEVELS, ANGLO AMERICAN MINES

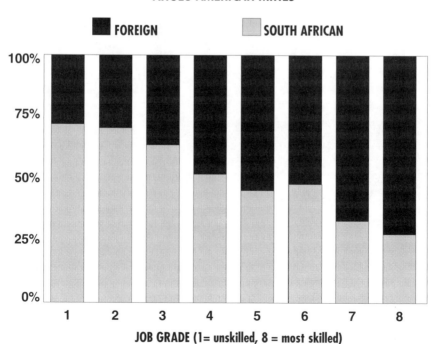

RESPONSE

DAVID COPLAN
Department of Social Anthropology,
University of Cape Town,
South Africa

Jonathan Crush and Alan Jeeves's contributions make me think of the French expression *"plus ça change, plus ça reste la meme chose"* – the more things change, the more they remain the same. The word "apartheid" comes immediately to mind – in the sense that it was a system, but not an entirely organised one.

Their papers outline the history of migrant labour in a way that makes clear the "systematised" nature of apartheid. It had its fractures, its internal contradictions and its ad hoceries, but it was not simply an odd patchwork of diabolical racist processes or practises.

The first paper points out the attempts to regulate labour and to continually control and undermine workers' alternatives. The implication of this is that whatever policy changes might be recommended, they must lead to more alternatives and greater flexibility.

Clearly now is a good time for innovation, for the people-centred transformation that Marcel Golding described. Transformation must aim to make life better for workers and not simply to continue a process of primitive accumulation at the expense of the majority of the population. Mine companies may still argue that they need to continue the process of primitive accumulation if they are to contribute to a successful new South Africa, but in reality, primitive accumulation takes place at the expense of black people in this country, and this must not be allowed to happen under the cover of financial discipline or any other guise.

While we do need financial discipline, we do not need sinister underlying strategies. We need innovations now, along the lines that Golding described. And we need to harmonise decency and economic justice with a viable economy.

Concerning the second paper, it seems that once again the contradictions within the apartheid government are still evident – with mine managers vacillating between the strategies of increasing internalisation of labour on the one hand and making greater use of foreign labour on the other. Yet it seems that both sides are being played off against the middle. The industry needs a large foreign complement of workers in order to deny South Africans their rights; and a large complement of South Africans in order to deny foreign workers their rights.

This diversity of supply is about choosing certain groups of workers at any given time in order to deny rights to other groups. I have observed the Basotho frequently used in this way because they can be repatriated and therefore cannot press their case. Sometimes management might want more Basotho because they can be used to undercut unity within organised labour, at other times they may become dispensable.

I would like to make a case for my Basotho friends – that they should continue to be employed. Mines should not be able to use the different kinds of perceptions, identities, plans, aspirations and projects of the different kinds of migrants to play both sides against the middle. When workers are thrown out of work, there is a tendency to rehire them at very low levels of pay and benefits, via labour contractors. These workers are then used to undercut the collective bargaining agreements the NUM has worked so hard to bring about.

Those rights are at risk. If we allow this sort of strategy to continue, the union is at risk and a decent South Africa for working people is at risk. To conclude, we certainly do need a coherent government policy, and, as Crush's paper implies, we need a certain kind of government intervention to bring about social and economic justice; this cannot be left to the market. If there is anything at all that our new government can do, it is to enforce or bring about fair labour practises. Workers must actually get what is protected by the Constitution and what is guaranteed by labour law. ◆

HOSTELS AND HOUSING

3

Housing as a Locus of Power

Ms Catherine Laburn-Peart
Department of Town and Regional Planning,
University of the Witwatersrand,
Johannesburg, South Africa

One of the most visible problems facing South Africa's newly elected Government of National Unity (GNU) is a country-wide crisis in housing. The elements of this crisis are: acute shortages of housing for those not classified white; affordability of low-income housing; availability of land for housing development to meet existing and projected needs; provision of infrastructure to service people at the lower end of the economic scale (SAIRR, 1989); and delivery of housing and housing finance.

A 1990 Urban Foundation study estimated that 1,8 million houses are needed to meet current shortages, with another 2,8 million needed by the year 2000 to accommodate projected population growth. This will require 400 000 units to be built each year, or approximately 1 096 units each day, at a cost of about R6,9 billion each year. This would represent 24 percent of gross domestic fixed investment at 1986 prices (SAIRR, 1992).

The National Housing Forum (NHF) pointed out in a 1993 study that the state spends only an estimated 2 percent of its annual budget on housing. The drain on the economy such an investment would make could only be made good by an annual growth rate of 17 percent, which is unrealistic given the current growth rate of 3 percent a year (SAIRR, 1992) and the Reconstruction and Development Programme's (RDP) projected growth rate of 5 percent. It is thus unlikely that the GNU will have the means to deal with the legacy of past neglect of housing provision for the poor. Past government policies expected the corporate economy and private industry to bear much of the responsibility for housing. However, with the election of a new national government, a great sense of expectation exists that houses will be built and that those who were previously excluded from the housing market will now somehow gain access to it.

There are few places in the world where systematic disempowerment is more evident than in South Africa, and none more so than in the mining industry and its hostels. Like all black people in South Africa, hostel residents have over the years been excluded from effective participation in the political and economic institutions of South Africa. But, in addition, the lives of mineworkers have been separated into mutually exclusive enclaves, and their living spaces, the single-sex hostels, "are neither acknowledged as legitimate extensions of the working environment nor defined as domestic space accessible to the families of those living there. For the majority of hostel dwellers, hostels have until recently represented non-decision areas" (Ramphele, 1993: 3). In the hostels most, if not all, potentially significant variables affecting the personal and working lives of the residents have been subjected to a hierarchy of command and control, a classic example of disempowerment. It is to the systematic disempowerment of mineworkers, through their lack of choice and alternatives in housing, that this paper now turns.

ENTITLEMENT AND THE CRISIS OF MINE HOUSING

For over a century, South Africa's economy has been dominated by the gold-mining industry, one of the largest employers of migrant labour in the country with a total work-force of about 500 000 in the late 1980s. This migrant system has operated since the first mines on the Witwatersrand were established, with the result that until very recently management and the state viewed mineworkers as temporary residents of urban industrial areas.

Migrants have traditionally been accommodated in single-sex, regimented, company-owned compounds or hostels, located close to the mine shafts on mine property. In the mid-1970s the mine hostels were racked by recurrent violence and disorder. Although the causes of mine conflict were complex, most observers agreed that the migrant labour system itself was heavily implicated, and that dissatisfaction with hostel accommodation was one of the major contributors to the problem. The largest mining corporations responded by upgrading some of their oldest hostels, building more rental housing units for married workers and designing new hostels in such a way that they could later be converted into married quarters.

The importance of housing issues increased with the unionisation of the work-force in the 1980s. Housing quickly became part of an overall management industrial relations strategy, and the establishment of the National Union of Mineworkers (NUM) in 1982 brought renewed pressure for more family accommodation to alleviate the worst effects of migrant labour. The NUM committed itself to the abolition of hostels, demanding "a broad range of flexible housing options which offer all workers the possibility of opting out of the migrant labour system, rather than a select few" (Motlatsi, 1987: 39-47).

Various reforms enacted by the state in the early 1980s significantly changed the housing policies of mine management. In 1983 the state finally recognised the permanence of African urbanisation, and introduced a 99-year leasehold system of tenure. The implications of this were that mining corporations could encourage their workers to buy rather than temporarily rent urban property. In 1986 the state abandoned many of its formal influx control regulations. Pass laws were repealed, and rights to permanent urban residence became dependent on access to approved housing. This meant that for the first time South African mineworkers could legally settle with their families in the townships close to the mines and were no longer restricted to single-sex hostel life.

INTRODUCTION OF HOME-OWNERSHIP SCHEMES

As a result of these changes, and because of considerable pressure from labour, mining corporations began to implement new housing policies. One such policy was home-ownership schemes for employees (Laburn-Peart, 1990). This involved either the development of a new village on mine property or, more preferable, negotiations with councils in existing townships near the mines for additional land for housing development. The mine would then encourage construction companies to build houses on this land for subsequent sale to qualifying mineworkers (married workers from South Africa, including the former homelands).

In 1986, soon after the launch of its scheme, the Anglo American Corporation commissioned a survey of the home-ownership market among all its qualifying black employees (Market Research Africa, 1986). The survey found that only 12 percent of the respondents knew that the company had launched a home-ownership scheme. Nevertheless, 34 percent of both married and unmarried interviewees were interested in moving permanently to the urban areas and acquiring homes. Half of the married men living in hostels said that they would like to bring their families with them; six out of 10 said that they would regard the move to town as permanent. On the basis of these findings, and without further consultation with individuals or union representatives about possible housing options, the corporation pressed ahead with its scheme, anticipating that as many as 13 000 workers would move to the new housing developments.

In terms of the scheme, the corporation secured agreements with building contractors for the construction of formal housing (Laburn-Peart, 1992). House prices ranged from R20 000 to R80 000. The corporation provided a heavily subsidised mortgage, reduced deposits from 5 percent to 2,5 percent of the purchase price, and pegged interest rates at 5 percent (paid off over 20 years). Workers were liable for the down payment (R500 on a R20 000 house), regular monthly mortgage payments, property taxes and maintenance costs. On termination of employment, the subsidies and benefits would fall away, leaving the home owners with the option to sell or repay the collateral as well as the mortgage at market rates (currently 13 to 16 percent).

The early results of the home-ownership scheme fell far short of management's optimistic forecasts. By October 1990, four years after the inception of the scheme and subsequent to further reforms by the De Klerk government, only 3 423 (less than 2 percent) of the corporation's 174 207 workers had joined the scheme. By December 1991 this figure had risen to only 2,85 percent.

There are a number of possible reasons for this unenthusiastic response among workers. The first and most obvious one is affordability. Given the notoriously low wages paid by the industry, even a very basic R20 000 house is too expensive for most mineworkers. In 1990 an NUM survey showed that 86 percent of the mine work-force could not afford the minimum price. In the current recessionary and inflationary climate, many of those who did join the scheme are now struggling to meet monthly mortgage payments. Respondents to a recent survey of home owners commented:

> (They should) decrease the amount of the bond because many people are having financial problems.

> Some people are not happy as they want to stay with their families, but they are fearful of being involved in paying the large amounts of bonds.

Another reason for the slow response to home-buying is linked to the burden of the past. Under apartheid, blacks in South Africa were disempowered and consistently denied both urban property rights and any form of residential choice. Hostels are part of this legacy of racial discrimination and economic exploitation. As a direct result of these discriminatory policies, neither the state nor the corporate economy felt obliged to provide housing or welfare benefits for families of migrant workers – "temporary sojourners" in urban areas. Under these circumstances, a culture of freehold individual property ownership failed to develop among migrants and their families. In the absence of alternatives, many mineworkers invested their wages in the overpopulated and impoverished rural reserves.

The migrant labour system allowed management to mistakenly assume that workers had viable, productive homes in the rural areas, and that migrants were "men of two worlds". The migrant labour system in fact offered workers no choice but to try to maintain their impoverished rural base as a place to which they could return between work contracts.

Communal land tenure predominates in most of the reserves, and this largely precludes accumulation through land purchase. However, communal tenure is only secure as long as the migrant or his family occupy the land. The home-ownership scheme effectively asks workers to abandon these traditional rural rights, and to cut their ties with the rural communities which are dependent on their remittances.

But the major reason for the failure of the scheme was the absence of consultation and participation – the continuing disempowerment of those most affected by the policy. Planners unilaterally designed and implemented the scheme, leaving no place for workers to exercise their own discretion. The NUM has demanded more flexibility in housing delivery, a greater variety of housing options, and cheaper and more accessible forms of housing finance. Had the corporation included consultation and negotiation in the planning process some of these issues might have been dealt with. The planners seem to have been ignorant of, or insensitive to, the real problems of affordability, the lack of a property ownership culture, existing commitments to rural and reserve areas and the need for participation in the planning process. Although these problems were identified as early as 1988, no action was taken to resolve them. The scheme as originally set up has been discontinued, and workers may now purchase houses through the NHF's first-time home-buyer's subsidy scheme.

It seems that the historical paternalistic planning ethos and power structure of the mining corporation has continued in the home-ownership scheme, and that corporate policy remains wedded to social control (Hunter, 1992). Having lived for so long in the total institution of the hostel, many new home owners have become accustomed to, and are dependent on, this paternalism through which, until very recently, "the mine" provided their basic needs of food, shelter and employment while they were away from their home base. This has continued to foster the culture of entitlement among the new home owners, some of whom expressed dismay and confusion when faced with costs and other obligations of home ownership. One employee interviewed in a study of the home-ownership scheme complained that "the mine has abandoned us" (Laburn-Peart, 1992). Others displayed misunderstandings in the matters of payment of rates to the local authority, or on transfer and other fees:

> Why do we still have to pay "rent" when we have bought the house?
> They should take care of facilities, like lights and water, because we also pay our bond promptly.

> We are not secure because the sales lady has now vanished. I am also confused because the bank's price was R53 000 and the contract price is R61 000 – so up to now I don't know what the real price is.

Many of the new home owners thus feel disillusioned with the home-ownership scheme, since to them the costs of home ownership outweigh the so-called benefits of tenure. The corporation may have tried to adopt a more socially responsible housing policy since the 1980s, which included the philosophy that career-minded mineworkers should be entitled to decent housing conditions, but the implicit assumption of the planners was that a detached, westernised house was the only acceptable form of accommodation.

Few mining executives contemplated the idea of allowing workers to have discretionary choice in the type of housing or of encouraging the much-needed development of a wider range of housing alternatives. No finance was made available under the home-ownership scheme for those who may have wanted to build their own structures. The corporation's policy also did not extend to low-cost site-and-service or self-help housing.

So the conclusion must be that merely erecting family housing units to replace existing hostels has not changed the nature of power relationships between those involved. The obligations of both the state and the corporation should not necessarily have been to build structures, but rather to have enabled workers to gain access to resources so long denied them, to create opportunities and to remove obstacles. Ramphele believes that "barriers to full participation by hostel dwellers in the planning ... programme should be removed, so that they (can) experience a sense of control over this area of their lives. (In this sense) empowerment ... is a process of acknowledging the humanity of those people who have been systematically dehumanised, thereby enabling them to stand up and challenge the status quo" (1993: 124). She further points out that while both the state and the corporate economy do have a major role to play, the individual also has to accept ultimate responsibility for successful performance: "Failure to ensure individual responsibility could lead to a situation in which society (or the corporation) would be seen as the agent for change, thereby disempowering the individual."

Hostels have historically been disempowering. They are institutions, not homes. There is no sense of choice or ownership, let alone responsibility for these environments, among those who live in them. But attempts to unilaterally move away from this type of company housing through the building of new houses in terms of the mine's home-ownership scheme have also become disempowering, for there has been almost no choice there either. Thousands of hostel workers have therefore rejected both hostel life and the expensive option of the corporation's home-ownership scheme by moving their families into informal settlements around townships near the mines. Few workers are inclined to live or house their families in scheme houses when cheaper, if more crowded, alternatives are available in existing townships. Regardless of state and company policy on urbanisation and housing, therefore, mineworkers have taken the initiative and empowered themselves. They have developed, and are likely to continue to develop, their own strategies and made their own decisions about where they live, and about the acquisition of affordable housing and shelter (Crush et al, 1992).

CONCLUSION

South Africans have to acknowledge the legacy of apartheid which, among many other evils, has generated a culture of dependency and of entitlement which will need to be overcome and transformed into one of choice and empowerment (Friedmann, 1992). For too long planners in this country have tried to hide behind an apolitical technical front, merely implementing state and corporate policy, but in so doing they have become associated with, and part of, the machinery of apartheid. There will be a great temptation to continue to do this under the RDP. Yet national transformation is going to result in demands for participation in the planning process and, in particular, participation by those formerly disempowered.

Implicit in this paper has been a criticism of the culture of entitlement, and the fact that, as defined by Ramphele (1993), this can perpetuate disempowerment. But there is, of course, an appropriate place for the culture of entitlement: if we are to be part of the transformation of this country and its mining industry, we must recognise that citizens and workers are entitled to make decisions over things which affect their lives and the lives of their families. We must foster this aspect of entitlement for the empowerment which it will bring will contribute to the transformation of power relations within both the industry and the country as a whole. ◆

REFERENCES

Crush, J, W James and AH Jeeves. 1992. "Introduction," in Labour, Capital and Society, Vol 25, No 1.

Davidoff, P and TA Reiner. 1962. "A choice theory of planning," in Journal of the American Institute of Planners, Vol 28, No 3.

Friedmann, J. 1992. Empowerment: The Politics of Alternative Development. Cambridge: Blackwell.

Hamdi, N. 1991. Housing without Houses: Participation, Flexibility, Enablement. New York: Van Nostrand Reinhold.

Hodge, N (ed). 1987. Killing a Man's Pride and Other Short Stories. Johannesburg: Ravan Press.

Hunter, P. 1992. "Housing, hostels and migrancy: a case study of accommodation practices at JCI's gold mines," in Labour, Capital and Society, Vol 25, No 1.

Laburn-Peart, CM. 1990. "Home-ownership schemes for black mineworkers: overestimating and underplanning," in Urban Forum, Vol 25, No 1.

Laburn-Peart, CM. 1992. "Transforming mine housing in South Africa: the Anglo American home-ownership scheme," in Labour, Capital and Society, Vol 25, No 1.

Market Research Africa. 1986. Accommodation Study, Target Group Report. No 1, Johannesburg.

Motlatsi, J. 1987. "1987 – the year mineworkers take control," in South African Labour Bulletin, Vol 12.

National Housing Forum. 1993. NHF Newsletter, No 4.

National Union of Mineworkers. 1990. Final Housing Survey. Johannesburg: NUM.

Ramphele, M. 1993. A Bed Called Home: Life in the Migrant Labour Hostels of Cape Town. Cape Town: David Philip.

South African Institute of Race Relations. 1988, 1989 and 1990. Annual Survey. Johannesburg: SAIRR.

Urban Foundation. 1990. Urban Debate 2010: Policies for a New Urban Future. Johannesburg: Urban Foundation.

4

VIOLENT CONFLICT IN MINE HOSTELS: POST-1990

DR ANTHONY MINNAAR
Conflict & Reconstruction Studies,
Centre for Socio-Political Analysis,
Human Sciences Research Council,
Pretoria, South Africa

High levels of conflict and violence between residents of public sector or industrial company-owned hostels and township residents have, since 1990, been specifically politically motivated. Stark battle lines have been drawn not only in territorial terms but also in terms of ongoing political competition, the struggle for resources, criminal activity and ethnic/tribal differences. Conflict has also been linked to calls for the demolition of these hostels.

Since 1990 a number of mine companies have feared that this kind of political violence would be exported to "their" mine hostels. Conflict in mine hostels, however, has revolved around right-wing militancy, racism, ethnicity and the launching of certain politically aligned unions at some mines.

QUANTIFYING HOSTELS IN SOUTH AFRICA

A Human Sciences Research Council (HSRC) study on hostels undertaken for the Goldstone Commission of Inquiry (completed in March 1993) identified 583 hostels countrywide (207 owned or controlled by municipalities/local authorities/provincial administrations and 333 privately owned, including mine hostels (Appendix A). Excluding those owned by the Anglo American Corporation (AAC), 63 hostels in the Transvaal qualified as mine hostels, 11 in Natal, 13 in the Orange Free State and 10 in the Cape (Appendix B). The AAC owns 35 hostels in its gold-mining division and eight in its coal-mining division (AAC refused to name or specify locations). This brings to 140 the total number of mine hostels in South Africa.

The exact number of hostel beds in South Africa cannot be pinpointed with complete accuracy. In 1991 the Department of Local Government & National Housing gave a total of 308 345 beds in the 402 hostels listed with them. According to the department, the Transvaal has the greatest number of hostel beds – 207 158 – followed by 50 158 in the Cape, 26 125 in Natal and 24 904 in the Orange Free State. A 1992 Council for Scientific and Industrial Research survey counted 529 784 beds for all hostels in South Africa, with a total of 312 581 beds for the former PWV region, which constitutes 59 percent of the total number of beds countrywide. The actual number of hostel residents in South Africa cannot be accurately counted either. Most beds are used for shift sleeping which means the total number of hostel residents could be more than a million.

BACKGROUND TO POLITICAL VIOLENCE AT HOSTELS

HOSTEL/TOWNSHIP CONFLICTS

Although there has always been a certain amount of social tension between hostel and township residents, the present conflict stems from mid-1990 after the unbanning of organisations like the ANC and the PAC. In the first six months after the unbanning, the ANC in particular established numerous branches in the townships. At the same time, trade unions and civic associations called for the eviction of hostel residents in order to create accommodation for returning exiles (Minnaar, 1993a).

The stayaway called by the Congress of South African Trade Unions (Cosatu) on 2 July 1990 to protest against the high levels of violence in KwaZulu/Natal considerably increased tensions on the Witwatersrand. Allied to this, a number of pro-ANC organisations such as the South African Youth Congress (Sayco) declared Inkatha, the Zulu cultural movement largely based in Natal, and its leader, Chief Gatsha Buthelezi, "enemies of the people". As a result, many Inkatha officials in the Transvaal were attacked and their houses fire-bombed (Seekings, 1991: 11).

In July 1990 Inkatha became the Inkatha Freedom Party (IFP). In an effort to gain more support it launched a number of branches in the Transvaal. It also started a recruitment campaign in the hostels which represented a natural power base as the majority of hostel residents were Zulu speakers. Hostel life tends to foster a group identity, and the IFP emphasised this sense of Zulu nationalism in its campaigns. The hostels became, not only centres for recruitment of Zulu-speaking residents, but also centres for political mobilisation.

During this recruitment and mobilisation period the IFP held a number of rallies. At one of them, held at the end of July 1990 in the East Rand township of

Thokoza, many participants were taunted by radical township youth. On their return from the rally, hostel residents indiscriminately attacked residents of Thokoza in retaliation for the insults they had received and a number of township residents were killed. This attack is considered to be the start of the Witwatersrand township war in areas like Katorus – the adjacent townships of Katlehong, Thokoza and Vosloorus on the Transvaal East Rand.

Various factors intensified this violence. The ongoing community struggles, particularly rent and consumer boycotts and work stayaways, often crystallised existing antagonisms between township inhabitants and hostel residents into stark battle lines. The public call for either the demolition of the hostels or their conversion into family units was seen by hostel residents as a ploy to destroy the IFP's power base in the hostels. IFP supporters also regarded these demands as an economic attack, as many of the Zulu-speaking migrant workers retain a piece of land in the homelands allocated to them by the local chief. If they brought their families to live in the urban areas they would lose their right to this land.

Furthermore, they feared that if the hostels were turned into family units, accommodation would be allocated to those workers already living with their wives and families in the nearby informal settlements. The hostel residents reasoned they would be evicted. With their accommodation would go their jobs, and they would be forced back to the homelands where there was no work.

Under these circumstances, attacks by township youths on the hostels, or on any hostel residents visiting shebeens or shops in the townships or travelling to work, were perceived by hostel residents as a direct threat. The hostel residents retaliated by targeting squatter settlements, which they believed presented the greatest challenge.

In the early stages of the Witwatersrand township war the IFP mobilised support by declaring that the calls for the demolition of the hostels were a direct threat to the hostel residents' "Zuluness" and therefore an attack on the Zulu nation. This mobilisation led to the expulsion from the hostels of many non-supporters of the IFP, who sought refuge in the surrounding squatter settlements. Since many migrants saw the ANC as a Xhosa-dominated organisation, and as the calls for demolition came from ANC-aligned organisations like the civic associations and the unions, Xhosa-dominated areas were targeted for attack.

At the same time, Zulu-speaking township residents, many of whom were not IFP supporters, were attacked by ANC "comrades" and were forced to seek refuge in the IFP-dominated hostels. Some of these hostels, originally designed as single-sex quarters, had to accommodate whole families. Many who had lived peacefully in the townships for years found themselves under attack just because they spoke Zulu. Some of them forcibly evicted township residents from the houses near to the hostels and moved in.

At the time of this study, hostels in the East Rand townships, particularly in the Katorus area, were practically under siege with no food deliveries unless under police or South African Defence Force escort. Large areas of the townships had become no-go areas for either political party – ANC or IFP. A state of perpetual armed conflict was in place. Opposing and armed combatants were engaged in defending their territory in this war zone, and people were dying on a regular basis. The proliferation of armaments has been astonishing – traditional spears, bushknives (*pangas*), home-made guns (*qwashas*), shotguns and automatic assault rifles like AK-47s and R1s. Grenades, mortars and rockets have also been used in attacks.

The four years since 1990 have been marked by retaliatory or revenge attacks between hostel residents and township residents. These have been interspersed with political assassinations, massacres, train attacks and taxi wars. During marches, stayaways and boycotts, houses have been fire-bombed and intimidators have been active. Both sides claim to be justified in arming themselves and repulsing any attacks.

Similar dynamics operate in the political violence in Natal. Workers who migrate to town from rural areas under Inkatha chiefs (chiefs are appointed by the KwaZulu government and loyalty to Inkatha is often a prerequisite) usually stay in the single-sex hostels. They are invariably assumed to be IFP supporters. The townships are likely to be controlled by ANC-aligned civic associations. Calls for loyalty to the ANC place the local hostel residents in a difficult position. They argue that they cannot be ANC supporters during the week and IFP supporters at weekends when they return home. They fear expulsion from the tribal area and the loss of their property and land if they do. If the local Inkatha chief suspects them of supporting the ANC they can even be killed. The hostel residents therefore refused to support the civics and so became the targets for abuse and sometimes physical attack by the comrades. Hostel residents have launched retaliatory or revenge attacks on the township residents, often killing women and children.

In this way a cycle of revenge was set in motion. The violence between IFP-supporting hostel residents and ANC-aligned civics and comrades has become a common feature of areas such as Bruntville and around the Umlazi and KwaMashu hostels near Durban (Minnaar, 1992; Zulu, 1992).

TAXI WARS AND TRAIN ATTACKS
One of the issues central to the hostel/township conflict is transport. In most Witwatersrand townships there are two minibus taxi associations – a local and a long-distance service. Some of the latter are Natal-based and financed. Long-distance Natal-based taxi associations ply the lucrative "home run" route, transporting migrants to and from the rural areas for weekend or monthly visits. When drivers found themselves idle during the week they began to transport hostel residents to work. This of course meant they were encroaching on the local taxi associations, who clearly resented this economic competition. Since these Natal-based associations mainly transported Zulu-speaking hostel residents they became associated politically with the IFP. The local taxi associations were linked with the township civics and, by extension, the ANC. The economic competition therefore was politicised.

With the escalation of the hostel/township violence after mid-1990, local associations began to suspect some of the long-distance operators of smuggling illegal firearms in their taxis, and began to single them out for attack. Long-distance operators began arming themselves (often with illegal guns) for protection. Rumours of an impending attack on long-distance operators would sometimes lead to pre-emptive attacks on rival local operators – and so the "taxi wars" began (Minnaar, 1993b; Minnaar and Torres, 1993).

Train attacks were another spin-off of this war. Hostel residents often retaliated by attacking train commuters, on the basis that all township residents were their enemies. After the assassination of ANC and South African Communist Party leader Chris Hani in April 1993 many of the rail lines serving the hostels were sabotaged, disrupting the transport of many hostel residents to and from work. This led in turn to an increase in the number of tit-for-tat attacks on township taxi passengers.

MINE HOSTEL CONFLICTS

Since 1990 conflict and violence has also flared in mine hostels. Mineworkers living in hostels close to high-conflict townships suffered the same fate as other migrant hostel residents. They found themselves denied access to township activities, sports functions, shops or *shebeens*, and experienced the same difficulties in using taxi transport. Like other Zulu-speaking hostel residents, Zulu mineworkers had the same concerns about losing their access to the single-sex hostels. They also preferred to retain their links with the rural areas where their families were accommodated.

Hostel accommodation has long been an issue with the National Union of Mineworkers (NUM). At its 1989 congress it passed a resolution demanding that control of mine hostels be handed over to the mineworkers. Hostel accommodation and the discriminatory allocation of family housing on the mines continue to be contentious issues.

In addition, the ongoing political competition between the IFP and the ANC has exacerbated the situation, in particular at mines where there is a Zulu-speaking contingent. The political rivalry is further complicated by the IFP's mobilisation around the notion of "Zuluness" which has intensified existing conflict along ethnic lines.

Furthermore, the penetration by the IFP-aligned trade union, the United Workers' Union of South Africa (Uwusa), into certain mines and its attempts to recruit members has increased political tensions not only between IFP and ANC supporters but between Uwusa and the NUM and other affiliates of the ANC-supporting Cosatu.

Another political issue for certain mine hostel residents is the militancy of white right wingers in areas such as the Orange Free State and western Transvaal, and blatant racism by white mineworkers toward fellow black miners.

During the NUM defiance campaign of March 1990, at the St Helena gold mine in Welkom, Orange Free State, there were numerous violent attacks on black miners, allegedly by right-wing vigilantes. In August 1990 the President Steyn gold mine in Welkom (No 4 shaft) was briefly closed following an outbreak of racial violence between black and white miners which left four dead and 18 injured. These racial attacks hastened the deliberations of a joint working group established by the NUM and the Chamber of Mines (COM). In November 1990 this committee drafted a race relations charter aimed at ending racism in the mining industry. One of the most important demands was for the allocation of resources to eliminate racial inequalities in the industry. Among other things, this meant training black mineworkers in skills that until the early 1990s had been closed to them by the colour bar included in the old Mines and Works Act. This charter was particularly important in that it was the first time that mine owners officially acknowledged that racism was a feature of the mining industry. Before this, they had consistently argued that their industry had been in the forefront of fighting racism.

'ETHNIC' CONFLICTS AND 'FACTION FIGHTS': POST-1990

Besides racism, the other prevailing factor in mine conflict, and one which has traditionally been cited by mine owners as the "sole" cause of conflict on certain mines, is ethnicity. However, a closer examination of such "ethnic" incidents of violence often reveals a political origin. Because mine management believed that faction fights were a result of the mineworkers' strong traditional tribal associations, miners were housed separately in the compounds along ethnic lines. These arrangements, management hoped, would not only prevent faction fights but would also prevent the mineworkers from forming a united front against management to enforce future demands.

This policy was officially abandoned by the gold-mining companies only in the 1970s. However, some mine companies continued to recruit men from particular areas for specific hostels. Furthermore, some mine managements still appointed *indunas* or tribal headmen on to hostel or liaison committees, thereby entrenching aspects of tribalism. The result has been a continuation of ethnically-driven conflict and a number of such faction fights erupted at various mine hostels during the 1990s.

One of the most serious clashes happened in September 1990 when allegedly ethnic conflict at the Durban Navigation Colliery (Durnacol) near Dundee in northern Natal left one worker dead and several injured. As a result, 1 500 Xhosa mineworkers were sent home to the Transkei for an eight-week "cooling off" period. This did not prevent ethnic tensions from spreading to other mine hostels in the area and a month later 10 miners were killed and 52 injured in sustained attacks on the Xhosa-speaking mineworkers' hostel at Iscor's Hlobane mine near Vryheid. The day after this clash, 350 Xhosa and Pondo workers fled the mine hostel and returned to their homes in the Transkei and Ciskei. Although management at the Hlobane mine had said that they were free to return at any time to apply for vacancies, the mine almost immediately began recruiting local Zulu speakers.

The NUM ascribed the violence at the Durnacol and Hlobane mines to deliberate attacks by Zulu-speaking IFP supporters on Xhosa-speaking miners. The union alleged that the attacks were part of an attempt by IFP leaders and the police to drive Cosatu activists and supporters from the area. However, IFP leaders maintained that the violence had its roots in rumours that Chief Buthelezi and the Zulu king, Goodwill Zwelethini, had been insulted by Xhosa miners failing to attend a rally addressed by them two months earlier. In response the NUM said that these rumours had been deliberately spread in order to sow dissent among Xhosa-speaking and Zulu-speaking miners in the area. Clearly these divisions were being exploited by certain people for political gain.

In addition, the NUM linked the clashes at Durnacol and Hlobane to the ongoing strike by miners at Iscor's Sishen, Thabazimbi and Grootegeluk mines. On the instructions of local IFP leaders, most of the Zulu-speaking miners had refused to participate in the strike for wage demands. This refusal was in line with the IFP's well publicised opposition to economic disruptions such as work stayaways, strikes and consumer boycotts.

In the aftermath of the violence at Durnacol the NUM called for the disarming of all Zulu miners, the disciplining of all instigators and their removal from mine property. They also demanded that all those miners driven from the mine by the conflict would be guaranteed re-employment. The mine conflict in northern Natal did have an element of ethnic rivalry (the attackers had shouted Zulu war slogans during the attack at Hlobane, and only known Xhosa-speakers were targeted by the attackers), but ongoing political mobilisation and economic competition had also played a role. At the time there had been considerable local resentment of "foreigners" and "outsiders" taking scarce jobs away from Zulu locals.

Also contributing to the conflict was the NUM call for mining companies to do away with hostels altogether. The NUM argued that miners living with their families should be integrated into the surrounding communities which would reduce the possibility of conflict. The NUM maintained that poor hostel conditions were the breeding grounds for intra-hostel conflicts, which were then labelled as ethnic or resulting from political antagonisms. Most mine companies insisted that the answer was not to destroy the hostel system but to improve the existing accommodation. Some mining houses hoped that subsidised home-ownership schemes would eventually lead to the depopulation of existing hostels, but for most, as long as there were single labourers seeking temporary work away from home, hostels would continue to be a feature of mining life.

Such "ethnic faction fighting" as took place at Durnacol in 1990 was widespread elsewhere. In the same month (October 1990) fighting between Xhosas and Basothos left nine miners dead and 42 injured at the Harmony gold mine hostel No 2 near Virginia in the Orange Free State.

The following year also saw its fair share of "faction fights" where ethnic rivalry was given as the initial cause of the violence. In August and September 1991 fighting broke out at the Wildebeestfontein North and Bafokeng North hostels of Impala Platinum's Bafokeng mine in what was then the homeland of Bophuthatswana. This fighting between Tswanas and Basothos left 19 miners dead and 26 injured. According to a mine spokesperson the fighting had started when some miners wanted to continue striking while others wanted to return to work.

Far more extensive "ethnic" violence occurred later in the year at the President Steyn gold mine in Welkom. After a week of attacks a total of 76 miners were killed and 180 injured. The presence of firearms was an ominous development and was linked to the increasing proliferation and accessibility of illegal firearms elsewhere in South Africa (Minnaar, 1994b).

In the aftermath of these bloody clashes the owners of the mine, Anglo American, sent all the miners back to their homes for a compulsory "cooling off" period.

Anglo American management requested the newly appointed Goldstone Commission to investigate the violence. However, then-President FW de Klerk blamed the NUM for the violence, saying it had "unilaterally called a stayaway which had nothing to do with employer-employee relations". He accused union members of widespread intimidation which he felt played a large role in the ensuing tensions and conflict. Cosatu and the NUM responded by blaming the hostel system which they said promoted and exacerbated tensions between residents. They also accused Anglo American of forcibly separating the mineworkers into hostel blocks along ethnic lines in order to deliberately bring the ethnic factor into the conflict. The NUM insisted that "the attempts to present the violence as a product of tribal tensions was simply a screen to cover the hidden hand in the violence".

In renewed violence at the mine at the end of November another 13 miners were killed and 35 injured. On the night of 24 November, miners who had returned from their compulsory "cooling off" period were attacked while they slept. The NUM alleged that the attackers had been allowed entry into the mine hostel through the connivance of certain mine security officials and did not have letters of identification. Mine management denied any such involvement.

Subsequently, in evidence laid before the Goldstone Commission, the NUM also accused certain mine security personnel of smuggling firearms to Basotho in the hostels prior to the violent clashes, and alleged that the attackers had been bused to the hostel. These attackers were also identified as belonging to the "Russians" gang – a criminal gang associated with Basotho from the nearby Thabong township.

The violent conflict at the President Steyn mine showed quite clearly that the underlying dynamics are multi-causal. While the symptoms are expressed in ethnic terms, the causes are usually intertwined with each other and cover a wide range of possible factors.

While mine hostels remain in use and their residents are drawn from differing tribal and cultural backgrounds, the nature of political competition in South Africa will in all probability ensure that violent conflict will continue at certain mine hostels. ◆

REFERENCES

Goldstone Commission. 1991. Report by the Commission of Inquiry into Public Violence and Intimidation into the Violent Events at the President Steyn Gold Mine, Welkom during November 1991.

McNamara, JK. 1985. Black Worker Conflicts on South African Gold Mines, 1973-1982, PhD dissertation, University of the Witwatersrand.

Minnaar, A. 1992. "Locked in a cycle of violence: the anatomy of conflict in Bruntville (1990-1992)," in A Minnaar, (ed,) Patterns of Violence: Case Studies of Conflict In Natal. Pretoria: HSRC.

Minnaar, A. 1993a. "Hostels and violent conflict on the Witwatersrand," in A Minnaar, (ed,) Communities in Isolation: Perspectives on Hostels in South Africa. Pretoria: HSRC.

Minnaar, A. 1993b. "Putting brakes on taxi wars," in Focus, Vol 2, No 6, July/August: 22-24.

Minnaar, A. 1993c. "East Rand townships under siege," in Indicator SA, Vol 10, No 4: 67-70.

Minnaar, A. 1993d. "'A tale of two hostels': hostel/township conflict in Bruntville and eSikhawini," unpublished research paper.

Minnaar, A. 1994a. "The arms of babes: an examination of the role and future of SDUs," Conflict Supplement, in Indicator SA, Vol 11, No 2: 2-5.

Minnaar, A. 1994b. "Guns galore!: the proliferation of illegal and other firearms," Conflict Supplement, in Indicator SA, Vol 11, No 3.

Minnaar, A and S Torres. 1993. "Riding the tiger: the taxi wars," in Indicator SA, Vol 11, No 1: 61-64.

Seekings, J. 1991. "Hostel hostilities: township wars on the Witwatersrand," in Indicator SA, Vol 8, No 3: 11-15.

Segal, L. 1991. "The human face of violence: hostel residents speak," in Journal of Southern African Studies, Vol 18, No 1, March: 190-231.

Union Government of South Africa. UG 37/1914. "Verslag van het onderzoek in zake naturelle-grieven, 1913-1914," Cape Town: Government Printer.

Zulu, P. 1992. "Hostels in the Greater Durban area: a case study of the KwaMashu and Umlazi hostels," In A Minnaar, (ed,) Communities in Isolation: Perspectives on Hostels in South Africa. Pretoria: HSRC.

APPENDIX A: HOSTELS IN SOUTH AFRICA: TOTALS

TRANSVAAL

Municipal/local authorities/provincial administration	109
Privately owned	102
Total:	**211**

NATAL

Municipal/local authorities/provincial administration	29
Privately owned	16
Total:	**45**

OFS

Municipal/local authorities/provincial administration	28
Privately owned	44
Total:	**72**

CAPE

Municipal/local authorities/provincial administration	41
Privately owned	171
Total:	**212**

TOTALS

Total: Municipal/local authorities/provincial administration	207
Total: Privately owned	333
Anglo-American Mines	43
Grand Total:	**583**

*This list is incomplete since not all privately owned hostels register themselves with local authorities. In addition, certain mining companies were reluctant to supply full figures or locations.

APPENDIX B:
LIST OF MINE HOSTELS IN SOUTH AFRICA

DISTRICT/NAME	SITE	BED/RESIDENT	OWNER
TRANSVAAL			
BARBERTON			
BARBERTON	AGNES GOLDMINE	335	E TVL CONSOLIDATED (ANGLOVAAL)
BARBERTON	NEWCONSORT	462	E TVL CONSOLIDATED (ANGLOVAAL)
BOKSBURG			
ANGELO	BOKSBURG	3 500	RANDGOLD
CENTRAL	BOKSBURG	5 000	RANDGOLD
CINDERELLA	BOKSBURG	5 722	RANDGOLD
FAR EAST	BOKSBURG	2 304	RANDGOLD
CULLINAN			
PREMIER	CULLINAN	1 255	DE BEERS
DELMAS			
DELMAS	DELMAS COALMINE	620	GENMIN (TRANSNATAL)
EASTERN CHROME MINE	DELMAS SILICA	90	SAMANCOR
ELLISRAS			
GROOTEGELUK	GROOTEGELUK COALMINE	1 542	ISCOR
EVANDER			
KINROSS GOLDMINE 1 & 2	KINROSS	*	GENMIN GOLD
LESLIE GOLDMINE	LESLIE	*	GENMIN GOLD
WINKELHAAK GOLDMINE	EVANDER	*	GENMIN GOLD
GERMISTON			
SOUTH WEST	GERMISTON	4 500	RANDGOLD
JOHANNESBURG			
VILLAGE MAIN	JOHANNESBURG	640	ANGLOVAAL
KLERKSDORP			
HOSTEL 2	HARTEBEESTFONTEIN	3 130	ANGLOVAAL
HOSTEL 4	HARTEBEESTFONTEIN	5 000	ANGLOVAAL
HOSTEL 5	HARTEBEESTFONTEIN	2 770	ANGLOVAAL
HOSTEL 6	HARTEBEESTFONTEIN	4 560	ANGLOVAAL
HOSTEL 7	HARTEBEESTFONTEIN	3 700	ANGLOVAAL
KRUGERSDORP			
MMC	KRUGERSDORP	*	SAMANCOR
PALMIET FERROCHROME	KRUGERSDORP	*	SAMANCOR
LYDENBURG			
TUBATSE FERROCHROME	LYDENBURG	*	SAMANCOR
MIDDELBURG			
MIDDELBURG	NALEDI	504	RANDCOAL
FERROCHROME	MIDDELBURG	*	SAMANCOR
NABOOMSPRUIT			
BUFFALO HOSTEL	BUFFALO FLUORSPAN	134	SAMANCOR
NELSPRUIT			
MMC	NELSPRUIT	*	SAMANCOR
OBERHOLZER			
BLYVOORTUITZICHT 1	CARLETONVILLE	3 904	RANDGOLD
BLYVOORTUITZICHT 2	CARLETONVILLE	1 864	RANDGOLD
PIET RETIEF			
PIET RETIEF	SAVMORE	250	GENMIN (TRANSNATAL)
POLANDSHOPE			
POLANDSHOPE	OPTIMUM COALMINE	900	GENMIN
PRETORIA			
LYTELLTON DOLOMITE	VERWOERDBURG	*	SAMANCOR

ROODEPOORT

DURBAN ROODE'PRT DEEP D	ROODEPOORT	2 476	RANDGOLD
DURBAN ROODEP'RT DEEP E	ROODEPOORT	1 576	RANDGOLD

RUSTENBURG

BAFOKENG NORTH	BAFOKENG	8 000	IMPALA PLATINUM (GENMIN)
BAFOKENG SOUTH	BAFOKENG	6 000	IMPALA PLATINUM (GENMIN)
WILDEBEESFONTEIN NORTH	WILDEBEESFONTEIN	10 000	IMPALA PLATINUM (GENMIN)
WILDEBEESFONTEIN SOUTH	WILDEBEESFONTEIN	4 000	IMPALA PLATINUM (GENMIN)
WESTERN CHROME MINES	MOOINOOI	*	SAMANCOR
JABULA	RUSTENBURG	3 500	JCI
KANANA	RUSTENBURG	2 900	JCI
ENTAMBENI HOSTEL	RUSTENBURG	4 000	JCI
C-HOSTEL	RUSTENBURG	1 000	JCI
PHULA HOSTEL	RUSTENBURG	3 800	JCI
B-HOSTEL	RUSTENBURG	1 000	JCI
BLESKOP HOSTEL	RUSTENBURG	3 800	JCI
RUIGHOEK	RUIGHOEK	*	SAMANCOR

SPRINGS

GROOTVLEI	SPRINGS	*	GENMIN GOLDMINES

STANDERTON

KRIEL	MATLA	1 400	GENMIN (TRANSNATAL)

STILFONTEIN

BUFFELSFONTEIN	STILFONTEIN	*	GENMIN GOLDMINES

STEELPOORT

LAVINO CHROME MINE	STEELPOORT	165	ANGLOVAAL
EASTERN CHROME MINES	STEELPOORT	*	SAMANCOR

THABAZIMBI

THABAZIMBI	THABAZIMBI MINE	1 087	ISCOR
THABAZIMBI	RHINO ANDALUSITE	150	ANGLOVAAL

WITBANK

KROONFONTEIN 1 & 2	BLINKPAN	1 400	GENMIN (TRANSNATAL)
TWEEFONTEIN COLLIERY	OGIES	12 000	LONRHO
WITBANK CONSOLIDATED	OGIES	650	LONRHO
WITBANK	DOUGLAS SECTION	1 456	RANDCOAL
RIETSPRUIT	RIETSPRUIT		
	OPENCAST SERVICES	448	RANDCOAL
KHUTALA	OGIES	1 011	RANDCOAL
LESEDI	DUVHA OPENCAST	526	RANDCOAL
WOLWEKRANS	WOLWEKRANS SECTION	335	RANDCOAL
X - SINGLE QUARTERS	VAN DYKSDRIF SECTION	1 320	RANDCOAL
Y - SINGLE QUARTERS	VAN DYKSDRIF SECTION	1 048	RANDCOAL

NATAL
HATTINGSPRUIT

HATTINGSPRUIT	SPRINGLAKE	*	KANGRA

NEWCASTLE

HOSTEL NO 2	DURNACOL COALMINE	NOT IN USE	ISCOR
HOSTEL NO 3	DURNACOL COALMINE	60 (SINCE 1991)	ISCOR
HOSTEL NO 5	DURNACOL COALMINE	*	ISCOR

PAULPIETERSBURG

PAULPIETERSBURG	LONGRIDGE	*	KANGRA

VRYHEID

HLOBANE 1	HLOBANE MINE	1 192	ISCOR
HLOBANE 3	HLOBANE MINE	1 328	ISCOR
VRYHEID	ALPHA ANTHROCYTE	250	LONRHO

ULUNDI			
ULUNDI	ZULULAND ANTHRACITE COLLIERY	500	GENMIN (TRANSNATAL)
UTRECH			
ZIMBUTU	WELGEDACHT EXPLORATION	258	RANDCOAL
UMGALA	WELGEDACHT EXPLORATION	748	RANDCOAL
OFS			
KOFFIEFONTEIN			
KOFFIEFONTEIN	KOFFIEFONTEIN	96	DE BEERS
ODENDAALSRUS			
LORAINE 1	ODENDAALSRUS	3 444	ANGLOVAAL
LORAINE 2	ODENDAALSRUS	3 500	ANGLOVAAL
THEUNISSEN			
THEUNISSEN	BEATRIX MINE	*	GENMIN GOLDMINES
THEUNISSEN	ORIX MINE	*	GENMIN GOLDMINES
VIRGINIA			
HARMONY GOLD MINE H2	VIRGINIA	6 632	RANDGOLD
HARMONY GOLD MINE H3	VIRGINIA	6 604	RANDGOLD
HARMONY GOLD MINE H4	VIRGINIA	3 960	RANDGOLD
HARMONY GOLD MINE V1	VIRGINIA	3 366	RANDGOLD
HARMONY GOLD MINE V2	VIRGINIA	3 740	RANDGOLD
HARMONY GOLD MINE M3	VIRGINIA	4 624	RANDGOLD
WELKOM			
ST HELENA GOLD MINE 1 & 2	ST HELENA GOLDMINE	*	GENMIN GOLDMINE
UNISEL GOLD MINE	UNISEL GOLDMINE	*	GENMIN GOLDMINE
CAPE			
KIMBERLEY			
DU TOITSPAN	KIMBERLEY	248	DE BEERS
FINSCH	LIMEACRES	378	DE BEERS
KURUMAN			
HOTAZEL	KURUMAN	*	SAMANCOR
NAMAQUALAND			
KLEINZEE	NAMAQUALAND	841	DE BEERS
KOINGNAAS	NAMAQUALAND	318	DE BEERS
POSTMASBURG			
BEESHOEK	SUIDELIKE PLASE	115	ACCOC. MANGANESE (ANGLOVAAL)
BLACKROCK	NOORDELIKE PLASE	1 130	ACCOC. MANGANESE (ANGLOVAAL)
SISHEN			
SESHENG HOSTEL	SISHEN IRON ORE MINE	1 896	ISCOR

ANGLO AMERICAN MINES		
GOLD DIVISION	35 HOSTELS	153 000 BEDS
COAL DIVISION	8 HOSTELS	7 846 BEDS

* = No. unavailable

Note: This list is incomplete since certain companies, such as the AAC, declined to give information. Others, such as Genmin and Samancor, supplied information on location but not size.

RESIDENTS' VIEWS IN THREE MINE HOSTELS

MS CATHARINE PAYZE
Conflict & Reconstruction Studies,
Centre for Socio-Political Analysis,
Human Sciences Research Council,
Pretoria, South Africa

The migrant labour system has to a large extent become synonymous with poor living conditions in mine hostels. This chapter examines the living conditions at three mine hostels – a gold, coal and diamond-mine hostel. The information was gathered in 1992 and 1993 as part of a research project on violence in South African hostels conducted for the Goldstone Commission of Inquiry[1]. Hostels are not named in order to protect the anonymity of the residents, and because some hostels only provided access on condition that they would not be mentioned by name. The researchers encountered various problems, including an unwillingness by some residents to participate. These residents were reluctant to speak because they felt that they neither had a mandate nor represented the hostel as a whole.

---

1. *The research team consisted of the author, another researcher and an interpreter. Although we tried to use interpreters trained in qualitative interviewing techniques, this was not always possible, especially since some of the trained interpreters were afraid to enter the hostels. Some of the interviews consisted of individual meetings, while others were meetings with large groups (up to 40 people). However, the majority were focus-group interviews, comprising eight to 16 residents. Only one question was asked, namely: "Tell us about life in the hostel."*

BACKGROUND INFORMATION

HOSTEL 1: A DIAMOND-MINE HOSTEL

A total of 624 men lived in this hostel at the time of research. No new admissions were being accepted because the hostel is being phased out. Privately owned by a diamond-mining company, it is situated in the Cape Province. The buildings were old but in good condition, and the rooms and grounds were clean and well maintained. Permanent employees of the mine did not pay rent, but contractors' workers living there paid R310 per month, including meals. Seven people shared a room, and each had their own bed and cupboard. All rooms had lights, fans and an electric plug, as well as a general living area with shelves and lockers. Cooking was discouraged in rooms for safety reasons, according to management, and all residents were given food prepared in the general kitchen. There were three communal bathrooms with functional ablution facilities and hot water, but the toilets had no seats as these were apparently frequently stolen. Lawns covered areas between blocks and there were benches and dustbins outside all the rooms.

This hostel had the most facilities of the hostels visited, but few were actually being used, partly because relatively few residents still lived there and most had access to township facilities. For example, the library, swimming pool and tailor shop were no longer in use. The soccer field was, however, well used, and music was broadcast over a public address system throughout the day. The hostel had a chapel and a meeting hall with a video recorder. Residents could also use the laundry and ironing facilities, a gym and a fenced car park. The privately owned beer hall situated just outside the hostel gate was very popular.

The general kitchen and dining hall were both clean and neat. Residents collected their food from a central outlet and either used the dining area or took their food to their rooms. Permanent employees participated in a coupon system, paying R2,80 per meal. A residents' committee had been established. Most residents were unhappy about the hostel being phased out. To them it implied an end to the migrant labour system, which provided them with a wage and low-cost accommodation. However, management believed that migrant labour would come to an end, and kept the hostel only for those residents who had been there for most of their lives, as well as to house contractors' workers.

HOSTEL 2: A COAL-MINE HOSTEL

This hostel consists of four hostel blocks, each housing between 380 and 1 600 men. It is owned by a coal-mining company and situated in the Transvaal. At the time of research, a brick wall surrounded the hostel and access was controlled. Four to five people shared a room. The mining company did provide some family units, but these only catered for about 2 percent of the total hostel population.

The hostel had a primary and secondary school and an adult education centre. However, teachers taught in only one language, which meant that children from different language groups experienced difficulties. A welfare store sold sports equipment to hostel residents at cost price, and there was a communal television room. Residents were responsible for cleaning their own rooms, but the mine company cleaned all outside areas. Lawns separated the hostel blocks, and a few trees provided shade. A public address system broadcast music. Residents paid R3 a month rent, with food costing extra and paid for by means of a coupon system. Meals were prepared centrally and the residents' committee negotiated yearly menu and price contracts with private companies. Profits collected from the hostel's beer garden were ploughed back into the surrounding black community.

Residents seemed to hate the hostel and, during interviews, frequently called for its demolition. One of their major complaints was that the mine had replaced statutory racial discrimination with structural racial discrimination. In other words, most black workers fitted into the only work category that did not qualify for housing benefits. Management denied that this was discriminatory, saying there were not enough houses for everyone and, therefore, the only practical solution was to exclude the largest category – into which most blacks fell. Hostel residents' dissatisfaction was exacerbated by the fact that whites in lower categories were allocated houses. They also said some houses on the mining property were unoccupied. A newly established hostel committee was attempting to mediate between management and residents over some of these difficulties.

HOSTEL 3: A GOLD-MINE HOSTEL

This hostel is situated in a right-wing stronghold in the Orange Free State. At the time of the investigation, it housed about 3 600 men. According to the workers, mine management was dissatisfied with the fact that 86 percent of workers reportedly belonged to the National Union of Mineworkers (NUM). The gold-mining group which owns the mine had made houses on mine property available to some black employees after the repeal of the Group Areas Act. The rest stayed in hostels where they did not pay rent and were given free meals at a central dining hall.

Living conditions varied according to the type of hostel room. The oldest rooms, or compounds (type A), housed 16 people on double concrete structures which were used as beds. Each room had electricity, lights and a small cupboard. The ablution facilities were of a very low standard. Toilets had a central flushing system, and all showers shared one water inlet. There were no partitions, doors or taps in the showers and the toilets had a pervasive foul smell. Some urinals were provided, but there were no basins.

In newer rooms (type B), 16 people shared a room which was equipped with bunk beds and lockers. These rooms were adjacent to communal areas which each served two rooms or 32 people. The ablution facilities were the same as those provided for type A rooms.

In the newest rooms (type C), four people shared a room and communal area. Type C rooms had built-on ablution facilities (serving several rooms), each equipped with two showers, two toilets, two urinals and two basins. These facilities were clean and functional.

All residents were able to cook their own food or eat at the dining hall which prepared food centrally. The dining hall was furnished with plastic furniture, crockery and utensils, as well as a television set. Food was served by the mine company's catering department according to menus chosen by the residents. However, during interviews many residents described their meals as "pig food".

The mine company had provided an information centre to which queries (for example about meal tickets or salaries) could be directed. There was also a post office, bank and dry-cleaner on the hostel grounds, as well as a beer hall (for residents only), a rugby field and soccer fields. Proceeds from the beer hall were ploughed back into the black community.

Residents resented the dehumanising effect the hostel had on them. They wanted accommodation which matched the standard of living enjoyed by white mineworkers and which allowed them to stay with their families. They were also unhappy about overt incidents of racism, many of which had been violent.

RESIDENTS' VIEWS

Residents from both the coal and gold-mine hostels saw the hostels as a manifestation of racism, discrimination and a general lack of concern by management for their well-being. Residents resented the fact that their white colleagues were given houses and could live with their families. One resident explained how bitter he felt about the way whites could afford to buy new cars while residents found it difficult to even borrow a car to take the remains of a deceased colleague back to his home in the rural area.

The coal-mine hostel residents had asked for houses in the townships and a living allowance in an attempt to improve their standard of living. Although this company did provide financial housing assistance to all its employees, hostel residents felt that it was inadequate and asked for higher allowances. Management rejected this, saying that residents simply refused to live within their means.

Residents of the coal-mine hostel complained about the white security patrols who accompanied management through the hostel, seeing this as a form of racism. These residents claimed that members of right-wing groups attacked them when they returned from the township, and alleged that armed white policemen also beat and harassed them. Some of these allegations had been reported in the daily press at the time.

RESIDENTS' ACCOMMODATION REQUIREMENTS

There was general agreement among all hostel residents that single quarters should be abolished and replaced by family units. Residents did not want to be separated from their families for long periods of time. One migrant worker told how he had returned home on leave only to learn that his daughter had died in his absence. Many residents were troubled by the fact that they could not participate properly in raising their children. They believed that a father was better equipped to make many of the decisions now left to their wives, and that their wives were often too lenient with deviant children. Visits by or to their families were at great expense, and travelling time made already short periods of leave even shorter. Some residents said that continual concerns about families far away caused accidents, even fatalities, at work.

Residents expressed deep regret at not being able to spend time with their wives. Some had taken mistresses, and this had led to family difficulties and often divorce, resulting in them losing their homes, and forcing them to remain in the hostels permanently. Many were concerned that remittances that should have been sent to families back home were being spent on mistresses in town. Residents also stated that forced separation resulted in a higher divorce rate.

Migrants wanted sports fields, libraries, recreational facilities and, most important, educational facilities for children and adults. Where these already existed calls were made for their upgrading. Residents from the gold mine had an amount deducted from their salaries each month for these facilities, but felt they were not getting their money's worth. All residents insisted that they should be consulted about family housing and the upgrading of facilities, not only before these processes began but during their implementation as well.

Crowding was a problem only for the residents of the coal-mine hostel, and they were concerned with lack of privacy and the forced sharing of facilities rather than overcrowding as such. These hostel residents found it difficult to sleep in a room with others who snored, played their radios, used the heater or worked different shifts. They were also woken up by a tractor which removed garbage from the dormitories early in the morning, and the central intercom system which could not be switched off. Management said that they had given residents the option of sharing rooms according to shift, but that this was turned down since residents said they would prefer to share rooms with people from the same home area rather than strangers.

Porridge instead of rice was the only change wanted by the diamond-mine hostel residents. They described their food as otherwise "delicious". In both other hostels the residents called their food "pig food" and said that it did not give them the strength to do their jobs properly. Generally, residents would rather prepare their own food and were unhappy about the ban on cooking in their rooms. Management at both mines said that this ban was a safety measure because residents used sub-standard equipment which caused electrical and fire hazards.

Residents from the coal-mine hostel wanted more influence in menu planning, and complained about the lack of variety on the menus. However, management replied that a hostel committee negotiated a menu at the beginning of each year, and blamed residents' dissatisfaction on a lack of communication between the committee and the residents.

The only specific crime mentioned was theft, and this was a problem at all three hostels. Residents claimed that the lack of access control enabled criminals to enter the hostels and that overcrowding and general living conditions were conducive to crime. Although no mention was made of violent crimes (excluding incidents of political violence), residents clearly did not feel safe.

Access control was only requested by members of the diamond-mine hostel, although they did not specify what this should entail. This request stemmed from the fact that their lockers had been opened while they were at work and valuables had been stolen.

Residents of the coal-mine hostel criticised the lack of maintenance of their buildings, saying no one was prepared to take responsibility for the upkeep of the property. They were also concerned about health hazards associated with the unhygienic conditions resulting from the lack of maintenance.

Visiting family members are usually accommodated in the visitors' quarters which are rooms on the hostel premises where men can stay with their wives and children for short periods (between one and two weeks). Amidst calls for improved visiting quarters was also a complaint by residents from the diamond-mine hostel that since a change of management they were no longer allowed access to these quarters. This may have been due to discrimination by the new hostel manager, or perhaps an attempt to curb the use of the services of local prostitutes. However, neither management nor residents were prepared to explain this prohibition.

CONCLUSION

Many hostel residents still accepted hostel life as their fate – the only way in which they can be economically active and secure low-cost housing which is in such short supply. Despite the fact that residents hated being subjected to hostel life they still thought of the hostel system as crucial to their survival and the only way in which they could have access to jobs.

It is obvious that workers in urban areas need low-cost accommodation, but none of the residents whose views are presented here wanted to continue living in these barracks-like structures. The problem needs to be addressed by a multi-pronged approach, and will necessarily involve protracted negotiations – as well as compromises on all sides. ◆

6

Gate Politics: Competing Interests in Mine Hostels

Dr Kent McNamara
*JKM Consultancy Services,
Johannesburg, South Africa*

For at least a century, mineworkers have been separated from their homes and families and cloistered in harsh, institutional mine hostels that have become synonymous with violence and deprivation. Despite their association with the "old" South Africa, hostels on the mines and in the townships remain a seemingly entrenched part of the new political and constitutional reality, partly because they are the subject of competing interests among the different stakeholders associated with them. At times the stakeholders themselves also reveal contradictory motives, which cloud the debate and inhibit the development of a consistent policy for the future.

Competing Interests

Mine managements say that the cost of financing alternative family accommodation for their employees is a crucial obstacle and the state has up to now been less than willing to help shoulder the burden (James, 1989). Yet paradoxically, mine managements also express their frustration with their continued responsibility for accommodating employees, seeing this as yet another addition to the already weighty list of issues and grievances with which the mines must grapple.

The unions, especially the National Union of Mineworkers (NUM), regard migrancy and hostels as highly exploitative and testimony to the hardships which their members have had to endure. Yet the NUM's meteoric rise in membership since its founding in 1982 has been due at least in part to the opportunity to recruit large numbers of supporters in the captive barracks-like environment of hostels. Hostels have also made it possible to sustain strike action – during the 1987 NUM strike the hostels were virtual "no-go" areas for management, which helped to prolong the action and extend it to its historic three-week duration.

Turning to the hostel residents themselves, they reveal a variety of circumstances, aims and interests. There is, for example, the question of "foreign" workers from Lesotho, Mozambique and elsewhere (over 40 percent of the total). Recently the distinction between foreigners and citizens has become unclear. In the 27 April 1994 elections foreign mineworkers were entitled to vote provided they had been employed in the country before November 1988. There has been some speculation that Lesotho could even become a 10th region of South Africa, but it is certainly not yet clear whether the citizens of that country would wish to give up their sovereignty.

However, even if foreign migrants were able to become permanent residents in South Africa, this does not necessarily mean that large numbers of them would choose this option. For many of the unskilled workers, hostel accommodation provides one of the cheapest ways of surviving the limits of a low wage. Living in a shack in the vicinity of the mine, for example, might mean low rent, but the hidden costs such as transport and water can be high. A single bucket of water in a shack settlement adjoining a gold mine in the Klerksdorp area is reported to cost R2 (Randall, 1994).

On the other hand, for upwardly mobile workers, hostels carry a social stigma. They are seen as a barrier excluding them from integration as equals into the social mainstream of mining communities. In the words of a worker at the Finsch diamond mine in the Northern Cape: "People in the hostel are not considered as human beings and live as prisoners (bandiete). We want to live among the people but we are separated and far away from the rest of the (mining) community."

With this range of individual motives and needs it is clear that hostel residents cannot easily be described as one stakeholder group. The diversity of interests among residents is apparent when we delve into the informal social and political life of mine hostels.

RESILIENCE AND ADAPTATION

To an outsider, a mine compound is the embodiment of deprivation and exploitation, what John Rex calls the "essential institution of labour exploitation" (1974: 4). Yet a series of anthropological and sociological studies conducted during the 1970s point to another side of compound life.

Pat Pearson's (1975) description of secondary adjustments in the "total institution", Rob Gordon's (1977) account of "brotherhood" among Namibian migrants, my own studies of home-friend networks (McNamara, 1980) and Dunbar Moodie's (1994) studies of miners' culture all reveal strong informal cultures of adaptation and support.

Migrants have established resilient, sometimes volatile, cultures of survival and identity which direct their energies away from underlying structural issues. For decades, groups of migrants have been involved in life-and-death struggles in hostels, a struggle waged at times against management and at times against other migrant groups. The hostel has become for many a resource to be fought over and controlled, primarily because it is linked to jobs and wages. Ownership of the hostel implies access to jobs, which are of greater significance for residents than ideological and structural questions about the hostel as an institution. This struggle for hostel ownership often finds expression in terms of what I call the "politics of the gate".

GATE POLITICS

Most mine hostels have one main entrance, usually guarded by security personnel who check incoming residents for weapons and contraband, but it would be a mistake to see the gate as being controlled solely by formal mine structures. Instead, it provides a focal point for underlying micro-political struggles among different groups of residents.

On a Sunday afternoon in 1980, a Pondo *induna* (the appointed head of the Pondo tribal group) placed a chair at the entrance to the Deelkraal mine hostel (on the West Rand). The Pondo dance team gathered around and started to dance in the entrance. (For many years tribal dancing has been practised on the mines, with each regional-linguistic group having a team which takes part in recognised dancing sessions every weekend.) Shortly thereafter, the Sotho dance team returned from dancing at another mine, accompanied by their own *induna*. They tried to enter the hostel, but were assaulted. The Pondo *induna* then assaulted the Sotho *induna*. The Sothos managed to force their way past, run into the hostel and collect weapons. The Pondos gained access to a garden shed and distributed implements. In the ensuing violence, 20 workers were killed (McNamara, 1988).

This clash took place on a newly established mine. The Basotho workers had been in the majority during the shaft-sinking and development phase, but their numbers were reduced as the mine brought in recruits from Transkei and Pondoland to make up the main labour-force. The Basothos had in effect become a dwindling minority.

The gate incident symbolised the changing political order in the hostel, with the Pondo *induna* moving to consolidate his group's dominant status and group "ownership" of the mine. The mine could now be secured to provide a reliable place of work for many men from Pondoland who could be recruited through a network of support and patronage. The vital importance of this rural-urban network for providing access to mine jobs was reflected in the wider conditions of unemployment and restricted recruitment to the mines from the late-1970s.

A similar saga was repeated at Leslie gold mine on the East Rand in 1987, where the Lesotho nationals had become outnumbered two to one by Transkeians.

Early that year, the Pondo *induna* was on duty at the hostel gate, and was alleged to have conducted "rough" body searches on Sothos returning to the hostel. Two months later a group of Sothos attacked the Pondo *induna's* room and tried to break down the door, but were intercepted by hostel security. Later, skirmishes broke out and eight men were killed, but violence continued for another month and the death toll reached 21.

During the previous few years, the number of Basotho workers had dropped as a result of the reduction of novice recruitment in Lesotho. This formed part of a strategy in the 1980s to reduce dependence on foreign sources of labour. The drop-off in recruits from Lesotho was noted by these men and raised in discussions with mine management. After the violence an independent attitude survey revealed that the Basotho felt they were poorly treated and that their future employment prospects on the mine were not good. By contrast, the Pondo interviewees approved of their treatment and believed they had job security (McNamara and Schlemmer, 1988).

The NUM's reaction to the violence was to demand the abolition of the *induna* system. However, the analysis presented here suggests that the incidents were merely the symptom of an underlying struggle for group dominance on the mine. The Basotho had clearly become a threatened minority and attacked the *induna* as a symbol of the privileged majority labour group.

CHANGING LABOUR TRADITIONS

This gate incident illustrates the interaction between two labour traditions, namely that between the long-established informal political culture of hostels and the new tradition of organised labour representation and "modernised" hostel management.

Since the 1980s, the *induna* system has been gradually dismantled, making way for new structures such as elected boards of representatives and governors which attempt to manage hostels on a democratic basis. Many of these changes to hostels have been introduced through pressure by the NUM, which has worked to remove "tribal" structures, notably *indunas* and tribal dancing. The union's view has been that tribal principles of accommodation and recreation divide the work-force and promote factional violence.

It is important, however, to appreciate that the union itself has become an integral part of the local-level political life of mine hostels. The *indunas* and dance teams have been singled out primarily because they present the union with rival structures of mobilisation. The union itself has also moved to control the politics of the gate – it is not uncommon for members of the union's "action committee" to station themselves at the gate to ensure that a strike call is observed.

We should also be wary of blaming tribal principles of hostel management for the apparently tribal character of hostel violence. My own research has found that attempts to break down so-called tribal networks by accommodating people in rooms on work-section lines merely resulted in the renewal of home-based ties in places such as the beer hall. Home-based regional networks of friendship among residents are symptomatic of the wider structure of migrant labour itself, and not of any local variations in hostel management (McNamara, 1980). Any future policy regarding mine hostels will need to take into account the deep-rooted underlife of informal political culture, together with the competing and some-times contradictory motivations of different interest groups and stakeholders in the hostel environment.

These issues are reflected in the NUM's recent demands. The union has at-tempted to reconcile different needs by simultaneously demanding advances in housing and the upgrading of hostels. The NUM has also recognised, as I believe has management, the importance of giving workers a range of choices between hostel accommodation, rented or purchased homes.

However, this approach will not necessarily resolve potential conflicts of in-terests between residents. On the collieries the union has been pressing for the conversion of hostels into family units. While such a strategy could be effective in areas with a high proportion of local labour, it could be threatening to long-distance migrants who still see benefits in hostel accommodation.

THE FUTURE: HOSTELS AS A RESOURCE

The micro-political struggles waged over the years in mine hostels suggest that many residents view them not as an impediment but as a valuable resource to be controlled.

The view of hostels as a resource is well illustrated by the changing fortunes of municipal hostels (providing accommodation for people engaged in munici-pal services and other urban industrial employment) as well as those previously under mine ownership and administration. Paul Kapelus (1994) has recently shown how the residents of the Mohlakeng municipal hostel (south of Randfontein) treat the hostel as a valued resource. Some individuals have im-proved their own living conditions by upgrading room blocks. Women have en-tered the hostel as a place of shelter. Entrepreneurs have started their own busi-nesses within its walls, selling meat and setting up shops, shebeens and tailoring services. Kapelus asks how changes and upgrading can take place in the hostel without breaking down the social structure already established there. The same question can be posed in respect of mine hostels.

Negotiation between the different interest groups who see hostels as a re-source will be essential. One negotiation model which has already emerged is a three-way one involving individual company managements, unions and local civic associations. Negotiations on these lines have taken place in the Potchefstroom area between businesses, civics and unions following the burning down of hostels in Ikageng township in 1990. These focused on reducing migrancy and improving housing in the area. The only missing stakeholders here were the hostel residents themselves. ◆

REFERENCES

Gordon, R. 1977. Mines, Masters and Migrants. Johannesburg: Ravan Press.

James, W. 1989. "The future of migrant labour in the gold-mining industry," in Industrial Relations Journal of SA, Vol 9, No 4.

Kapelus, P. 1994. Here to Stay: Negotiating Space and Forming Identities in the Mohlakeng Hostel. Honours dissertation, University of the Witwatersrand.

McNamara, JK. 1980. "Brothers and workmates: home-friend networks in the social life of black migrant workers in a gold-mine hostel," in P Mayer, (ed,) Black Villagers in an Industrial Society. Cape Town: Oxford University Press.

McNamara, JK. 1988. "Inter-group violence among black employees in the SA gold-mining industry – 1974 to 1986," in South African Sociological Review, Vol 1, No 1.

McNamara, JK and L Schlemmer. 1988. Black Employees' Attitudes to Inter-Group Violence on Gold Mines of the Evander Area. Unpublished consultancy report.

Moodie, TD. 1994. Going for Gold. Berkeley: University of California Press.

Pearson, P. 1975. The Social Structure of a South African Gold Mine Hostel. Honours dissertation, University of the Witwatersrand.

Randall, C. 1994. Personal communication, AAC Gold and Uranium Division.

Rex, J. 1974. "The essential institutions of southern African labour exploitation," in SA Labour Bulletin, Vol 1, No 4.

7

Town Women and Country Wives: Housing Preferences at Vaal Reefs Mine

Professor Dunbar Moodie
(with Vivienne Ndatshe)
Department of Sociology,
Hobart and William Smith Colleges,
New York, USA

In previously published work on sexuality and gender on the South African gold mines, we attempted to present the point of view of the male migrants (Moodie, with Ndatshe and Sibuyi, 1988: 228-56). For men with rural land on which to establish homesteads, country women and homosexual "mine wives" provided the sexual intimacy least threatening to their life purposes. "Town women" remained potentially disastrous temptations to self-indulgence. While some men did enter into sexual relationships with such women, their descriptions of them revealed their fear of the commitments those relationships might involve. "Beware the breasts of the Tswana women," go the words of one Mozambican miners' song[1]. For migrants intending to return to build their homesteads, "town women" represented an inducement to abandon

---

1. *I am indebted to Leroy Vail for this reference.*

country life.

With the rise in mine workers' wages during the 1970s and the subsequent recruitment of miners from urban and peri-urban townships, resettlement areas and rural slums within South Africa, the work-force on the mines became more proletarian (Crush et al, 1991). Fewer miners now have country proprietorships from which to be tempted. As a result, many are turning to relationships with women living in townships near the mines. We know little of the views and lives of these women, although a recent article by Jochelson, Mothibeli and Leger (1991) touches peripherally on the sorts of sexual relationships they develop with migrant miners. This study explores major themes in such relationships, and is written from the testimony of some of the women involved, focusing specifically on housing policy.

The research focuses on the attitudes of the women and their partners to the various housing options currently available. The choices on the mines include the traditionally free but crowded compound rooms, extremely low rental houses in the mine married quarters (mine village or *skomplas*) which are available to black supervisors whose occupancy is completely dependent on continued mine employment and miner-owned and company-subsidised mortgaged homes in suburban-type subdivisions. In addition, the mines provide up to one month's free accommodation for black miners' wives in closely supervised "visiting wives quarters".

Off-mine alternatives include homes in nearby black townships (not often available to mine workers), galvanised iron shacks in township backyards (with rentals payable to township landlords and landladies), galvanised iron shacks in site-and-service settlements now being erected adjacent to the townships with municipal assent and shacks in unregulated shanty towns springing up on farms or near existing townships.

Extensive interviews conducted by Vivienne Ndatshe with Xhosa-speaking women over a six-month period (June-December 1990) revealed their views on these various options.

Her informants came from a range of sending areas, including the extremely impoverished Ciskei, the still agriculturally productive Pondoland (a traditional sending area for the mines) and the western region of the Transkei (the economy of which varies from unproductive Mfenguland to the better-maintained Gcaleka and Bomvana coastal areas, and from economically mixed areas in Tembuland and the Tsolo/Qumbu/Mount Frere district to the rapidly urbanising Umtata area). Xhosa-speakers are at present the largest group of workers on the western Transvaal mines.

URBAN SETTLERS

Differences in women's life choices and in their preferences for permanent urban settlement seem to depend in part on their age but largely on whether they have access to workable rural land. The better-schooled, unmarried or recently married younger women were more likely to want to stay in town. In general, however, women of all ages who came from the still productive areas like Pondoland were more reluctant to settle in town than those from impoverished regions such as the Ciskei. Several of the Ciskeian women interviewed came from Mdantsane (near East London) and were already committed to urban life. However, rural Ciskeian women who came to the mines to visit were also more likely to stay. Given that hunger was a common reason for their coming, their reluctance to leave is hardly surprising.

One of them told a typical story:

> I came to visit my husband who was not coming home, even on his leave. His parents sent me and told me to take my two children with me. I was thin and ugly and the children were poorly dressed. When he was called and found out I was there, he asked why I was there without telling him. Mind you, I hadn't travelled before and I was afraid. I told him his parents sent me and gave him a letter from home. He left me in the waiting room and went to the compound and I thought he was going to ask people to kill me. He brought food for us. I gave it to the children. I was angry and at the same time scared. My brother was working here on the mines. I asked my husband if it was very far to where he worked. "Have you come to your brother or me?" he asked. I lied and said my mother gave me a message for him. My husband said nothing about where to find my brother. He took me to a house in the married quarters and I stayed there with the owner who was also from Ciskei.
>
> My husband visited from time to time. Other days he said he was working. I didn't mind. As long as he was feeding my children, let alone myself, I was prepared to do whatever he said. I stayed a month in the married quarters. My brother was working in Stilfontein and my husband brought him to see me. I told him the whole story and asked him for money in case my husband didn't give me enough to get home. I also told him I would be coming back to look for work, leaving the children with my mother-in-law. He promised to help.
>
> I had heard that my husband had another woman. Other women told me what was happening to our husbands when we stayed at home. There are women who don't stay long in the country but visit their husbands regularly. One woman said she would never stay at home for long. She and her husband would rather have no home in the country. She would not give him a chance with those town women. She also said she loves her husband and doesn't want to be separated from him by the job.
>
> My brother came and gave me money which I hid from my husband. After three weeks he did give me money to go home. I went back to the country knowing to myself that I was coming back, but not to him. I told my mother-

in-law what had happened and how her son treated me – even the money he gave me was too little. I loved my mother-in-law, but I had no choice because I was not married to her and she couldn't support me and the children needed school uniforms.

When I arrived home I went to see my own mother. I told her that I was going to work in Johannesburg for my children. My mother understood but she was against my going to Johannesburg because she thought my husband would make trouble for us both. I left a letter on my mother-in-law's bed, so that when I had gone she could know where and why I left. I went with my friend to my brother in Stilfontein. He took us to Khuma (Stilfontein township) to a friend's backyard shack. The place was reserved for the friend's wife but she had gone back to the country.

My friend and I stayed there and looked for work in town, sometimes visiting my brother on the mine. We soon got boyfriends. It was not difficult to find a boyfriend. Miners love women. My boyfriend gave me money which I sent to my mother. Sometimes I sent clothes to my children. I wasn't going around much because I didn't want my husband to know my whereabouts.

Money is a temptation. I say this because another man really attracted me. He was a Shangaan. I left my old boyfriend for this man and am still staying with him. This Shangaan took me to Kanana and we have lost contact with my friend but I keep in touch with my brother. He tells me that my husband works in Carletonville now. When his mother told him that I had left, he went home and married another girl in the country. Now I feel free. I sell beers around the mine now. We make good money. I support my mother and my children. I would rather stay here with my man than go back to the country. He had a wife but does not correspond with her. He is very straight. From work he comes home. He doesn't care or tell me not to sell so I do what I like. We are busy applying for a house or we shall build our own. If I own a house I will bring my children here.

This story contains all the important themes mentioned by other landless, married women from the former Ciskei and western Transkei. They said they came to the mines because their children were sick or hungry. Sometimes the problem was that the mother-in-law, with whom the young wife invariably resided, received money from the husband but did not share it. In such cases, the wife came to beg the husband to send money directly to her. Most often, however, the man had stopped remitting altogether or sent money very occasionally and never enough to support the country household.

In the past, when there was a more self-sufficient rural homestead, or *umzi*, producing at least some basic family maintenance, men had an incentive to keep in touch and to subsidise the women's agricultural activities. This was because the country homestead, essentially a semi-subsistence small-holding, represented hope of a dignified old age for both men and women – especially when daughters were married off well and sons migrated to work. The latter remitted wages for investment in agriculture and eventually brought home young wives who helped the older women work the land. They bore daughters to work in the homestead and to herd cattle purchased from mine wages.

With the collapse of agriculture in the old Ciskei and much of what used to be known as the western Transkei, remittances were devoted increasingly to consumption rather than investment. Men had much less incentive to remain faithful to wives and families whom they rarely saw during their prime years. Until the mid-1970s however, few men from these areas went to the mines simply because wages were so low. Workers from underdeveloped Xhosa-speaking areas thus tended to migrate to better-paid employment in Cape Town or elsewhere (Jochelson et al, 1991).

When the mines raised wages and set out to recruit "South African" labour from the mid-1970s many of these men were drawn to the Transvaal. A number of the older women interviewed mentioned that their husbands had shifted jobs in the early 1980s from Cape Town to Vaal Reefs mine.

Although some men did remain supportive of their wives, more of them were attracted to town women as the rewards of faithfulness to their rural families diminished. Rural women thus had to come to the mines in search of the support that no longer came in the form of remittances. Often repudiated by their husbands, they in turn drew more men into town relationships. Family attachments aside, however, repudiation of a visiting wife led to outspoken condemnation from workmates and other women.

Wives who were abandoned moved through a series of dependent relationships, often ending up in long-term relationships with "Shangaan" men. Mozambican workers seem to have the least bargaining power in relation to South African women (informants told Ndatshe that it was they who were most likely to visit prostitutes). The women found these workers less controlling and more generous if they consented to live with them. Women in relationships with Mozambicans often engaged in some sort of small-scale entrepreneurial activity (most often brewing or retailing of beer – sometimes with sex on the side – but also dressmaking, sale of cooked meat and vegetables, or retailing of clothing).

Both men and women hid details about their earnings from their partners, even in marriage, and there is little notion of a joint or family budget. Mozambicans tended to be especially tolerant of women with incomes on the side, perhaps because they had to be. Nonetheless, few women sought complete financial independence. Even if they could support themselves, they expected assistance from the men with whom they lived and did not hesitate to leave them if such help was not forthcoming.

The transient nature of rural women's early urban liaisons underlines the importance of mine married quarters and township backyard shacks. Houses in the mine married quarters, where rents are ridiculously low, are usually full of visiting friends and relatives. Management has banned rental charges for such visitors, but charges by the householder for "groceries" tend to be two or three times what it costs to rent a backyard shack. Mine married quarters are, therefore, temporary stopping points en route to township backyards. When country women finally settle down, whether with their husbands or, more usually, in new relationships, those from the impoverished rural areas rarely want to return home or to settle in the mine married quarters. At this point, they are most likely to persuade their men to take out mortgages on mine-subsidised homes if they qualify or – if they do not – to build in the new site-and service shack settlements.

These are the families, along with the progeny of long-time urban residents, who have been squeezed into the backyards by South Africa's urban housing shortage. They will benefit most from various home-ownership schemes in townships around the mines. For the present, however, given the uncertainty of South African township life and job insecurities, a sizeable majority of the women interviewed in this study did not want to give up completely on their rural homes.

Even Nokwandisa, a 27-year-old from Flagstaff, whose husband, a survey assistant, has bought a mine-subsidised suburban house at Kanana and whose children are at school in town, had doubts about cutting her ties with the country:

> At home I have no fields and only a few sheep which are kept by a relative. (Nonetheless) I would like to have two homes. For the future we don't know what is going to happen in this country. Moreover, if we don't keep our home in Pondoland, people will laugh at us, and the chief will give our place to other people and we will have no land. That is why we keep both places. When I am here my health is much better than in the country and I am happy to stay with my husband and children, all living together. But I also want to keep in contact with my husband's family.

VISITING WIVES

Women from Pondoland – and indeed areas of the Ciskei and western Transkei where it is still possible to build an *umzi* – maintain a firm affiliation to country life. Take the case of Nolulamile, a 22-year-old Pondo woman, as described by Ndatshe:

> Nolulamile has got two sisters and one brother. The elder sister and herself are married. Younger ones are still at school. She passed Std 3 and left school because there was no boy to look after the cattle. So she looked after her father's stock. She grew up with boys and was fighting with sticks on the veld. There were other girls who also looked after their parents' stock, but not as many as boys ... Nolulamile's father worked on the mines. Now he has stopped and stays at home to help his young son look after the few cattle remaining after the drought.

> In 1986 she married her lover. She left with him for his home in the night so that no one knew where she had gone. At first she was afraid to be with the new family. But there were other brother-in-laws' wives who were nice to her and she quickly felt at home. Her mother-in-law was also nice to her. She showed or told her all the customs of her new home.

> Nolulamile is a real farm girl. She doesn't like to stay long on the mines, where people don't respect each other and where money is used every day. At home there is maize and other vegetable from the fields. She talked about wild vegetables which grow in the forest where you haven't planted them. If she could conceive and have children she would never come here, she said. When she is at home her husband sends money to her and she is satisfied.

This story depicts the tenacity and satisfaction with which country people hang onto their rural patrimony and gives evidence of the contemporary strains on the *umzi* system. Nolulamile's father's lonely struggle to establish a viable *umzi* (even to the extent of having his daughter herd cattle, which would have been unheard of in the past when brothers and clan-relatives would have helped) contrasts with the greater resources of the larger family into which she married.

Nolulamile, like many women from traditional *umzis*, joined her husband on the mine in order to conceive. By all accounts, parents-in-law heartily oppose these visits since they lose their daughter-in-laws' company and their labour. However, mine managements' current policy of stabilising migrancy, which ties job security to steady employment and permits only short leave, makes wives' visits inevitable. The availability of proper medical attention at the mine hospital often keeps them there until they come to term, despite the tradition for women to return to their own mothers to have their first baby, and for a month or two longer if the home area has a history of infant mortality.

The case of Nomkhonzi is typical. She was only 18 when she came for the first time to her husband on Vaal Reefs mine in August 1990, after she had conceived:

> Her mother is a pensioner. Her father died in 1976. The only people still alive and helping her mother are the mother's brothers and their wives. The brothers help her mother on the fields. They plough for her and their wives come at harvest time to help her. Nomkhonzi also goes and helps her mother.

> She got married in 1989. Her husband is the only son with two sisters and his parents are both alive. So he will inherit the *umzi* when his parents die... Her husband wants her to be near him when she has a baby in November. It is unusual for a young woman to leave her parents and come to her husband to have a first child, because the first child is always delivered at her mother's home. But Nomkhonzi considers that an old-fashioned custom. Also she says that her mother cannot afford to buy all the things she

will need when she returns to her in-laws after the delivery. Her husband also feels sorry for her mother. That's why he prefers to have his wife with him, he says.

Nomkhonzi took a taxi from the country. Her husband told the taxi driver to bring his wife ... to No 6 Vaal Reefs where he works. Her husband then took her to Mandela Park, the site-and-service shanty town where his clan-brother has a shack. This man doesn't stay in Mandela Park but lives in the compound. He lets the shack to his home friends' wives. Then when his wife visits she has somewhere to stay. There are two women now occupying the shack.

Nomkhonzi will stay for a month after she has the baby. The couple write letters to her mother-in-law, who lives with her daughters' children because their mothers migrate to work. Nomkhonzi doesn't like the house in town. She likes country life very much. "In town money is used too much whereas at home where we grow maize we don't have to buy much," she said. "Even if my husband does want to have a house here, I will never stay in it, but will visit. Or if we have a house we will let it to people visiting the mines."

Repeatedly in the accounts of visiting wives, rural social networks and the uncertainties of dependence on the urban economy emerge as reasons for giving priority to the country home. Several young woman did admit that life for women was easier in town and that they rather enjoyed it, although some were bored without work on the *umzi*. Older women whose husbands have access to land in the country hold different attitudes to life in town:

There are those who say they don't like to live in townships because their husbands might lose their jobs on the mines. Others say they want to have houses on the mines and at home. They prefer to go backwards and for-wards until their husbands resign ... Yet others said if their husbands could build big nice houses like those on the mines it would make a big differ-ence because they wouldn't have to pay rent every month as they do on the mines. They would plant vegetables and they would have their own cattle on their own land. In townships people have big houses and little or no food or cattle. They buy everything. That's why most visiting wives are not really interested in staying permanently on the fields in the country. After hoeing and harvest time when the maize and other vegetables have been gathered in at home, then she visits her husband. "It's like when you are in boarding school," she said. "When it's school holidays children go home to rest after studying hard. Even so for us married women, we must rest near our husbands, as children rest near their parents."

Some "superwomen" manage to live in both worlds. Usually these are wives who rent homes in the mine villages at very low rates. Regina Mkhazi, for instance, has 10 children who go to school and live on their land in the country near Lusikisiki. She is in regular telephone contact with them. She goes home at the time of ploughing and works with the children on their land until the crops are in and then returns to her husband. In the *skomplas* she has her own sideline, selling sheep heads, which she buys from local farmers and resells to other residents. On weekends she also sells cooked meat to visitors at the *shebeen* next door (and perhaps manages to dispense a little liquid refreshment herself to regular customers). At the end of the interview, she returned to a theme which seems almost universal amongst country women:

> Men are delicate (fickle) people. The women of Johannesburg (*Egoli*, the city of gold) are a temptation to our husbands. There are women whose husbands were taken away by these women of the township, or sometimes these women have run away from their husbands and come here to the mines to take our men away from us. And they do take them – some win them. So I want to be near my husband so that he will have no chance for these women. When he retires we are both going home and will stay together in our house at Lusikisiki.

There are two major themes which emerge from the accounts provided by women with ongoing rural attachments. The first is the tension between the uncertainties of urban life and mine employment and the struggle to maintain a viable rural existence. The second is their fear of the seductive potential of so-called "town women". The latter concern keeps older women in happy marriages and with viable rural *umzis* constantly moving back and forth between country and town, quite apart from their desire to be with their husbands. For those women, inexpensive rental accommodation, whether in mine village or township shacks, remains essential.

TOWN WOMEN

Who are the "town women" so universally feared by country wives? Historically, they were Tswana women from farms and townships around the mines, or impoverished Sotho women seeking economic security (Bonner, 1990). Increasingly, however, they include young Xhosa-speakers. Many, but by no means all, come from the former Ciskei, which rivals Lesotho in its poverty. Even Pondoland supplies its quota of young town women who despise farm work and country ways. Many of them take up with miners and live in mine housing. Conversations with management representatives at both Welkom and Vaal Reefs suggest that a very high percentage of men moving into the *skomplas* (and even the suburban-style mortgaged housing) with their "wives" married quickly, often within a week of being offered a house.

There seems to be considerable variety of "town women". We shall examine three different personal accounts, moving from a clear case of "serial marriage" to one in which the frequency of relationships is suggestive of prostitution, although the woman in question rejects that characterisation. "Cynthia," aged 36, comes from Matatiele:

> The daughter of a woman who died when she was in first grade, she went to live with clan people in Matatiele because her grandparents were in Port Elizabeth. Her grandfather worked in secondary industry. Her grandmother sold liquor. However, on her mother's death, the grandmother had to come home and her grandparents separated. The grandmother took Cynthia to her place of origin in Mount Frere and went back to Port Elizabeth to earn enough to support her and her brother. However, Cynthia's uncle, her grandmother's son, who worked for Standard Bank, finally took over the support of both his mother and his niece. To his chagrin, when Cynthia was in Standard 6 she became pregnant, had a baby girl, and ran away to marry the father and live with him in Carletonville. They moved to Potchefstroom where her husband killed a man in a *shebeen* brawl and was jailed. A year later, she married a lover in Potchefstroom. She stayed with him for four years and then moved to work in Klerksdorp, leaving him because "he liked women". Two years later she moved in with a new boyfriend who at that time worked on the mines. She lives with him in Klerksdorp.
>
> Her boyfriend has a car and he is now self-employed. He is very jealous. He stopped her from working and gives her whatever she wants. But she says, "I have my *inyatsi* (lover) in Vereeniging, whom I visit. Whenever I fight with my boyfriend, I go and visit him and he makes me happy when I am miserable. My boyfriend is good in support, but my sport is the Ethiopian Church because I travel all over the country with church members."

This woman has moved from one more or less steady relationship to others, with occasional casual encounters in addition. She typifies the type of town woman most feared by country wives and the ease with which she has been able to find men in the townships around the mines is typical. So far she has not had to resort to the "Shangaans" (Mozambicans), lowest on the scale of desirable partners.

The second person represents a different type of town woman, one who is younger and has had more sexual partners. "Marianne" is 30 and comes from Cofimvaba, former Transkei:

> The daughter of an unmarried domestic servant in Johannesburg with four other siblings, Marianne was raised by her grandmother in an unloving home and eventually married by abduction (*ukuthwala*) at age 16 to an older man in Thembuland. She had three children by him, but he took a lover and eventually married her. Marianne left him and went back to her mother, who by now had returned to the country after the death of the grandmother. Her brother was working on the mines.

Marianne moved to Butterworth and got a job in a shoe factory. She was in love with a man from Kentani who worked at Vaal Reefs. After a year he took her to the mines as his "wife". "He didn't want me to work, so we lived in a backyard shack happily here," she said. He gave her money which she sent back to her mother for the children. She went to a doctor to ensure that there would be no more children. One of the children was injured so she had to go home for three months.

On her return she discovered that her "husband" had moved another woman into her *umkhukhu* (shack) and thrown out all her belongings. "That was a second blow in my love life," she said. She was furious and turned to her brother who took her to the *umkhukhu* of his girlfriend. By her account, she "stayed there for two weeks. Then I got this new boyfriend – a Shangaan. After all my trouble with Xhosa men, I said to myself, `I will never love a home-boy again!' I enjoy him more than I have ever enjoyed any man but I am not married to him. He is my *masihlalisane* (meaning "stay together"). He does everything for me. He goes back to his country for leave and I also go to my home and visit sometimes. I stay home for two months and come back to him."

When asked if her boyfriend has ever visited her home, she smiled and said "No". Her brother visits her every weekend. They keep in touch with their mother. Her other brother, who works at Stilfontein, has lost contact with their mother but still visits his sister. She would like to have a house in town so that her children could stay with her. Her mother could also come and visit. "Life here is very relaxing, free. You do what you want to do and go where you want to go." She would also like a shack in the site-and-service scheme but she and her boyfriend have not got the necessary identification documents, so it is not possible.

This account repeats many of the themes in the first story. However, as Ndatshe noted: "The landlady where I went to talk with Marianne herself drinks very badly. There are many pretty girls staying in her backyard *imikhukhu*. They wear makeup and are very smartly dressed. None of these girls are working and they have Shangaan boyfriends. The old lady I talked to told me that all those girls do not have steady boyfriends. They are being paid by men, but they don't go around the mines for sex. Rather the men come to their shacks. According to a neighbour the place is rotten. The people of that house are all very rude, always drunk and swearing and fighting. They hardly sleep, especially on weekends. When I returned to the house for a further interview, I was warned off by the son of the landlady."

At places like these, town women obtain Shangaan regulars who may eventually move them out to their own quarters. However, that does not seem to prevent their also engaging in paid sex. The Shangaan relationships provide a certain stability and respectability (at least in their own eyes) for these women.

Some town women are completely without stable relationships. "Ntombi," an Mpondo women from Port St Johns, is 27:

> She was married by abduction to a widower at her father's insistence. She had four children by this man and then left him on her father's death because, she said, her husband's older children didn't like her and he refused to build her a separate house from his daughter-in-law. She moved back to her own mother with the children. At first she worked for a bus company in Lusikisiki but left after four months because of poor wages and went to Umtata to work as a domestic servant for her own sister. After a while she returned home and sold fruit and vegetables from her mother's garden.
>
> She moved to the mines when her uncle's daughter (married to a mine worker) came home for her annual visit and offered to take her back with her to look for a job. They left with her mother's approval but her cousin's husband disapproved because she and her cousin went out drinking together and were not at home when he arrived from work. So she had to leave and move in with other relatives from Port St Johns. The owner of that house lost the house because of their behaviour.
>
> Meanwhile, Ntombi had made friends in a *shebeen* and they found a Shangaan man for her. They lived in a backyard shack for a few months until he found her with another man and threw her out, nearly killing her in the process. She now lives with a group of young unmarried women from the Transkei (including one from Tsolo, one from Bizana, one from Ngqeleni and one from Butterworth), sharing a shack with another woman. When Ndatshe asked who pays her rent, she said that they have different boyfriends who each pay a certain amount because the women asked for help from them since they were not working. "So now you are prostitutes?" I asked. "Not really, because we don't sell sex," she said laughing. "Men just help us. They are our boyfriends." "But you said such friendships last only a day," I told her. "But sometimes longer than a day, if one is lucky," Ntombi said. "Paying us if there is no food, or buying beer for us."

Acknowledged prostitution thus seems to be a matter only for the most down-and-out of town women, who proposition miners at shopping centres or in the bushes near the mines. Most men reject such coldly commercial transactions. "That is for animals," one of them said. Men seem to feel a need to seduce the women with whom they have sexual relations.

But along with seduction goes responsibility for maintaining the women and their children. This is what is most feared by country wives. However, as more and more young women come to the mines from the rural areas to see their husbands or simply to look for work, the distinction between town women and country wives may become quite hazy, especially given the common pattern of "serial marriages".

CONCLUSION

Given the complexity of urban dwelling patterns around the mines, simple solutions to eliminate migrant labour for South African mine workers will be difficult, especially if the migrant system is retained for "foreign labour," and the gender imbalance around the mines is thus perpetuated. In view of population pressures on urban facilities in contemporary South Africa, mine workers with homes in the countryside should be enabled to maintain them. Investment by mine management, the union and the state in low-cost housing alternatives of the site-and-service type and also subsidised rental accommodations will help such workers maintain their rural links.

Provision of such housing options, however, will also encourage the type of "serial marriages" described above. Furthermore, as long as "foreign labour" on the mines ensures a gender imbalance, site-and-service housing will continue to act as a lure for town women. The relative independence of such women, along with a sort of "serial dependency" in their relationships, will continue not only to attract migrant husbands who are without their wives, but also to draw some visiting wives and girlfriends wanting to escape the strenuous labour, family responsibilities and dependency on in-laws that accompany life in the rural areas. Once having experienced the excitement of the townships, these women may abandon their country lives entirely and join the growing numbers of town women.

Attempts by middle-class moralisers to legislate their own standards of sexual or "family" morality have invariably failed. People want to live their own lives and make their own choices within the structures constraining them. While it is desirable to develop housing policies which give individuals a wider range of options (in this case to provide a number of inexpensive, decent and sanitary housing alternatives), the results, which some may reject as immoral, will seem emancipatory to those who are the beneficiaries. The basic objectives should be to widen opportunities for people to make their own decisions about how they conduct their lives.

If policy makers are worried about the instability of marriages of black mine-workers, the most constructive approach would be to extend the right of mine visits to "foreign" wives and girlfriends. This would certainly lead to massive permanent immigration, particularly from the areas which have been most impoverished by many generations of mine labour and more recently by destabilisation. It would, however, be a way for the South African state and the mining industry to pay back some of the wealth expropriated from "foreign" labour supply areas through reliance on generations of under-paid migrants, and would lead to some of the wealth of South Africa being shared with those "foreigners" who actually earned it, rather than with their governments.

One final policy consideration emerges from the experience of these women. The tenacity with which people struggle to work agricultural land in such areas as Pondoland suggests that capital investment in peasants' agricultural produc-

tion and the provision of marketing infrastructures might produce valuable results, especially given the tremendously high level of unemployment in South
Africa. Typically, investment in rural development has pushed people off the
land. Is this exodus a necessary corollary of any model for rural development or
merely a result of current economic assumptions? Certainly, more viable peasant
production would cut down the pressure on permanent urban housing and on
urban wage labourers themselves.

Utopian suggestions aside, the conclusion of this study of the attitudes of
"miners' women" to housing is that flexible housing options are needed on and
around the mines. A range of home-ownership schemes and several rental alternatives will be required in order to provide for complex migration and urbanisation patterns and family and marital relations of greatly varying stability. At
present, the greatest demand is for cheap but comfortable accommodation both
for visiting spouses and girlfriends, wives and families who are living permanently or semi-permanently in the urban areas. ◆

This paper first appeared in Labour, Capital & Society, Vol 25, No 1, 1992. The editors
wish to thank the publishers, the Centre for Developing-Area Studies, McGill University,
Montreal, Quebec, Canada, for granting permission to publish this version.

REFERENCES

Bonner, P. 1990. "Desirable or undesirable Basotho women? Liquor, prostitution and the migration of
Basotho women to the Rand, 1920-1945," in C Walker, (ed,) Women and Gender in Southern
Africa to 1945. Cape Town: David Philip.

Crush, J, AH Jeeves and D Yudelman. 1991. South Africa's Labour Empire: A History of Black
Migrancy to the Gold Mines. Boulder and Cape Town: Westview Press and David Philip.

Jochelson, K, M Mothibeli and J Leger. 1991. "Human Immunodeficiency Virus and migrant labour in
South Africa," in International Journal of Health Studies, Vol 21.

Moodie, TD with V Ndatshe and B Sibuyi. 1988. "Migrancy and male sexuality on the South African
gold mines," in Journal of Southern African Studies, Vol 14.

8

Housing: the Role of the Employer

Ms Sue Moorhead
Housing Unit,
National Union of Mineworkers,
Johannesburg, South Africa

Since its 1987 congress, the National Union of Mineworkers (NUM) has called for the dismantling of the migrant labour system. The system has ensured the maintenance of a cheap labour-force housed in single-sex hostels which are, by any decent standards, unfit for human habitation. This has been, by and large, the major housing policy directive of the union.

We recognise that the dismantling of the migrant labour system is going to be a long process. It involves dealing with the culture of circulatory migration, the massive provision of resources in terms of bulk supply of services and community facilities and, most importantly, the projected life span of a particular mine and the economic viability of a mine and/or mine town.

NUM Housing Policy

The policy approach of the NUM is the following:
◆ Mines must ensure that there is a wide range of flexible, low-cost housing options for the vast majority of the workers. This includes single or family accommodation.
◆ Wages must be restructured so that they are decent living wages. Historically

mine wages have been very low and have excluded the costs of accommodation, food and transport for the family, on the basis that these were provided for the miner at the mine.

◆ Until workers have a decent living wage, employers must provide a housing allowance which is an equal amount across the board for all workers. It must be enough to cover the cost of a bond repayment or rental on a decent house.

◆ Mines must upgrade or convert hostels into decent single and/or family accommodation.

◆ There must be a wide range of tenure options that will allow workers freedom of choice. This includes rental, individual home ownership and social housing.

◆ There must be effective participation of workers in all aspects of housing decisions, including the housing delivery process.

◆ Hostels must be democratised so that residents participate jointly with management in all areas of decision-making around the running of the hostels.

The NUM's approach is in line with the new government's Reconstruction and Development Programme (RDP) which encourages local players to work together on local problems and solutions. The proposals are also in line with the guidelines for the National Housing Subsidy Scheme where "social compacts" of local players are required to put forward project proposals.

Each mine may have different housing policies and situations. The NUM is therefore proposing a process involving housing committees at mine and company level, rather than making detailed proposals for specific company housing benefits. (With a specific company, the NUM will also make specific proposals on the basis of the company's existing housing policies.)

Firstly, the company should agree to recognise housing committees appointed by the NUM branch committee at each mine. Secondly, each mine should undertake a survey of existing housing and hostel facilities and workers' needs in conjunction with the housing committee. The survey would ask whether workers want family or single accommodation; rental, ownership or social housing; whether workers intend settling near the mine permanently or temporarily; what they can afford to pay; and whether the workers' priority is housing in their place of origin and what their needs there would be. The survey would also look at the need for community facilities.

Mine management and the housing committees should plan and implement a programme that would allow workers a real choice between living in (upgraded) hostel accommodation, social housing, or rented or purchased single or family accommodation.

Social housing is a relatively new idea in South Africa. Based on the principles of collective ownership and democratic control, it promotes integration and non-discrimination and aims to make housing affordable. The notion of social housing is gradually being recognised in South Africa as an alternative to owning your own home or renting from a private owner. There is still very little experience of it, but it is an option that is worth exploring.

There are two models. First, community ownership/rental where the land and housing are owned by the community and rented to individuals. Or second, limited ownership in a community housing context. A community-based housing institution is formed to access subsidy and loan funds and individuals are able to gain access to freehold title after they have made some or all of their contribution to repaying the blanket loan.

NUM's housing programme will investigate company housing assistance, including subsidies, living out allowances, loans, bonds, collateral security for loans and bonds, and so on. It will also look at various ways that the company could assist in the provision of affordable housing for its employees, including making land, material, equipment or resources available.

The mine management should ensure that mine employees are, where possible, able to benefit to the fullest extent from national and regional initiatives to make decent housing available to all people. This could include applying jointly with the other local players to the Regional Housing Board for subsidies available under the new Housing Subsidy Scheme. It could also include putting together RDP proposals jointly with the other local stakeholders.

The local surveys and programmes should be reviewed at group level meetings between the NUM and the management of the various mines. This would be in order to monitor the process, share information and experience and identify common problems and issues that could be addressed at group level, such as revision of company housing policy and so on.

As an alternative, a housing committee or forum should be established as a first step at head office level to establish broad policy and parameters. Housing committees would then be set up at mine/business unit level. Where applicable, representatives of the neighbouring communities, relevant public authorities, and so on should be involved in housing planning.

GUIDING PRINCIPLES

◆ Workers must be fully involved, through democratic means, in all levels of decision-making on hostels and housing including formulating and changing company housing policies around housing allowances, home-ownership schemes, personal housing loans, rental of company housing and so on.
◆ Hostel upgrading and conversion and new housing must be planned within the development requirements for the surrounding community, where applicable. Provision of services and facilities must be done in an integrated manner to take into account the needs and existing facilities of the overall workforce and the broader community where applicable (eg recreation facilities, schools, clinic, transport).
◆ Acceptable alternative housing must be provided for hostel residents who move out because of hostel upgrading or conversion.
◆ Workers must not be subjected to any extra cost for basic standards.

◆ Job creation and training for retrenched workers must be built into the programme.

◆ Education and information about housing must be disseminated. There must
be information and training to fully equip workers to participate in all aspects
of housing.

◆ Family housing must be provided by the company. There must be no discrimination on the basis of job grade or any other basis and there must be an
acceptable number of family units that are affordable for the lowest paid workers. Allocation criteria must be decided jointly by the company and the NUM
and the allocation process must be fair and transparent.

◆ Where the company sells its housing, all employees must have access to buying the houses. If the company sells at a discount, then mechanisms must be
put in place to ensure that the discount will be passed on to future employees
who may buy at a later date. This is to ensure that the discount does not
simply find its way into the pockets of the employees that buy first.

◆ Freedom of choice; there should be no restriction on where workers live.

◆ There must be no connection between workers' performance on the job and
their housing. For example, access to a company house or to the company
home-ownership subsidy should not depend on a supervisor's recommenda-
tion. Disciplinary procedures related to housing and hostels should have no
connection to work.

◆ If workers lose their jobs or are retrenched, the company housing subsidy
must be phased out over a period of time.

◆ Workers from other countries should get help, if they so require, to obtain
legal residents' status for themselves and their families.

◆ Proper steps must be taken in the registration of voters to ensure that migrant
workers within and outside South Africa are entitled to vote. Boundaries for
local government must include neighbouring mine hostels or smaller communities which are economically dependent on the major town.

Finally, the NUM firmly believes that workers must be fully involved, through
democratic means, in running the hostels in which they live. The key objective of
the NUM is to establish a system at mine level that facilitates good hostel management and maximises the participation of residents in determining the quality
of their life through effective communication channels and joint decision-making
with management. ◆

RESPONSE

PROFESSOR WILMOT JAMES
Executive Director,
Institute for Democracy in South Africa,
Cape Town, South Africa

The various chapters on hostels reveal many of the unacceptable and intractable problems associated with single-sex life on the mines, and how these have continued into a democratic South Africa. Black mineworkers lead isolated, alienated and often violent lives. They are cut off from broader society, their families, in a huge industry that demands so much and gives so little.

The chapters also indicate how slow and partial progress has been. Family housing, the only alternative finally to hostels, remains the preserve of a small elite. Neither management nor the National Union of Mineworkers seem able to make a decisive shift in how the majority of the black miners are housed.

Two possible avenues of change need further exploration. One is to test whether hostels and their practices are consistent with the democratic constitutional principles South Africa has just adopted. Certainly, hostels seem to violate important democratic values, such as freedom of association, assembly and the right to a family life. It would be interesting to see how the Constitutional Court might respond to the status of mine hostels in relation to the Bill of Rights and constitutional provisions.

A second avenue is to look very carefully at the incentive structure that governs managerial behaviour. The new government has inherited, for example, a tax regime that does not reward companies for innovations in the housing field, or in other areas of reform for that matter. The housing situation on the mines would change rapidly if companies had to pay tax penalties for keeping hostels and tax relief if innovative housing developments were initiated. ◆

HEALTH AND INSECURITY

JOB STRESS, HEALTH AND PERCEPTIONS OF MIGRANT MINEWORKERS

MS MATSHELISO PALESA MOLAPO
Department of Anthropology,
Emory University,
Atlanta, Georgia, USA

The life of the migrant mineworker is a difficult one in which the stresses of dangerous underground work are exacerbated by the alienation of living away from home and family. These strains have a negative effect on the health of the migrant worker: several studies have revealed a link between psychological strains, social strains and job stress on the one hand and high blood pressure on the other (Ahmed, 1991: 288-291). Other outcomes related to stressful situations are the development of peptic ulceration, diabetes and cardiovascular diseases (McQueen and Celentano, 1982: 397-418; Levin et al, 1981: 5-8). Also relevant to the position of the migrant miner are studies showing that individuals who suffer from psycho-social stress usually have low socioeconomic status, poor education and boring but stressful jobs lacking in scope for promotion and decision-making (Bjorntorp, 1991: 195-201). A strong social support system – which migrant mineworkers lack – is found to act as a buffer against these stresses (Dressler, 1990).

This study explores the social risk factors that may make migrant mineworkers vulnerable to non-infectious chronic diseases such as cardiovascular diseases. Data is drawn from ongoing research. To date more than 800 workers have been screened for high blood pressure and 400 interviewed at Western Deep Levels gold mine. The interviewees were healthy Basotho mineworkers aged between 25 and 45 who spend their days and/or nights working in shifts underground. Interviews were also conducted with doctors, nurses and psychologists, as well as social workers and hostel managers.

STRESSES OF UNDERGROUND MINING

Western Deep Levels, owned by the Anglo American Corporation, is the deepest in the world at 3,6km. To reach the maximum depth – levels 100 to 122 – workers must take three sets of elevators down into the earth before continuing their arduous journey by train and on foot to the working face. The toughest working conditions are to be found in the tunnel from which the gold-bearing ore is re-moved, the stope-panel. Here work takes place in an extremely confined space and miners may have to squat for eight hours in order to drill holes in rocks prior to blasting; all this time they are subjected to an almost unbearable combination of heat, noise and humidity that causes discomfort, anxiety and fear. The stress of working under such conditions is exacerbated by the need to watch constantly for signs of imminent/impending accidents. Rockfalls (the fall of unstable rock) and rockbursts (violent movement of rock resulting from a seismic event) are common and increase in frequency at the deepest levels. Fires and explosions pose further risks.

Most miners fear working underground: 95 percent of those interviewed for this study were afraid of dying or being crippled in mine accidents, particularly rockfalls. Degrees of fear, however, ranged from extreme cases of post-traumatic stress disorder and claustrophobia to a resigned attitude that death is the fate of all living creatures. Most of the workers who showed signs of fear abhorred everything connected to mining: the underground work, compound life and (human) labour relations on the mine. Only a minority thought mining was a source of pride, identity and security.

The constant fear felt by miners was described by 25-year-old Phakiso from Lesotho, who had been working at Western Deep Levels for 11 months at the time of the interview[1]. Like many other miners he does not like mine work but feels he has little choice because his family is desperately poor. He feels that as a timber member he labours hard in difficult and dangerous conditions and that in return he is paid little. Phakiso lives in fear of a rockfall and is haunted by the memories of his first accident:

> At Christmas I witnessed a horrible accident underground in which six people died. Their limbs were cut off and some were buried alive. I could not eat nor sleep that night ... You are never sure if you will make it safely back (to the) surface each day you descend.

---

1. *The names in this article are pseudonyms to protect the subjects.*

Long-time miners share similar fears. Phehello, aged 43, who has been working at Western Deep Levels for more than 13 years, says:

> You are most likely to die or to become crippled by the time you leave this place ... I have been working here for years but I cannot get used to underground accidents, particularly rockfalls ... I have seen just too many horrible accidents underground. While underground we worry too much because we are never sure if we will make it back to the surface alive and well. All the time we are down there we pray silently.

In extreme cases, mineworkers suffer from such severe post-traumatic stress that they can no longer work underground and must undergo extensive therapy. Dumiso, 34, from Lesotho, is one such victim. A mineworker for six years and the sole survivor of a major rockfall a year ago, he watched five co-workers die while nearby rescuers battled to reach the group. In haphazard speech, Dumiso explains haltingly that he never wants to work underground again because he fears that rocks will kill him. He has nightmares in which he is hit by rocks or in which women bury him by covering his corpse, not with soil, but with rocks that fall with great force upon him. Though he is already dead in his dream, he feels as if he is dying again.

Many workers have experienced accidents so often that they claim to have gained visual skill and a sixth sense that enables them to foresee underground accidents (Leger and Mothibeli, 1988). Before starting work, they examine the shape of the rocks in the face to see if changes have taken place overnight. If they find anything suspicious they notify their team leaders and other supervisors, saying that they do not want to work in a dangerous area. Miners claim that supervisors often do not take these fears seriously and force them to work anyway. At times, accidents occur after the supervisors have been warned, the miners say. Sello, who has been a mineworker for the past 22 years, describes the chilling sensation he has experienced before an accident:

> Before the rocks fall and hit the ground there is a wind that blows. At first the wind is very mild and once it has gained strength the rocks burst and fall simultaneously. When they fall they hit from angles ... There is no way one can escape them ... Everything happens so fast that it is hard to warn people in advance so they can protect themselves ... The wind is so strong that it blows helmets off our heads. That is how we sustain head injuries. At times it displaces the person by blowing him to another area. In other situations, the rocks blow the victim into pieces (so) that it is hard to distinguish human flesh or body parts from one another.

Workers think of seismic movements as an animal or monster that moves from shaft to shaft causing accidents. Tales about the "creature" are common at Western Deep Levels because of the many accidents that occur there. Says Oupa from the Orange Free State:

> There is something alive that moves underground here at Western Deep. It
> is like an animal and unique to Western Deep. When it hits it kills instantly.
> I remember one time when it hit at number three shaft, five people died at
> once; hours later it hit at number two shaft and three people died.

Some miners resign immediately after an accident but others cope by developing psychological survival skills. Samuel, 41, from Lesotho, who has been working at Western Deep Levels for 16 years, says:

> I have witnessed too many mine accidents underground. I have seen 40 to
> 60 people that I know very well die. Some of them were very close friends
> of mine. I do not have fear of the underground any more; I am hardened.

Belief in prayer and ancestral powers and a sense of omnipotence enable some miners to recover quickly from an ordeal underground. Thami, who was trapped underground for three days, says God decided it was not yet his time to die. Another worker says that he is protected underground by "doctoring" powers which he inherited from his grandfather, a powerful traditional doctor, and he believes he will never be killed in an underground accident. This worker also copes by eliciting a sense of humour, constantly joking and laughing.

Many workers want to resign but stay on in part because they believe they will lose all the benefits due to them if they do so. But the main reason they face the daily perils of underground mining is so that their families do not starve. Workers who are proud of mining are usually older (20-30 years of experience of mining) and have seen and been involved in all kinds of accidents, but have survived. Mining makes them feel younger and stronger.

STRESSES CAUSED BY HUMAN AND LABOUR RELATIONS

Adding to the stresses endured by miners as a result of underground work are problems in labour and human relations. Interviewees complained about the lack of respect from their seniors underground and from mining authorities; little or no prospect of promotion; threat of retrenchment; boredom; a sense of exploitation by the mining industry; unfair compensation; living away from their family; limits on lengths of visits by wives; and too many expectations from families back home. Mineworkers feel they have no say in decision-making and that their lives are therefore akin to those of prisoners. They say a supervisor will make a worker's life miserable if the worker voices his opinions. Comments Khutso:

> I do not feel free and happy at my work because nobody listens to me. I
> feel like a prisoner here. We cannot even speak for ourselves. The white
> supervisors at Western Deep ... treat us like slaves and nonentities just
> because we are black.

Another worker voiced similar complaints:

> I feel like a prisoner who is serving a long sentence here at Western Deep
> because for most of my life I do not live with my family. The mine also
> treats us as though we have no right to live our lives as we wish. Our wives
> can only visit for a short while. I visit home once a month. If I try to go
> home for six days the management gets angry ... We always have to lie and
> say somebody died at home. Even when we are due for leave we have
> problems because there are some individuals that we have to bribe so that
> our leave forms can be processed.

There is no outlet for the anger and suspicion that miners experience. Some-
times their lack of trust is so deep-seated that they do not even trust their spouses.
Personal problems are only compounded by their stressful work environment.
As Samuel explained:

> I have a serious problem and that is to do with my temper. I usually feel
> angry and feel like fighting. My blood would boil. My supervisors have
> advised me against my violent temper. For the sake of my children I am
> trying to control my temper. I share my problems with no one, not even
> with my wife. There are a lot of things that happen at work that make me
> very unhappy but I keep them to myself.

Miners feel they have no control over their lives and are at the mercy of the
mine authorities who can, for example, keep the miners waiting for long hours
underground for transport to the surface after they have finished their work.
(Workers on the morning shift clock-in at 5am and are supposed to clock-out at
2pm, but even if they finish what needs to be done by 11am they are kept in an
enclosure until 2pm.) Miners also say they are not allowed to leave the work site
until the supervisor feels the work has been done. Some people work double
shifts without being paid for their second shift. Workers on evening shift de-
scend at 8pm and are supposed to knock off at about 4am. But often they work
beyond that up to midday or 2pm and are not paid for the extra time.

Miners complain about a general lack of respect from underground supervisors and clerks at the hospital and pay office. They resent being cursed and being
referred to as "stupid" men who know about nothing except work underground.
Says Khutso:

> People generally undermine mineworkers. They think we are stupid. It does
> not mean that if we have never been to school and cannot speak English we
> are stupid. God gave us knowledge, all of us.

Mineworkers are particularly aggrieved when they are treated with disrespect by those who were previously their equals. Khutso complains that black
workers who are promoted to team leader positions sometimes "mimic the white

supervisors" and "try to please them at our expense". These frustrations are echoed by Samuel, whose comment shows scant sympathy for a retrenched team leader:

> The team leader that I work with right now is a good man. But the previous one had no respect for us. He was a newcomer; we taught him the job and thereafter he looked down upon us. He used to tell us that we [were] "not men enough". That used to hurt our feelings and we would be very angry to the extent that going to work was such great effort each time we think of this man. He lost his job; he is now in Lesotho doing nothing.

Team leaders often feel quite differently about their work. Mosioa, a 33-year-old stoping team leader with a Std 7 qualification, does not mind working hard because he earns more than many others. Though he dreads underground explosions and accidents caused by machines and elevators, he does not have any serious work-related problems.

The issue of unpaid overtime is seen as being symptomatic of the indifference of mine authorities. Workers say they are promised bonuses for working in excess of the standard eight-hour shift. But when their pay slips arrive there is usually no extra money, or only R5 extra, they say. Tax deductions are often given as an excuse, but these are not shown on the pay slip. Mineworkers who question this are sometimes threatened with losing their jobs. Authorities also play on the ignorance of the workers. Continues Khutso:

> When the union tries to follow up on such an unfair matter, the mine plays some tricks. What it does is that it retrenches workers and organise(s) with contractors to bring workers for cheap labour. We are always scared that we will lose our jobs.

Confusion surrounds the criteria for promotion at the mine. Many workers believe they are not promoted because of their poor relations with their seniors. They say inexperienced newcomers often get promotions more easily and earn more than long-timers. Telekiso, who was injured underground, said:

> I have been working at Western Deep for 12 years and I have never been promoted. I do not feel respected in any way. My existence as a mine employee and my services are not recognised nor appreciated ... When are these people going to realise that we are human beings too?

Some workers feel that the only way to secure one's job or to get a promotion is to be submissive. Thuto's approach is as follows:

> In order to survive here on the mines you just have to act stupid ... When you get a promotion you will earn more money and that money is going to quieten you. Those people who receive more money do not even partici-

pate in the meetings organised by the union because they do not want to say anything counter to the system; they now become part of the system. Those who keep on challenging the workings of the mine management by conscientising the workers are most likely to be dismissed.

Workers complain that their illnesses are not taken seriously and that sometimes they are sent underground even if they have fractures. The medical staff always think they are malingering, they say. Only extreme cases – such as when a miner collapses underground due to heat exhaustion – receive urgent attention. Workers say they are supposed to be compensated for illnesses arising from heat exhaustion, but they never get that compensation. They believe that the mine cares only about the labour they provide. They say a healthy miner is regarded as marketable but that he is abandoned as soon he develops serious occupationally related health problems. This attitude is demonstrated by the poor compensation that workers get in the event of injury or permanent disability. Miners still harbour bitter memories about past refusals by mine management to pay the costs of transporting home the corpses of employees who had died underground. Among both surface and underground workers, Western Deep Levels is known as *hamatsotsi* – the place where a person can be robbed of money, good health and life[2].

All the complaints mentioned above have serious effects on workers' health, effects that can even develop into serious long-term physiological risk factors. Jobs characterised by a combination of high demands, low control, low decision-making and a poor employer-employee working relationship have been shown to be associated with an increase in blood pressure (Schall, 1992: 488-494). Studies have also established a link between noise and several diseases including cardiovascular diseases, hypertension and peptic ulceration (Godlee, 1992: 110-113).

OTHER SOCIAL STRESSES

Migrant workers are subject to social strains resulting from the fact that they live far from their families. Many work on the mines only because jobs are scarce back home. The rural domestic economy of Lesotho, for example, is largely dependent on miners' remittances (Murray, 1981). Migrants who have never been to school find that mining is one of the few employment opportunities open to them. Others come to the mines to earn enough money to buy cattle for brideprice, to build a home, buy livestock or educate their children.

Most miners do not want to live permanently in the city or on the mines: they have established homes in the rural areas. They find city life extremely expensive because they are forced to buy all their requirements. On the other hand, however, kinship relations place a big financial burden on the migrant miner. His earnings usually have to support several people and households – his own, that

---

2. *Tsotsi is a word derived from South African street lingo referring to a thug or a crook.*

of his parents and possibly an unmarried sister and unemployed brother and their children. This is a way of returning favours to members of the extended family who help their wives in the fields all year. Workers say that their extended families will suffer if the miner's nuclear family relocates permanently to the city.

REPORTING AND RECORDING ACCIDENTS AND DISEASE

A monthly report of one of the medical stations at Western Deep Levels, shows that out of a total of 1 218 patients, 173 were hurt in mine accidents, 118 treated for acute upper respiratory infections and 84 had sexually transmitted diseases (STDs). These statistics probably under-report the prevalence of all three since not all workers visit a medical station when they are sick. The reason for this is in part because of the way reporting of injuries takes place: it is up to white supervisors or shift bosses to decide whether workers injured underground should report to the medical station. In most cases supervisors do not send workers for treatment so that they do not lose the bonus awarded for an "accident-free" shift. Injured workers do not benefit from these bonuses; only their supervisors do.

Shift bosses have other methods of making sure they get these bonuses: they have been known to remove hospitalised workers before they have received any treatment so that there are no records of the accident. They have also taken injured workers to outside hospitals for the same reason. The mine management is trying to curb these practices and apparently is having some success. Workers feel that if they go against the word of their shift boss by reporting sick, they will be subjected to unbearable working conditions and probably lose their jobs. When the mining houses introduced bonuses for injury-free shifts, they probably had good intentions of minimising accidents by promoting and encouraging safety underground. It would seem these safety measures are not being properly implemented by the supervisors, who compromise the health and safety of workers for their own gain.

The incidence of TB on the mines is increasing, particularly among underground workers. Workers interpret TB – as well as any chest pains, gastric pains or stomach cramps – as "food poisoning" or *sejeso*, and do not believe that modern medicine can cure them. As a result, they consult traditional healers back home to remove the "poison". After such treatments, some of the workers do not complete their TB treatments as scheduled by a medical doctor.

Most of the patients who have STDs are too embarrassed or scared to go to the medical stations and prefer to consult a private doctor. The medical stations routinely test for HIV on patients reporting STDs, and some patients are probably afraid to take this routine HIV check. This may also keep them away from the medical stations.

Patients who test positive for HIV usually receive counselling, which includes Aids education programmes, one-on-one counselling and group counselling at a

TABLE 1: HOSTEL AND SHAFT PRESENTING PROBLEMS, JAN-DEC 1992

MINE	PROB 1	PROB 2	PROB 3	PROB 4	PROB 5	PROB 6
SOUTH MINE						
NO 1 HOSTEL	SEXUAL	STDS	HIV	FAMILIAL	PSYCHOSOMA	STRESS
NO 1 SHAFT	DEPRESSION	ALCOHOL	*PTSD	MARITAL	FAMILIAL	ANXIETY
EAST MINE						
NO 3 HOSTEL	HIV	ALCOHOL	FAMILY & WORK	PSYCHOSOMA	DEPRESSION	PSYCHOSOMA
NO 3 SHAFT	ALCOHOL	PTSD	DEPRESSION	MARITAL	FINANCIAL	ANXIETY
WEST MINE						
NO 2 HOSTEL	HIV	DEPRESSION	STDS	MARITAL	FAMILIAL	DRUGS
NO 2 SHAFT	ALCOHOL	DEPRESSION	MARITAL	PSYCHOSOMA &PTSD	STRESS	FAMILIAL
NO 9 HOSTEL	HIV & STRESS	STDS	MARITAL	DEPRESSION	BEHAVIOURAL	DEPRESSION
REGIONAL	ALCOHOL	MARITAL	DEPRESSION	CHILDHOOD DISORD	PSYCHOSOMA	FAMILIAL
ELANDSRAND						
HOSTEL	ALCOHOL	PTSD	DEPRESSION	MARITAL	PSYCHOSOMA	ANXIETY
SHAFT	FAMILIAL	FINANCIAL	HIV	WORK RELATED	ALCOHOL	DEPRESSION
EAC	ALCOHOL	DEPRESSION	MARITAL	PTSD	PSYCHOSOMA	ANXIETY

* PTSD – Post Traumatic Stress Disorder
  Source – Employee Assistance Centre (EAC) Annual Report 1992

clinic run by the Employee Assistance Programme. Medical staff and therapists are, however, frustrated by the fact that the very people who test positive and receive Aids education are usually the ones who report to the medical stations with new STDs.

Another problem for Aids counsellors and educationists on the mine is that as soon as some workers learn that they are HIV positive they consult their traditional healers who claim to have a cure for Aids. The patients are treated with *muti* to "cleanse" the blood and flush the virus out of the system. After such treatment the workers have the healer's assurance and truly believe they are free of the virus and resume unprotected sex. They also discontinue counselling sessions. Clearly, there is a long way to go in convincing workers about the dangers to which they are exposing themselves and others, and in educating them in making use of the system of traditional healing more wisely.

THE MINERS' EXPLANATORY MODELS OF ILLNESS

If treatment for any condition is to be effective, the cultural explanations and perceptions of illness, disease and well-being – as understood by the workers in this case – must be taken into consideration. This is crucial in the sense that workers' views will determine the compliance with and effectiveness of treatment as well as implementation of health care. It is not only medicine that contributes to healing: the mental state and cultural beliefs of an individual make a tremendous contribution to his or her well-being. An example of this lies in miners' explanatory models of illnesses associated with blood. Generally, Africans perceive blood to be the source of life. Thus one needs healthy blood and circulation in order to lead a healthy life. If an individual does not have "healthy blood" he is likely to be constantly sick and will eventually die.

Because of these views, clinical withdrawal of blood for testing is a sensitive issue for workers. The removed blood is considered to be part of the body and irreplaceable; it must at some stage be reinfused into the system as the body cannot function without it. Workers also fear that blood may become contaminated while it is in the laboratory and that this in turn will make them sick. When some patients test positive for HIV they conclude that their blood was contaminated or bewitched while in the laboratory.

The fact that workers do not know what happens to the blood after tests affects every aspect of their well-being: they complain of general malaise, weakness and dizziness. Molise has this to say about the withdrawal of his blood:

> Since my blood was taken five months ago I have not been myself. My blood is weak and as a result I feel weak. This weakness is also affecting my sexual performance. I do not know what they have done to my blood. Nobody wants to tell me where my blood is. I want it back. I am sure that I will feel better and be myself again once it has been reinfused.

Most workers believe that high blood pressure is a sexually-related disease and that it is likely to develop in individuals who do not engage in sexual intercourse. The assumption behind this is that sex activates blood and keeps it circulating; a lack of sex will cause the blood to accumulate and to become motionless, resulting in illness. It is believed that people with "high blood" feel listless and suffer from headaches. The workers say "high blood" can be prevented and cured by regular sexual intercourse and less worry; certainly this is the opinion of many of the men in the compound who exchange money for sex. Some believe that "high blood" can develop into serious mental illness and insanity. In this case, they say, the blood has "gone to the head".

Another common opinion among mineworkers is that an individual who worries too much is likely to develop "high blood" because the heart will pump blood extremely fast and as a result an oversupply of blood will accumulate in the head and body. Workers say that they are prone to high blood pressure because they worry a lot about their absent families and the infrequent contact with their wives.

The life of the average worker alternates between work and over-indulgence in alcohol. High rates of alcohol abuse among mineworkers present serious behavioural and medical problems. In the 1992 annual report of the Employee Assistance Centre, alcohol was named the biggest problem. Also on the list were STDs, HIV, sexual problems and depression (Table 1). Some sexual problems, such as weak libido, may be associated with heavy alcohol intake and stress. When asked what the reasons were for their excessive drinking, workers listed worry, fatigue, anger, thirst and a need to kill time. Some said they were able to sleep "peacefully" when drunk and that this allowed them to escape from their worries about their families and underground work.

Few workers believe that overconsumption of alcohol is bad: alcoholism is not seen as a disease, merely as a habit. The reason for this is that mineworkers consider it normal for every community to have a certain number of alcoholics. Some workers say alcohol is a form of food while others see it as therapeutic in that it makes one forget one's problems and provides enjoyment. Mineworkers believe that too much alcohol intake will overpower the amount of blood in the bloodstream; an individual who reaches this point cannot live without alcohol because it has become part of his or her identity. Such an individual will only look "normal" when drunk.

CONCLUSION

The overconsumption of alcohol is just one of a range of serious behavioural problems manifested on the mines as a direct result of job stress and other social strains endured by migrant underground workers. Underground work in itself is very strenuous and poor human and labour relations only exacerbate the stress felt by workers. It may be true that little can be done to reduce the strain of underground work, but improved labour relations could limit additional stress, and increase productivity.

It is crucial for perceived injustices, for example non-payment for overtime and the unfairness of the system of bonuses for accident-free shifts, to be addressed immediately. These issues pose serious risk factors to chronic psychological and physiological disease outcomes such as depression, anxiety, alcoholism, psychosomatic problems and cardiovascular diseases.

The issue of housing preferences for migrant labourers must also be examined. Mining houses are starting to experiment with alternative housing programmes, such as home-ownership schemes, rent subsidies, living-out allowances and the upgrading of hostels, which could provide an alternative for migrant workers who wish to live with their families either temporarily or permanently near the mines (Crush and Jeeves, 1992). The proximity of families should curb miners' interaction with prostitutes which would in turn limit the escalating cases of STDs and HIV. The presence of spouses and family will also provide a better social support system from which the miner will be able to draw some psychological strength in trying times. ◆

REFERENCES

Ahmed, LE. 1991. "Clinical presentation of high blood pressure," in Ethnicity and Disease, Vol 2, No 1.

Bjorntorp, P. 1991. "Visceral fat accumulation: the missing link between psychosocial factors and cardiovascular disease," in Journal of Internal Medicine, Vol 230.

Dressler, WW. 1990. "Culture, stress and disease," in T Johnson and C Sargent, (eds,) Medical Anthropology: Contemporary Theory and Method. New York: Praeger.

Crush, J and AH Jeeves. 1992. "The failure of stabilisation experiments and the entrenchment of migrancy to the South African gold mines," in Labour, Capital and Society, Vol 25, No 1.

Godlee, F. 1992. "Noise: breaking the silence," in British Medical Journal, Vol 304.

James, W. 1992. "Capital, African labour and housing at South Africa's gold mines," in Labour, Capital and Society, Vol 25, No 1.

Leger, J. 1987. "From Hlobane to Kinross: disasters and the struggle for health and safety on the mines," in G Moss and I Obery, (eds,) South African Review, Vol 4, Johannesburg: Ravan Press.

Leger, J. 1990. "Key issues in safety and health in South African mines," in South African Sociological Review, Vol 2.

Leger, J and M Mothibeli. 1988. "Talking rocks: pit sense amongst South African miners," in Labour, Capital and Society, Vol 21.

Levin A, L Schlebusch, F Katzeff, K Naidoo, I Goolam-Hoosan and MG Moshel. 1981. "Psychosituational factors and duodenal ulceration in South African blacks and Indians," in South African Medical Journal, Vol 59, No 5.

Marks, S and N Andersson. 1989. "The state, class and the allocation of health resources in southern Africa," in Social Science and Medicine, Vol 28, No 5.

Marks, S and N Andersson. 1989. "Diseases of Apartheid," in John Londale, (ed,) South Africa in Question. Cambridge: African Studies Centre.

McQueen DV and J Siegrist. 1982. "Social factors in the etiology of chronic disease: an overview," in Social Science and Medicine, Vol 16.

McQueen DV and DD Celentano. 1982. "Social factors in the etiology of multiple outcomes: the case of blood pressure and alcohol consumption patterns," in Social Science and Medicine, Vol 16.

Moodie, TD with V Ndantshe. 1992. "Town women and country wives: migrant labour, family politics and housing preferences at Vaal Reefs mine," in Labour, Capital and Society, Vol 25, No 1.

Murray, C. 1981. Families Divided: The Impact of Migrant Labour in Lesotho. Cambridge: Cambridge University Press.

Packard, R. 1989. "Industrial production, health and disease in sub-Saharan Africa," in Social Science and Medicine, Vol 28, No 5.

Packard, R. 1989. White Plague, Black Labour: Tuberculosis and the Political Economy of Health and Disease in South Africa. Berkeley: University of California Press.

Seedat, YK. 1981. "High blood pressure – the silent killer," in South African Medical Journal, Vol 59.

Schall, PL. 1992. "Relation between job strain, alcohol and ambulatory blood pressure," in Hypertension, Vol 19.

WHITE PLAGUE, BLACK LABOUR REVISITED: TB AND THE MINING INDUSTRY

PROFESSOR RANDALL M PACKARD
Department of Public Health,
Emory University,
Atlanta, Georgia, USA

DR DAVID COETZEE
Department of Community Health,
University of the Witwatersrand,
Johannesburg, South Africa

In 1989, when *White Plague, Black Labour: Tuberculosis and the Political Economy of Health and Disease in South Africa* was published, few could have predicted the rapid political transformations that are now under way in South Africa. The political climate in the late 1980s did not seem to hold much promise for significant political change. In fact there were signs of growing conservatism within the white population, accompanied by increasingly oppressive security measures. The book concluded with the following pessimistic prediction:

The current push by conservative whites for stronger segregation and the stiffer laws aimed at controlling the spread of illegal squatter communities would seem to indicate that a 1950s-like exercise in wall-building is in the offing. If this course is chosen, the next generation of South African leaders, whatever their political or racial complexion, is likely to face an even greater epidemic of the "white plague" (Packard, 1989: 319).

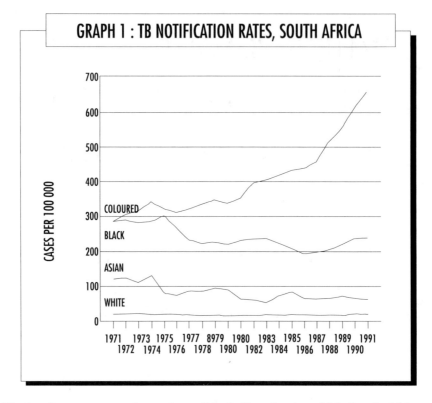

GRAPH 1 : TB NOTIFICATION RATES, SOUTH AFRICA

The book was wrong about the political direction in which South Africa was about to move. Yet it was tragically correct about the future of TB. South Africa is today facing a rising TB epidemic (Graph 1).

The current rise in TB incidence, while broad-based, is not distributed evenly. Whites continue to exhibit the lowest rates of TB, although cohort studies suggest that small increases have occurred between 1986 and 1991. The most affected group, as defined by South Africa's racial categories, are "coloureds", among whom a virtual epidemic has been under way for over a decade, with a dramatic increase since 1986 in the rates recorded for every age group (*Epidemiological Comments*, 1992: 184) (Graphs 2 and 3).

The high incidence figures for coloureds, when compared to the lower figures for Africans, have raised questions about the validity of both sets of data. Some have argued that considerable over-diagnosing of TB among coloureds has occurred in the Western Cape[1]. Yet studies that have examined the specificity of TB

---

1. *Derek Yach, Director, Research, Medical Research Council, Pretoria – Personal Communication.*

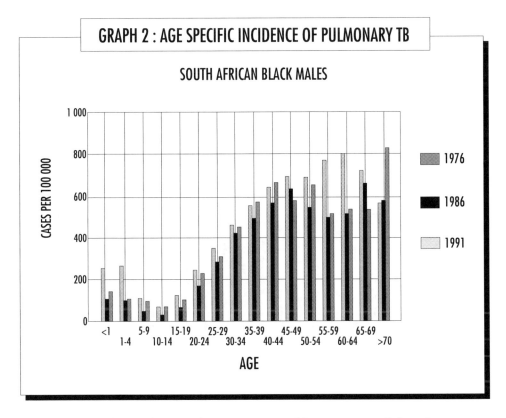

GRAPH 2 : AGE SPECIFIC INCIDENCE OF PULMONARY TB

SOUTH AFRICAN BLACK MALES

diagnoses in all populations do not support this argument. Others have suggested that the high level of TB among coloureds reflects the fact that the majority live in the Western Cape Health Region which has the most efficient health services and record-keeping. Coloureds with TB are, in effect, more likely to be diagnosed than are Africans living in areas with less efficient or non-existent health services (Packard, 1989: 301). Implicit in this argument is the suggestion that the African incidence rates are artificially low due to under-reporting.

There may be some truth in both suggestions. The Western Cape Health Region does have the highest reported incidence and prevalence of TB, although the Orange Free State is a close second. The Western Cape also investigates more suspects and contacts per case than any other region (*Epidemiological Comments,* 1993: 3).

Conversely the region with the lowest prevalence and incidence rates, Lebowa, has what are arguably the least efficient TB services. Official notification figures show that in 1991 Lebowa had a low prevalence of 145/100 000 compared to an average for the seven health districts of 662/100 000. But Lebowa's cure rate is only 41 percent compared to an average of 72 percent for the seven health regions. The estimated case fatality rate is 8 percent compared to 3 percent for the seven regions, an indication that cases are being identified late in their disease experience. Lebowa's "absconding rate", that is the percentage of people who are lost to treatment, is 53 percent, compared to 18 percent for the seven regions. Case finding activities are even more revealing. Only 0,36 new suspects are

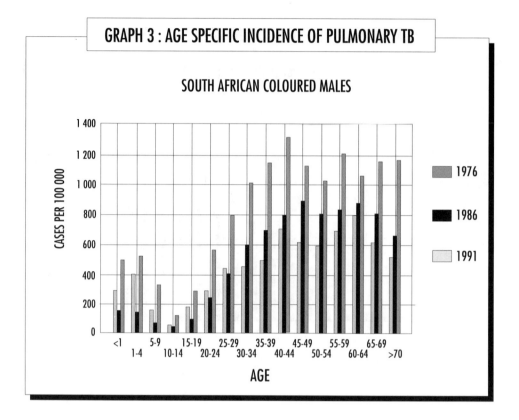

GRAPH 3 : AGE SPECIFIC INCIDENCE OF PULMONARY TB

SOUTH AFRICAN COLOURED MALES

investigated for every new TB case, compared to an average of 3,3 for the seven health districts. No mass X-rays are conducted. However, the case yield from X-rays performed in clinics is an astounding 585/1 000 compared to an average of 135/1 000. These figures lead one to believe that there is far more TB in Lebowa than is reported.

There are other reasons for suspecting that African TB rates may be closer to those of coloureds than the official notification figures reveal. Populations at greatest risk of contracting TB have the least access to health services. Health services in the country's booming squatter communities and overcrowded townships are either non-existent or have broken down under the weight of financial constraints or ongoing violence. In 1993 local political activists in squatter camps in Gazankulu, near the prosperous white farming community of Tzaneen, refused to recognise any state authorities including those responsible for health. Health officers were therefore unable to gain access to the inhabitants of these camps to identify TB cases or trace contacts.

The current rise in TB cases in South Africa is part of a world-wide increase. Yet it must also be seen as a product of specific political and economic processes. Some of these, described in *White Plague, Black Labour*, were set in motion decades ago. The impoverishment of rural former homelands combined with low-wage policies in industry and a series of repressive measures exposed the vast majority of African men and women to unhealthy and unsafe living and working

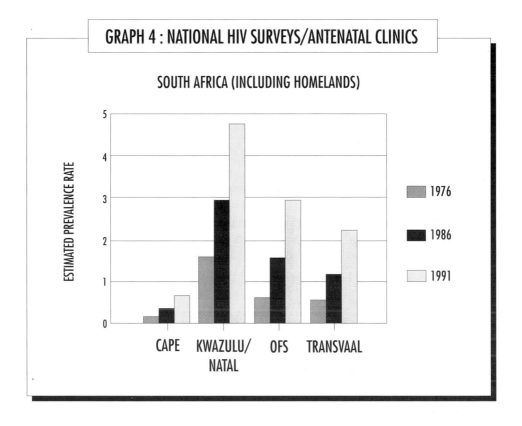

GRAPH 4 : NATIONAL HIV SURVEYS/ANTENATAL CLINICS

SOUTH AFRICA (INCLUDING HOMELANDS)

ESTIMATED PREVALENCE RATE

CAPE KWAZULU/ OFS TRANSVAAL
NATAL

1976

1986

1991

conditions, and prevented them from maintaining the health and well-being of their families.

Yet the epidemic also has more proximate causes. One of the most important of these is the scrapping of influx control laws in 1987. For decades influx control laws, regulated through the compulsory carrying of passes and the use of police-state monitoring and control of population movements, had restricted rural African families from settling in urban areas and enforced the separation of men and women from their families. The removal of influx controls was viewed by many as a progressive move.

Yet it occurred during a sustained economic recession that continues today and it coincided with the worst drought of this century. In this context thousands of Africans have moved away from the impoverishment of rural areas to seek a better life in and near the urban centres. But they have found that there is no better life because there are few jobs and the former government's adoption of a free market approach to housing, withdrawing from the provision of state-owned housing, meant that there was no place for the people fleeing rural poverty.

The result has been the emergence of huge squatter communities throughout the country. In addition, population densities in existing townships, such as Daveyton and Thokoza on the East Rand, or KwaMashu outside Durban, have greatly increased. The Urban Foundation estimates that the size of the shack-dwelling population, a euphemism for those people who piece together shelters

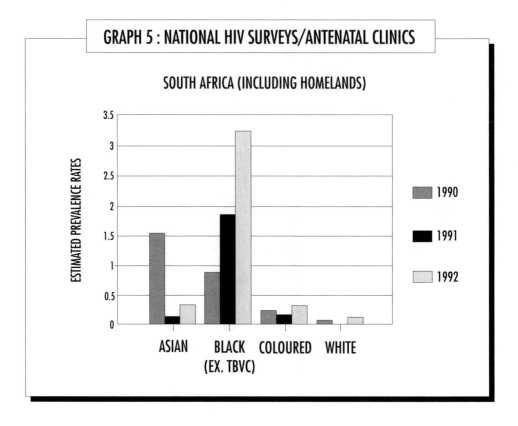

GRAPH 5 : NATIONAL HIV SURVEYS/ANTENATAL CLINICS

SOUTH AFRICA (INCLUDING HOMELANDS)

from packing crates, car parts or whatever they can scavenge, constitutes 64 percent of the total African population of the Durban region. While the new state is
trying to rationalise this squatter process and provide some basic amenities (la-
trines, water pipes), these camps are marked by overcrowding and lack of sani-
tation in combination with poor nutrition and outright hunger.

In 1992 about 40 percent of shack dwellers and 13 percent of township dwellers lived on R30 a month (Hambridge, 1992: 1). The high levels of disease in such
communities are indicated in the existence of two squatter camps outside East
London named by their residents "TB" and "TB 2". The lack of adequate health
services and monitoring facilities prevent us from documenting the true extent
of the problem.

On top of the social and economic conditions existing in overcrowded townships and squatter camps, there is the political turmoil and violence that has
racked many of these areas. In the year preceding the recent elections, political
and other forms of violence and ongoing feuds between the ANC comrades and
the *impis* of the Inkatha Freedom Party, between township residents and the residents of the migrant hostels, between rival gangs made up of young men who
have long since given up hope of an economic future, between the better off and
the poorest of the poor, racked the East Rand townships in the Transvaal on a
daily basis. These conflicts were undoubtedly heightened by the flood of new
residents that accompanied the lifting of influx controls, and greatly increased

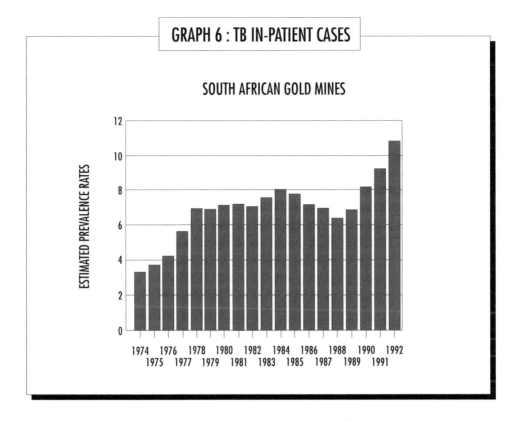

GRAPH 6 : TB IN-PATIENT CASES

SOUTH AFRICAN GOLD MINES

pressure on the limited resources available to township residents. This violence, which during much of 1993 claimed about 100 lives a week on the East Rand, created high levels of stress, disrupted social life and prevented people from going to work for fear of being attacked or killed. These people were at risk of losing the jobs that kept them from sinking even deeper into poverty. The violence also disrupted, and in some cases closed down, existing medical services, as noted above, and has no doubt contributed to the high "absconding" rates reported in the region.

Finally, one must add to the political and economic mix the effects of HIV and Aids which is accelerating among certain segments of the African population. Estimates of the time it takes for the prevalence of HIV to double range from six to 12 months depending on the population being studied (*Epidemiological Comments*, 1992: 35) (Graphs 4 and 5).

Many of the same conditions which have apparently contributed to the rising tide of TB in South Africa have also increased exposure to HIV. Migrant labour and family separation, combined with high levels of background infections and malnutrition, as well as political violence, have facilitated the transmission and progression of HIV. A study of HIV in KwaZulu/Natal in 1990 revealed that among people in the 15-44 year age group, those who were most mobile (defined as having moved once in the previous year) had nearly three times the incidence of HIV infection as their more stable counterparts. The study concluded that this

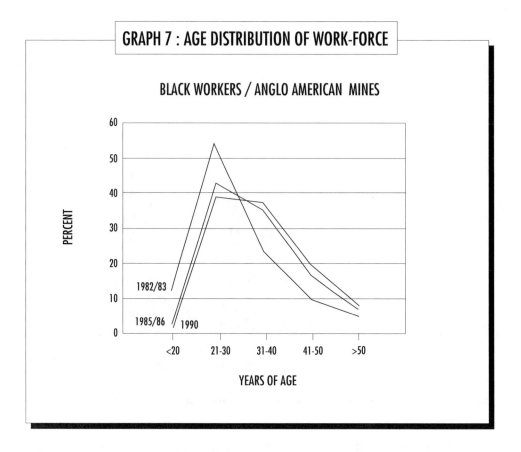

GRAPH 7 : AGE DISTRIBUTION OF WORK-FORCE

BLACK WORKERS / ANGLO AMERICAN MINES

mobile group, although small (313 people out of a total study population of 2 678, or 11,8 percent), constituted an important source of infection in the study area (Abdool-Karim, nd).

Hambridge (1992: 2), in his study of HIV and Aids in Natal, noted that among youth gangs in the townships and squatter camps, sexual mores had disintegrated and in their place a youth culture of sexual promiscuity bound up with anti-apartheid struggle placed young women in a situation where refusing sexual activity was equated with being unpatriotic. Although such claims echo sexual stereotypes that have been too closely associated with discussions of Aids in Africa, studies of youth gangs in the United States also point to an association between high levels of sexual activity and gang membership. Women in general are at a much higher risk of HIV infection than men in Natal and elsewhere. In KwaZulu/Natal in 1990, 2,3 percent of rural women aged between 15 and 44 were infected with HIV. Only 0,5 percent of rural men in the same age group were infected (Abdool-Karim, nd: 24).

Prior to the transition, controlling the growth of the HIV epidemic was extremely difficult due to the existence of these underlying social and economic conditions and within a political climate where health workers preaching abstinence and condom use were viewed with suspicion.

The combination of all these factors has produced an ideal breeding ground for TB. Yet it is important to realise that the recent increase in TB incidence may be due to other causes. The removal of influx controls not only created conditions conducive to the spread of TB, it also reversed practices which had led to the systematic removal of African TB cases from the view of the government health statisticians. Years of forced removals, the repatriation of sick workers and the creation of nation states that were excluded from South Africa's statistical boundaries had contributed to a decline in South Africa's TB notification rates. With the removal of influx controls and the reincorporation of homeland populations into the official statistical boundaries of South Africa, TB may simply have become more visible.

In addition, there is evidence of a new consciousness among some regional health authorities of the need to take a more aggressive stance in dealing with TB. The Orange Free State Health Region has greatly increased its surveillance activities, extending case finding and prevalence surveys to white farming areas for the first time. An independent survey among blacks living on farms revealed a TB prevalence of 681/100 000 among children aged two to 16 years, and 879 per 100 000 for adults 17 years and older (*Epidemiological Comments*, 1991: 176). For all intents and purposes these cases were previously invisible, appearing in the health statistics of neighbouring homelands outside South Africa. It is in fact difficult to sort out the extent to which the current rise of TB is a product of changing social and economic conditions in the country, or the growing visibility of the problem, or both.

TB AND THE SOUTH AFRICAN MINING INDUSTRY

The rising tide of TB in South Africa has been particularly acute among black workers in South Africa's gold-mining industry. TB has long been a major source of morbidity among black workers in the South Africa gold mines. Improvements in case finding and treatment led to a steady decline in the incidence between 1960 and 1968 and then after a brief rise in 1969-70, through the early 1970s. The incidence of TB (simple and with silicosis) then rose sharply from the mid-1970s. Industry-wide TB rates for black miners rose from roughly 4/1 000 to over 10/1 000 between 1976 and 1979. By contrast the incidence of TB among white and coloured workers declined during this period (Leger, 1992: 197).

TB incidence figures for black mineworkers declined somewhat from 1984 to 1988, only to rise again in the next four years. The Chamber of Mines (COM) reported that the incidence of in-patient cases was 10,6/1 000 in 1992 (Annual Health Department report, 1992). Overall incidence (in-patients and out-patients) is estimated to be around 16/1 000. This level has not been seen on the mines since the 1920s. It should be noted that within this general pattern one can see considerable variation among mines. Thus on both the Free Gold Mines in the Orange Free State and on Gold Fields West, TB rates appear to have peaked in 1989 and then declined. Even so, rates for these mines remain considerably higher than in the 1970s (Graph 6).

Mine medical authorities have attributed the rise in TB on the mines to four factors: 1) increasing background levels of TB in the areas from which they draw their labour; 2) better case detection; 3) the introduction of HIV on to the mines; and 4) the increasing age of their work-force.

BACKGROUND INFECTION

The rise in TB on the mines parallels the nation-wide increase in TB since the mid-1980s and is no doubt linked to the fact that the broader population from which the mines are drawing their labour has higher TB rates. Moreover, the mines are drawing more of their labour from areas within South Africa where TB infection rates are extremely high[2]. The sharp rise in 1977 was no doubt exacerbated further by the mines being forced to recruit workers who were less fit from those internal sources to make up for the loss of foreign labour.

On the other hand, the incidence rates on the mines are considerably higher than those for the African populations from which labour is currently being drawn. In addition, age specific TB incidence rates for all black males in South Africa indicate that while there was an increase in incidence between 1986 and 1991, 1991 rates are in most cases equal to, or lower than, 1976 rates. By comparison, the TB rates among black mineworkers in 1991 are nearly twice those recorded in 1976 (Graph 2).

Now it may well be that the rates for the wider black male population are artificially low due to poor case-finding. Yet this effect should to a certain extent be countered by the fact that miners are a select population of healthy men and that the mining population does not contain older segments of the African population that have high TB morbidity rates. In other words, as a sample population they should exhibit a healthy worker bias.

In addition, the mines have instituted rigorous screening methods to prevent the entrance of workers who have active TB, or even the hint of active TB, on to the mines[3]. In a number of mines, miners returning from leave and showing signs of TB are treated for the disease before being returned to work. In addition, suspected apical lesions are treated even in the absence of sputum positivity. Thus, although high background levels of infection exist in recruitment areas for the mines, it is unlikely that mineworkers are bringing active disease onto the mines. But it must be acknowledged that both examination and treatment practices vary considerably from mine to mine and that some mines may be less efficient in excluding diseased miners. In general, the TB occurring on the mines today is the result of either previous dormant and undetectable infections progressing to active TB under the stress of mine work or from new or reinfections acquired on the mines. (It is generally assumed by mine medical authorities that

2. *In this regard it is interesting to note that the Gold Fields Mines Medical Report for 1980 attributed the group's lower than average TB incidence in part to their greater use of workers from tropical areas "who have a history of producing less tubercule". Annual Medical Report. 1980. Gold Field Mines: 5.*
3. *The following discussion of mine examination practices is based on interviews with medical officers for three different mining groups during August 1993.*

TABLE 1 : AGE SPECIFIC MORBIDITY FOR TB AMONG EXISTING EMPLOYEES

AGE	INCIDENCE PER 1 000 WORKERS
UNDER 17	0
18-20	2,9
21-25	2,5
26-30	4,4
31-35	6,1
36-40	10,4
41-45	15,5
46-50	13,0
51-55	23,0
OVER 55	0,5

virtually all African mineworkers have been infected, though routine testing is not conducted.) All things being equal, mineworker rates should be lower than those of the general population whereas in actual fact they appear to be considerably higher. It is thus unlikely that the high rates on the mines are simply a reflection of the general trend in TB, although they are certainly affected by it.

CASE-FINDING

Better case-finding may have contributed to the initial sharp rise in TB notifications although to date no one has shown exactly what improvements occurred in case-finding in the mid-1970s which would have led to such a sharp increase in cases. Moreover, the question remains why this rate has not been reduced. If the population was highly unstable with the yearly introduction of new workers, as occurred in the 1960s, then one might expect the case level to remain high, assuming that the new recruits were a source of TB. Yet the African work-force has been increasingly stabilised since the late 1970s. Today there is relatively little turnover. In this situation, better case-finding should have led to effective treatment and a reduction in TB rates over time. The drop in rates in the early 1980s may in fact reflect this treatment effect. Yet the trend has been reversed since 1988 and rates continue to climb.

HIV

The introduction of HIV infection on to the mines in the mid-1980s may be contributing to the current rise in TB cases and it will almost certainly complicate the TB problem on the mines in the future. A comparison of HIV prevalence studies conducted on one group of mines in 1990 and 1992 revealed an increase in overall prevalence from 1,28 percent to 4,78 percent, or nearly 400 percent[4]. Obviously, HIV could not account for the initial rise in cases in the mid-1970s. Moreover, the extent to which HIV is contributing to current TB rates varies from mine to mine. The percentage of all culture positive M. TB patients with HIV ranged from 3,6 percent to 16,6 percent on three groups of mines visited in 1993[5]. If one assumes the worst case and takes the highest figure as an average for the mining industry, then one could argue that HIV may have increased TB incidence on the mines by 16 percent. (This assumes that TB is an opportunistic infection following on HIV infection among mineworkers, and not a concurrent infection, a fact which has not been demonstrated.) Given that TB rates have risen by roughly 43 percent since 1986, HIV must be seen as but one of the causes of this increase.

The impact of HIV on TB on the mines, however, goes beyond its role in the production of TB. It has also restricted the ability of health authorities to cope with the disease. One of the most problematic impacts of HIV in the mines, as elsewhere, is its interaction with drug resistance. Data from one mine hospital in 1992 indicated that 31,1 percent of all culture positive TB patients showed resistance to one or more drugs. Of these drug resistant patients 14,7 percent were HIV positive. Among the small proportion of patients who were resistant to four drugs, and thus virtually untreatable (6 percent of all resistant patients), 33,3 percent were HIV positive. In effect, increased levels of HIV infection on the mines are likely to reduce immunity and resistance to TB, increasing TB incidence, while making it more difficult to treat those patients who are diagnosed.

AGE OF WORK-FORCE

The increasing age of the work-force may well be an important factor in increased rates of TB. The policy of labour stabilisation reduced the recruitment of first time mineworkers to a small fraction of the total work-force. This increased the average age of the work-force from 26 years in the mid-1970s to 36 years today. Risk of TB among blacks in South Africa, as elsewhere, increases with age as shown in age specific rates. Thus an older work-force can be expected to suffer from increased levels of TB (Graph 7).

The relationship between age and incidence of TB on the mines reported in the late 1960s would suggest that a large portion of the rise in TB on the mines

---

4. *National Centre for Occupational Health. Epidemiology Section, Research Proposal.*
5. *Some of the variation among the three mines may reflect differences in criteria.*

may be due to the increasing age of the work-force[6] (Table 1).

This data, if consistent with current trends, would indicate that nearly all of the increase in TB between the mid-1970s and today could be accounted for by the increase in the average age for the work-force.

Yet even if the 1980s data is comparable to current trends, this conclusion needs to be modified. If one looks at age specific TB rates for the general African male population one finds that increasing age has a less dramatic effect on TB incidence, increasing from approximately 3/1 000 for age 25-29 to 5/1 000 for men aged 35-39. These rates may be artificially low, but there is no reason to suspect that the trend in age specific rates is wrong. Thus while increasing age heightens the TB risk of all African men, the scale of this increase appears greater in mineworkers than in the general population of black males. In other words, age may be a greater risk factor in mineworkers than in non-mineworkers. This suggests that there may be a synergistic relation between age and mine employment. Since the vast majority of TB in older men appears to result from the reactivation of existing infections, one may speculate that the factors which contribute to reactivation in older age are strengthened or stronger in mineworkers. Just what these factors may be needs to be clarified.

There is evidence that the longer a man works on the mines the greater his chance of contracting TB. The 1932 TB Commission Report indicated that African mineworkers experienced a heightened risk of contracting TB during their first year of employment. This risk decreased after the first year and until year five, when the risk of TB increased dramatically. This increase in later years was assumed to be related to the accumulated effect of exposure to silica dust.

The positive correlation of years of employment with the incidence of TB is supported by more recent data from the Pathaut study which is currently being conducted at the National Centre for Occupational Health[7] (NCOH). The Pathaut study involves the examination of autopsy data collated over a 17-year period, from 1975-1991. From the approximately 60 000 autopsies that have been done on workers who have died while on the mines or who have had their hearts and lungs examined if they died after leaving mine service, some 17 000 cases involved men who died of "unnatural causes", primarily traumatic injuries. This population represents something approaching a random sample of mineworkers with which one can trace trends in disease prevalence[8]. There is a correlation between years of service and prevalence of TB. When viewed alongside data on the changing composition of the African work-force in terms of the distribution of years of service, it suggests that the increasing average years of service since

---

6. *In the mid-1980s it was not yet apparent how dramatic an effect stabilisation would have on the average age of the work-force.*

7. *The project is being directed by Danatu Kielkowaki, Peter Reid, Jill Murray and Roslyn Lowe, of the NCOH Epidemiology staff. We greatly appreciate their having shared their data with us.*

8. *An unknown number of TB cases would have been lost from this sample on account of deaths without autopsies. However, this would affect the levels of disease reflected in the population rather than the trend.*

1977 may be linked to the increased incidence of TB. This data clearly needs to be adjusted to account for the role of increased age in increasing risk of TB.

Again it is assumed that the primary factor in mediating years of mine service and risk of contracting TB is exposure to silica dust and the coexistence of silicosis. Thus the Pathaut study also indicates a correlation between silicosis and years of service. Yet the correlation between silicosis, or pneumoconiosis, is difficult to demonstrate from the incidence data. In fact official data on the incidence of silicosis in black miners since 1975, when compared to data on the incidence of TB for the same period, indicates a negative relationship. TB rates go up while pneumoconiosis rates decline and vice versa. This is exactly the opposite of what one would expect if exposure to silicosis was a contributing factor to TB in older miners with long histories of employment (Leger, 1992: 197).

This contradiction, however, appears to be created by changes in diagnostic practice in combination with changing mining regulations regarding the fitness of miners with both silicosis and TB. An occupational health officer at one of the largest mine hospitals explained that prior to 1983 the law prohibited the employment of silicotic workers underground. They had to be given above ground employment which paid less and in most cases meant they would lose their jobs. Mine officers held back silicosis claims. X-rays were labelled as having irregularities, but silicosis was not mentioned. Once the law changed and it became possible to return silicotics to work, medical officers began identifying cases as silicosis. This contributed to a sharp rise in silicosis cases at the same time that overall TB rates were declining[9].

More generally it is still the case that miners identified as having TB *and* silicosis must be removed from underground mining. Two other medical officers said they felt that this was unfair to the old-time employees of the mines. While identification of silicosis could lead to compensation, the level of awards hardly compensates for the loss of employment. So the medical officers ignore the silicosis until the miner is ready to retire. He is then diagnosed and given compensation. Clearly, this humanitarian instinct also serves the interests of the mining industry, since it allows the mines to keep experienced and valued workers underground for a longer period of time than would be possible if the laws were strictly enforced. The practice makes it difficult to determine from existing records the extent to which exposure to silicosis is the mediating factor between increased years of employment and increased risk of TB.

Clearly, further research needs to be carried out on the mines to determine what factors are contributing to the production of TB. Scant research of this type has been carried out since the 1930s. It is in this context that the authors, with the assistance of the NCOH and the University of the Witwatersrand Department of Community Health, have initiated a pilot case-control study of co-factors for TB on the Gold Fields West mines. The study will involve 300 incident cases of TB and 300 controls drawn from the same mineworker population. The study is being supported by the Migrant Labour Project, which in turn is funded by the

---

9. *Interview, 9 August 1993.*

International Development Research Centre of Canada, and by a grant from Gloxo Pharmaceuticals.

CONCLUSION

The current rise in TB in South Africa is unlikely to change soon for the better. The underlying causes of TB are likely to persist for years regardless of political change. Some improvements can occur in health care delivery as the violence subsides and with a greater commitment to building up primary health care facilities and improving TB services. A democratically elected government may also provide those at greatest risk with confidence in their health services, allowing for the development of greater popular participation in health programmes.

But the underlying economic problems will be more difficult to solve. TB is a social disease, sensitive to shifts in economic conditions. Improvements in the general health and welfare of all South Africans will bring about a reduction in TB, whether or not health services improve. Improvements in health services, in the absence of real economic reform, will do little to reduce the toll inflicted by this disease.

Finally, given the extraordinarily high levels of TB infection among all segments of the South African population, HIV/Aids will assuredly continue to produce active cases of TB and limit the capacity of medical officers to treat TB. This effect, moreover, is independent of improvements in the general welfare of the populations at risk or in health services. The problem of the growing spread of HIV/Aids must be tackled if South Africa is to finally gain the upper hand in combatting the white plague. ◆

REFERENCES

Hambridge, J. 1992. "Aids/HIV and social dislocation in Natal," in Aids Analysis Africa, Vol 1, No 3.

Leger, JP. 1992. "Occupational disease in South African mines: a neglected epidemic?" in South African Medical Journal, Vol 91.

Packard, R. 1989. White Plague, Black Labour: Tuberculosis and the Political Economy of Health and Disease in South Africa. Berkeley: University of California Press.

Abdool-Karim, Q. "Aids in SA: Epidemiology," Unpublished data, nd.

"The trend in tuberculosis through the eyes of cohorts," 1992. in Epidemiological Comments, Vol 19, No 11.

"Third national HIV survey of women attending antenatal clinics, South Africa, October/November 1992," 1993 in Epidemiological Comments, Vol 20, No 3.

"Tuberculosis control programme – 1990," 1991 in Epidemiological Comments, Vol 18, No 8.

"Tuberculosis control programme – 1991," 1993 in Epidemiological Comments, Vol 20, No 1.

Tuberculosis Research Committee. 1932. Tuberculosis in South African natives with special reference to the disease among mine labourers on the Witwatersrand. Johannesburg: South African Institute for Medical Research, Publication No 30.

RESPONSE

DR JUDITH HEAD
Department of Sociology,
University of Cape Town,
South Africa

Many studies have focused on the macro-level of mine migrancy and the gold-mining industry. These have examined the structural and global changes taking place in the industry, their effect on regional relations, trends in recruitment and so on. Far less research has been done into workers' perceptions of the situation, their day-to-day preoccupations and the direct effects of changes in the industry on their lives.

The strength of Matsheliso Molapo's contribution is that workers' views are paramount. This type of research draws workers into the debate in an era of greater transparency and worker involvement in the affairs of their organisations and government. It is interesting that a number of companies dealing with issues of racism or sexism start by canvassing every worker – from the lowest in the hierarchy to the managing director – on how they think the organisation should change. There would seem to be a lesson here for mining houses: start taking seriously what workers believe.

Ms Molapo examines workers' resistance to aspects of hospital treatment and this is a problematic area: my research on a sugar plantation in Zambezia indicates that workers fear hospitalisation because they believe that one goes to hospital only to die. That tradition seems to exist on the mines too. Ms Molapo describes mineworkers' beliefs about blood, among these the fear that one will become ill if a sample of blood is removed. Difficulties arise because workers do not necessarily believe or understand what they are told in hospitals. It seems there is a need for much more discussion about these and other beliefs and perceptions about health if health programmes are to be effective.

The second contribution, by David Coetzee and Randall Packard, is a model case-study in health detection: it shows how the real roots of a problem can be traced, and faulty hypotheses demolished, by asking the right questions, looking carefully at the answers and scrutinising records and autopsy reports.

The growing preoccupation with health and safety on South Africa's gold mines is also not co-incidental; rather, it flows from greater worker mobilisation and unionisation.

This research suggests that workers will have longer working lives. This will have important consequences. In the past, health problems have been exported back to rural areas where they have remained untreated. In the future these illnesses may become apparent while the worker is still on the mine. The connection between industrial history and health may be easier to make and for the individual man it opens up the possibility of having industrial injury/illness recognised and hence compensated. ◆

MIGRANCY IN SOUTHERN AFRICA

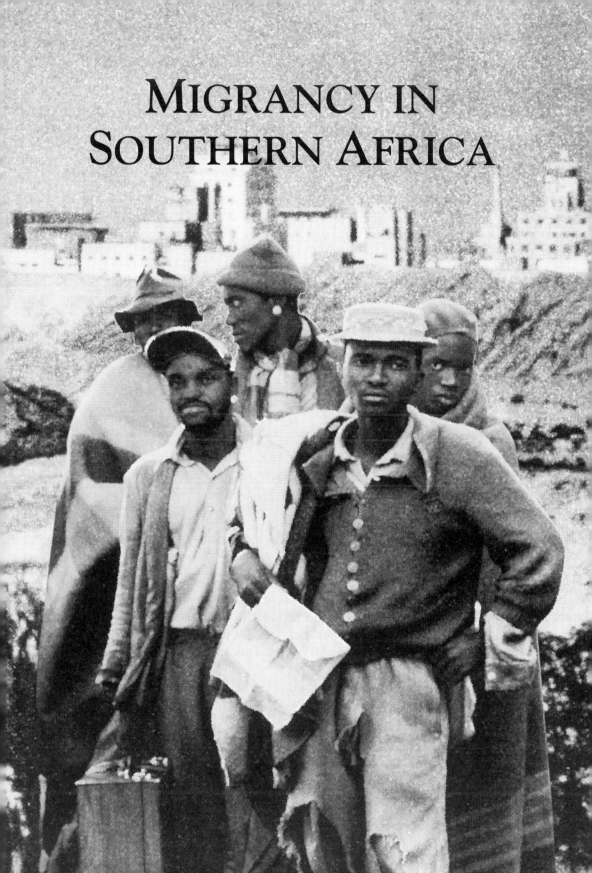

Malawian Migrant Labour and the Politics of Hiv/Aids, 1985 to 1993

PROFESSOR WISEMAN CHIJERE CHIRWA
Department of History,
University of Malawi,
Zomba, Malawi

In October 1987 the South African government prohibited HIV carriers and Aids sufferers from immigrating to the Republic. Those already in the country faced possible deportation. It became an offence for an individual or an institution to knowingly help an HIV carrier or Aids sufferer to enter or stay in South Africa. All those entering the country to work or study had to produce an HIV-free certificate issued not more than two weeks prior to their entry.

Malawian workers interviewed for this study said that many Malawian migrants in South Africa had tested HIV positive before this declaration, and some had already developed Aids. In February 1988, 101 Malawian mining recruits were repatriated from South Africa for being HIV positive and a month later the Chamber of Mines stopped importing labour from Malawi altogether. This decision caused a great deal of tension between the Malawian government and The Employment Bureau of Africa (Teba) and between the Malawian government and migrant labourers. Migrants said they were not given reasons for these decisions and they wanted either an official explanation or the resumption of recruiting by Teba.

Using information from interviews and documentary evidence, this chapter demonstrates the connection between labour migration and the risk of contracting and spreading the HIV/Aids virus in both Malawi and South Africa. Migrant labourers are a high-risk group, and as such they stand a good chance of contracting and spreading HIV/Aids in both countries, but it would be wrong to single out the migrant labour system as being particularly instrumental in spreading the disease in the southern Africa region. Long-distance road haulage, itinerant trade, tourism and prostitution may play an equally important role.

HIGH-RISK GROUPS AND THE SPREAD OF AIDS

Malawi is land-locked and heavily dependent on long-distance road haulage. With its large road network, Malawi bridges southern and eastern Africa. Historical studies have shown that there is a direct connection between improvements in communication networks and the spread of infectious diseases (Davies, 1979; Hartwig and Petterson, 1978; David and David, 1981). Recently, Orubuloye et al (1994: 6) argued that "everywhere in Africa, long-distance lorry drivers are a source of sexually transmitted diseases (STDs) and Aids infection, and levels of disease are consequently higher along the most densely trafficked routes". They further noted that "most of the research on the incidence of HIV infection among the people along the roads pertains to the west-east axis from middle Africa to the Indian Ocean, the Zaire–Rwanda–Uganda–Kenya route". This route traverses areas where HIV first appeared and which are now the most heavily infected parts of Africa (Orubuloye et al, 1994: 89). Malawi has connections with these areas through Tanzania and Zambia. The patterns observed by these authors therefore affect Malawi and possibly the whole of the southern Africa region from which the South African mines have for a long time drawn large numbers of labourers.

Malawi is also an important tourist destination in the region, with the number of visitors having steadily, if not rapidly, increased over the last five years. This has been partly because of improvements in communications, but is also due to the declining value of the Kwacha (Malawian currency) which has made Malawi a relatively cheap tourist location. Most of these tourists are from Zambia, Zimbabwe, Mozambique, South Africa and the eastern African countries.

The Malawian tourist industry therefore provides contact between the high-incidence area of east Africa and the supposedly low-incidence areas of southern Africa. (Although there have been numerous reports in the media that Aids is also entrenched in southern Africa.)

Transport nodes and tourist attractions tend to be centres of itinerant trade and night entertainment, where traders and prostitutes conduct business with truck drivers, passengers and tourists. Studies conducted elsewhere in Africa have shown that many female itinerant traders sell sexual favours in addition to their trade goods (Orubuloye et al, 1994: 90-92), often in competition with full-time prostitutes. Recent studies in Malawi have expressed fears that the expanding tourist sector will be accompanied by a high HIV/Aids incidence (Derman et al, 1993; Chirwa, 1994).

There is also a direct relationship between migrant labour and itinerant trade. Up to the 1970s, migrant labourers and/or their relatives dominated the cross-border "informal" trade between Malawi and its neighbours (Chirwa, 1992). In the 1970s and early 1980s this trade moved into the hands of itinerant traders on both sides of the country's borders. The majority of the Tanzanian and Zambian traders operate independently in and out of Malawi, while those from within Malawi tend to utilize migrant labour connections. This difference arises from the fact that there are a lot of Malawians working in both Tanzania and Zambia who give material support to their relatives and friends engaged in cross-border trade. Of late, there has been a marked increase in the "informal" trafficking of consumer and capital goods between Malawi and South Africa and Malawi and Zimbabwe, especially by former migrants and those who have relatives working in the two countries. The point to emphasise here is that all those involved in the above economic activities are connected to, or fall into, the high-risk category, and could therefore be instrumental in spreading HIV/Aids in the eastern and southern Africa regions.

The refugee problem also contributes substantially to the spread of HIV/Aids. Political disturbances in the region have resulted in millions of people fleeing from their homes to neighbouring countries where their living conditions are conducive to the spread of infectious diseases. When they return to their countries the risk of spreading these diseases is high. With the current political changes in South Africa, Mozambique and Malawi, increasing numbers of refugees will return home. The health implications of this need to be taken very seriously.

THE HISTORICAL AND SOCIAL CONTEXT OF AIDS IN MALAWI

The first case of Aids in Malawi was diagnosed in 1985. By June 1993, some 29 194 cumulative cases of HIV/Aids had been reported from various hospitals in the country's 24 districts. The Aids Secretariat in Lilongwe (1994) estimates that by 1995, 700 000 to 1,1 million of the nine to 10 million people in Malawi will have tested HIV positive. "This scenario," they report, "is predominantly the result of ... sex with multiple partners, low acceptance of use of condoms and a high prevalence of other sexually transmitted diseases" (1994: iii).

Paul Kishindo has argued that social and cultural practices play an important role in the transmission of HIV/Aids in Malawi. He claims that "it is a commonly held view by both men and women in this country that sexual satisfaction comes from the natural contact of genital organs: the use of condoms during sexual intercourse is therefore seen as unnatural and making intercourse less satisfying" (Kishindo, 1993: 7).

Citing evidence from a survey conducted for the Ministry of Health in 1989, Kishindo observed that less than 1 percent of the 2 000 informants interviewed used condoms. Many prostitutes said they did not insist on condoms, and would rather risk contracting Aids than losing a client and some earnings. "Losing clients could spell real economic hardship for a prostitute who lives solely on the sale of sexual services," according to Kishindo (1993: 8). Some female informants for this study confirmed these observations. Cultural concepts of sexual intercourse are transmitted to young men and women through initiation rites such as *jando*, male circumcision, and *chinawali*, female initiation. Both boys and girls are taught that sex is penetrative because procreation is their prescribed role in society.

Kishindo further notes that in some societies in the southern and central districts, and among adherents of the Muslim faith, all boys are circumcised. One instrument may be used several times without sterilisation. If the instrument became infected with HIV, the virus would be transmitted to several boys. After initiation, a boy is regarded as a social adult and may be encouraged to experiment with and exercise his adulthood by having sex with girls of his age. "It is during this sexual experimentation that the Aids infection acquired during circumcision may be transmitted to young girls in the villages," says Kishindo (1993). In this way young boys and girls could contract the Aids virus at a very early age. Given that the disease is a slow killer, the chances of these boys and girls spreading it to several partners as they grow up is very high.

Official records suggest that Malawi experienced a rapid spread of HIV/Aids between 1986 and 1991. It is estimated that one in three adults in the urban areas may be carrying the Aids virus. The ratio is slightly lower in the rural areas. The rise in reported cases may be a result of the vigorous testing and reporting campaign by the National Aids Control Programme (NACP) established by the Ministry of Health in 1989, but it could also be caused by the repatriation of some 2 000 Malawian migrants who had tested positive. The decline in new reported cases between 1991 and 1993 could be a result of the activities of the NACP, but the shortage of trained personnel has reduced the potential for successful programme implementation (Kishindo, 1993). The effectiveness of the NACP is therefore questionable. It could be that new cases are simply not being reported, or that a number of the earlier victims were dead by 1993.

Testing and data collection methods are not always reliable, and this should be taken into account when interpreting the above figures. Official records are often based on rough estimates and generalisations which lead to inaccurate predictions and conclusions. In addition, the above figures would make more sense if a breakdown was provided on age, gender, economic occupation or background, level of education, district of origin (rural or urban), length of infection and numbers of infected people dying during the period covered. The last point would be helpful in determining cumulative cases.

The Aids Secretariat notes the social consequences of the HIV/Aids epidemic in Malawi:

> The selective deaths of young adults is leading to an alarming increase in
> the number of orphaned children and destitute old people which threatens

to overwhelm the usual societal coping mechanisms. The health care services are overstretched as epidemics of previously controlled diseases such as tuberculosis have soared. The improvements in social indicators gained during the last two decades are threatened by Aids (The Aids Secretariat, 1994: iii).

HIV/AIDS AND MALAWIAN MIGRANCY

Two conclusions can be drawn from the preceding account about the relationship between labour migration and the spread of the disease: firstly, that Aids was already entrenched in Malawi by the time the South African government took the decision to prohibit carriers and sufferers from entering the Republic, and secondly, that the possibility of some Malawian migrants being HIV carriers and Aids carriers did indeed exist.

The politics of disease has always been at the centre of labour migration agreements between Malawi and recruiting organisations. The 1913 ban on migrants from north of latitude 22°S was prompted by the high death rate among northern migrants, the majority of whom were Malawians and Mozambicans. Missionaries, chiefs, settlers, colonial administrators and some scholars in the northern territories pointed out the relationship between labour migration and the spread of infectious diseases, linking these to social and moral "degradation" in the migrants' villages. Often these arguments were not backed by concrete evidence. In 1987/88 the South Africans used the politics of disease in a manner reminiscent of the old colonial attitudes on the relationship between migrant labour and the spread of deadly infectious diseases.

The decision to prohibit HIV carriers and Aids sufferers from working in South Africa came at a time when unemployment in both Malawi and South Africa was increasing. It was also a period of major change in the regional labour supply for the South African mines. After a plane crash in 1974 in Francistown, Botswana, in which 74 Malawian migrant workers died, the Malawian government took the political decision to temporarily ban recruiting for South African mines. Two factors influenced the decision. Malawi needed adequate supplies of labour for the expanding tobacco and tea estates, the building of the new capital city in Lilongwe and the construction of roads to open up the country to agricultural production. The plane crash gave President Hastings Banda a good excuse for restricting migration in order to divert the flow of labour to these sectors. At the same time, there was increasing pressure on him from the Women's League of the ruling Malawi Congress Party to restrict the outflow of men and divert their labour to the peasant sector. The flow of Malawian labour to the South African mines thus began to decline from the mid-1970s.

Throughout the 1980s, the major suppliers of mine labour were the so-called homelands within South Africa and the neighbouring countries of Lesotho, Botswana, Swaziland and Mozambique (Crush et al, 1991). Malawi, though regarded as South Africa's "friendly neighbour", was no longer a major supplier of mine labour – the country's value as a supplier of mine labour underwent a steady decline.

However, the mining industry wanted to retain Malawi as a labour supplier, for three reasons. Firstly, the mining industry valued its Malawian employees, who were more experienced and less militant than their South African counterparts. Secondly, through labour agreements the mining industry and the South African government had established good political relations with Malawi and these needed to be maintained. Thirdly, it was essential to keep Malawi open to recruiting in case of sudden changes in domestic labour supplies. However, the industry was concerned about the political and health risks involved in recruiting workers from a "high-incidence" and "high-risk" area such as Malawi.

It would have been preferable for both the mining industry and the South African government to deal with HIV/Aids no differently from any other infectious disease and to allow employers and recruiters to exercise their discretion in hiring. After all, testing for infectious diseases was already an important aspect of the agreement between Teba and supplying countries. Mining employers and their recruiting agents had the capacity to reject those who were HIV positive without government regulations.

The Malawian government had three concerns: the ethical or moral justification for HIV/Aids testing as a pre-condition to employment; compensation for repatriates; and the legality of the decision to repatriate those who had tested positive. The government understood HIV/Aids testing as a pre-condition to employment on the South African mines to be contrary to the policy of the World Health Organisation on Aids. In fact, South Africa would be the only country in Africa to impose such a requirement. Although Aids testing is a pre-condition to immigration into some countries – and even in these cases regulations are not usually forcefully implemented – it is ethically and morally unjustifiable to deny people access to employment just because they are HIV/Aids positive. The Malawian government therefore rejected the idea of screening the migrants within the country before they left for South Africa.

The repatriation of HIV-infected recruits in 1988 was also an issue. Migrants said they did not know they would be tested in South Africa, and therefore wanted to be compensated for their repatriation. However, neither Teba nor the employing mines accepted responsibility for the repatriations as they were simply responding to legislative provisions over which they had no control. Technically they had not violated the terms of contract with the recruits, complicating the issue of compensation. Neither Teba nor the employing mines are legally obliged to pay compensation to any employee repatriated because of HIV/Aids, but the employee is entitled to compensation on the basis of having signed an employment contract prior to leaving his country. The contract, offering termination benefits, is valid from the date of signature by the recruit, which in the case of the Malawian migrants was prior to leaving for South Africa.

Malawians also felt that neither the testing nor the repatriation was part of the terms of the agreement signed with Teba, and that the South Africans were therefore unilaterally introducing new terms into the agreement. However, there was a provision in the agreement stating that terms of employment would be interpreted and applied according to South African employment laws. If these provided for testing for infectious diseases and repatriation of those found positive, there was no violation of the terms of the agreement.

To the Malawian migrants, taking blood samples for HIV/Aids testing without their informed consent was an insult. They said they were not told why blood samples were being taken, nor who would have access to the results (Crush et al 1991: 114-17). To the migrants the prohibition on employing HIV carriers and Aids sufferers in South Africa was an unfortunate and unfair decision that placed unnecessary conditions and restrictions on their right to choose where to work[1]. They feared that the requirement of an HIV-free certificate would result in the invasion of individual privacy during the process of testing.

However, more than three-quarters of the 163 migrants interviewed for this study were willing to be tested. They said that in this way they would gain "a clear conscience" and be able to migrate freely. The rising unemployment in Malawi makes testing an acceptable option. Many returned migrants have not yet found employment at home. Those with savings started small businesses, but because of the deteriorating economic situation in the country over the last five years these businesses have performed very badly. Small trucks bought by the migrants are grounded because of rising maintenance costs. Many small grocery shops and bars have closed because of the rising prices of consumer goods and low wages and poor agricultural incomes. Returning migrants are often poorer now than they were a few years ago. The investments they had made at home are failing, and they want to migrate again to earn money to boost their enterprises. This worsening economic plight, aggravated by the closure of labour recruitment, will force many workers to accept pre-employment HIV/Aids screening.

Most potential migrants are concerned about the stigma attached to the disease, and would certainly not like to see their names appear in official documents as carriers or victims, or even as people who have been tested[2]. This concern is not unique to Malawian migrants. Studies conducted elsewhere in Africa have shown that interviewees are particularly sensitive about the topic of sexual relations, especially sexual relations outside marriage. Since Aids is a sexually transmitted disease, the identification of a person as a carrier or patient is often taken as an indication of promiscuity, despite the awareness that the disease can be transmitted in other ways (National Statistical Office, 1994: chapter 10).

What Malawian migrants hated most was being stigmatised as a high-risk group and their country being categorised as a high-incidence area. "If the South Africans thought we brought Aids with us to their country they were mistaken," said one. "The chances of contracting the disease within South Africa are very high." He claimed that truck drivers, urban women (especially *"shebeen queens"*)

---

1. *Interviews with George Tondoli, Liwaladzi, Nkhota-Kota, 21 December 1993; Nathan Friday, Kasitu, Nkhota-Kota, 22 December 1993; Lloyd Chilewe, Misanjo, Mulanje, 4 April 1994; G Mulile, Namanja Village, Mulanje, 8 April 1994.*
2. *Interviews with Isaac Nyirenda, Mpamba, Nkhata Bay, 16 December 1993; John Kaunda, Nthulinga, 18 December 1993.*

and homosexuals – *mathanyula* – in the compounds play a more significant role in spreading Aids within South Africa. In his opinion, the whole Aids issue was a ploy aimed at barring Malawians from employment in South Africa to solve the local unemployment problem[3]. Many more Malawian migrants have similar views[4]. But they do identify the compounds and *shebeens* within South Africa, and the bars and despatching points within Malawi, as places where the Aids virus could easily be contracted.

However, in practice it is also entirely possible for migrants to have contracted HIV/Aids in their areas of origin. The money they brought home was usually far above the average rural income, which often led to conspicuous consumption and spending. In this way migrants became "a big attraction to women in the villages" (Kishindo, 1993: 5; Chirwa, 1992: chapter 10). If these men or women were HIV carriers and Aids sufferers, the disease would spread rapidly in the villages.

Three-fifths of the returned migrants who were interviewed had had more than two sexual partners within the first 24 months of their return. Some of them had as many as five to 10 partners. It is this sexual behaviour that places migrants in the high-risk category alongside truck drivers, prostitutes and itinerant traders. What is particularly disturbing is that the majority of the Malawian migrants come from rural areas, and with their return, rural women have probably become increasingly vulnerable to contracting HIV/Aids. This means that the prevalence of Aids in the country will no longer be confined to urban areas. If anything, in subsequent decades, the disease will be concentrated in the rural areas, and the returning migrant labourers will have played a significant role in this shift.

CONCLUSION

The connection between migrant labour and the spread of HIV/Aids has implications for both Malawi and South Africa. The threats that migrants pose to the mining labour supply are not any different to those they pose to their village communities. This chapter has argued that it is wrong to single out the migrant labour system as solely responsible in spreading HIV/Aids in the southern Africa region. Long-distance road haulage, tourism, prostitution, cross-border itinerant trade and the return of refugees may play a more significant role in spreading the disease. If these factors are taken into consideration, Malawi would not be seen as the only high-risk and high-incidence area in the region. The decision taken in 1987 by the South African government to bar immigrants with HIV/Aids was a product of unnecessary disease phobia, if not xenophobia. ◆

---

3. *Interview with Mwazeni Mtira, Chia, Nkhota-Kota, 29 September 1989.*
4. *Interview with Mwazeni Mtira, Chia, Nkhota-Kota, 29 September 1989; Lloyd Chilewa, Msanjo, Mulanje, 4 April 1994.*

REFERENCES

Chirwa, WC. 1992. Theba is Power: Rural Labour, Migrancy and Fishing in Malawi, 1890s - 1985. PhD dissertation, Queen's University, Kingston, Canada.

Chirwa, WC. 1994. "Tourism, commercial fishing and the dispossession of fishing communities in Malawi," paper prepared for the National Environmental Action Plan (NEAP), Blantyre, Malawi, February.

Crush, J, AH Jeeves and D Yudelman. 1991. South Africa's Labour Empire: A History of Black Migrancy to the Gold Mines. Boulder and Cape Town: Westview Press and David Phillip.

David, N and V David. 1981. "Social causes of infertility and population decline among the settled Fulani of north Cameroon," in Man, Vol 16.

Davies, JNP. 1979. Pestilence and Disease in the History of Africa. Johannesburg: Witwatersrand University Press.

Dawson, M. 1988. "Aids in Africa: historical roots," in N Miller and RC Rockell, (eds,) Aids in Africa: The Social and Policy Impact. Lewiston: Edwin Mellen Press.

Derman, B, A Ferguson and R Mkandawire. 1993. "Human rights, environment and development: the dispossession of fishing communities on Lake Malawi," unpublished paper.

Hartwig, GW and KD Petterson, (eds,) 1978. Disease in African History: An Introductory Survey and Case Studies. Durhan: Duke University Press.

House, W and G Zimalirana. 1992. "Rapid population growth and poverty in Malawi," in Journal of Modern African Studies, Vol 30, No 1.

Kishindo, PA. 1993. "The social context of Aids in Malawi," paper presented at the Regional Conference on Ethical and Social Issues Surrounding Aids, Lusaka, Zambia.

National Statistical Office (NSO). 1994. Demographic and Health Survey, 1992. Zomba: NSO.

Orubuloye, IO, JC Caldwell and G Santow (eds,) 1994. Sexual Networking and Aids in Sub-Saharan Africa: Behavioural Research and the Social Context. Canberra: The Australian National University.

The Aids Secretariat (Malawi). 1994. Malawi Aids Control Programme: Medium-Term Plan II, 1994 - 1998. Lilongwe: The Aids Secretariat.

MIGRANT MINE LABOUR FROM MOZAMBIQUE: WHAT PROSPECTS?

DR JUDITH HEAD

*Department of Sociology,
University of Cape Town,
South Africa*

Mozambican men have been migrating to the Witwatersrand ever since mining first began there in the 1880s. Until 1971 they were consistently the largest contingent of foreign labour employed on the mines (Centro de Estudos Africanos [CEA], 1987a: 24-25; Crush et al, 1991: 234-5). Mine wages have historically played an important role in the reproduction of peasant households in southern Mozambique, and foreign exchange receipts from remitted wages have been of great importance to the country's balance of payments (CEA, 1987a: 144; Wuyts, 1989: 86-87).

However, since the mid-1970s the number of Mozambican workers employed on the gold mines has declined dramatically. Between 1965 and 1975, 89 923 men were employed on average each year, but between 1976 and 1986 this fell to only 45 474. Between 1987 and 1993 the figure stood at 43 176.

The relative position of Mozambican workers has also declined. In 1975, the year of Mozambique's independence and the peak year in the employment of Mozambicans, they constituted 30,2 percent of the total labour-force and 40,9 percent of the foreign labour-force. Today they make up only 13,6 percent of the total labour-force and 28,4 percent of the foreign labour-force on the gold mines (Crush et al, 1991: 234-5; Chamber of Mines [COM] 1990, 1991, 1992 and 1993). A similar pattern can be seen on the coal mines.

This decline has to be seen in the context of a general decline in employment on the mines. In the five years between 1987 and 1992 a total of 173 957 jobs were lost in the gold and coal-mining industry. Of these, 52 145 were those of foreign migrants (COM, 1992). Many marginal mines are struggling for survival and the industry as a whole is battling with a stagnating real gold price and increased working costs, in part due to inflation and increased competition from low-cost producers elsewhere (COM, 1993: 2-7). The heady days of the 1970s, which saw massive capital investment and significant expenditure on research and development, have given way to "belt-tightening" strategies[1]. Further reductions in the labour-force therefore appear likely (COM, 1992: 52).

The critical questions are how will this reduction in the labour-force happen and who will be most affected? For reasons related to the South African and southern African regional economies it seems likely that foreign labour will be particularly hard hit. In years to come, the foreign labour-force will probably continue to decline until it is virtually insignificant. The need for the COM to maintain an expensive recruiting organisation and infrastructure to contract labour from neighbouring countries is rapidly diminishing when they can be hired more cheaply at the gates of the mine.

This reduction in employment opportunities comes at a time when the economies of regional supplier states, and especially Lesotho and Mozambique, are in crisis. Growing unemployment, particularly among the young, has in turn fuelled growing social unrest and illegal migration to South Africa. These tendencies are likely to continue unless there is a real commitment to investment in employment-creating strategies in the supplier states.

CHANGING PATTERNS OF LABOUR DEMAND IN THE GOLD-MINING INDUSTRY

By the 1980s the Employment Bureau of Africa (Teba), still known as the Witwatersrand Native Labour Recruiting Organisation (Wenela) in Mozambique, increasingly began to focus on processing applicants for mine contracts rather than actively recruiting men.

In the heyday of "active" recruiting Wenela agents used to seek out men and try to persuade them to sign on at the mines (Manghezi, 1987: 7-8), sometimes by offering various material incentives (CEA, 1987b: 33). By the mid-1980s Wenela in Mozambique and Teba in Lesotho and elsewhere had hundreds, sometimes thousands, of men camped on their doorsteps for months waiting for a chance to go to the mines. This situation persists today. The informal settlement outside the Wenela offices in Maputo has gone, but thousands of men turn up if word gets out that novices are being signed on. This restructuring has enabled Wenela to cut its costs. Between 1975 and 1993 Teba/Wenela reduced the number of its

---

1. *Interviews with Mr Greeff, General Manager, Safety and Technical Services, COM, 14 December 1993 and Mr Moloney, Manager of Operations, Teba, 14 December 1993.*

stations in southern Africa by almost half[2]. Wenela no longer provides food and transport to men from all over southern Mozambique on their way to the mines. Today it is only at the border post of Ressano Garcia (Komatipoort) that Wenela assumes the cost of the train fare to the mines.

These changes suggest that there has been a fundamental shift in the economic situation of migrant labourers. For the vast majority of peasants, farming does not generate sufficient income to dispense with wage labour employment. On the contrary, access to wages sustains peasant agriculture. The decline in employment on the mines has meant that the traditional source of cash income has dried up for thousands of families. Little wonder then that men are desperate for work and Wenela no longer needs to recruit them.

Hence, structural changes within the organisation of labour-use in the mining industry were in part made possible by structural changes in the broader southern African regional economy. The availability of men seeking work meant that longer contracts with shorter periods of leave could be imposed. The mines could hire better educated men, and they could begin to consider sources of supply from within South Africa. Recruiting operations could therefore be streamlined.

The impact this had on the structure of the labour-force is reflected in comparisons between surveys of the Anglo American Corporation's (AAC) gold-mining force conducted in 1986 and 1993. The surveys indicate that the Mozambican labour-force is serving longer; that more Mozambican workers are older than South Africans, who are more represented in the lower wage bands. This suggests that newer entrants to the industry tend to be South Africans and better educated (De Vletter, 1986; AAC, 1993).

THE CURRENT SITUATION

The origins of current patterns of labour demand date back to the mid-1980s with the repeal of influx control legislation and the last of the job colour bars. These changes represent possibly the most significant break to date with the historical organisation of mine labour recruitment and supply.

A gradual move away from the institutionalised system of migrant labour is now discernible. For the first time since its inception the mining industry can hire men at the gates of the mine in an unfettered and "free" labour market. This does not mean that men will cease to migrate. Individual men are already travelling to the mines under their own steam from the historical labour reserve areas. They will continue to come to the mines. They will probably not, however, come through Teba. The need to maintain an expensive recruiting organisation and infrastructure is declining.

The importance of Teba's reorganisation cannot be overemphasised. Teba is no longer simply the recruiting arm of the COM. On the contrary. It is now a "stand-alone" company which no longer survives on subsidies from the industry. It now has to charge for services rendered. Its labour processing activities are now only one of its functions. It manages Teba-Cash, a banking service offered to

---

2. *Interview with Mr Moloney, 14 December 1993.*

mine employees. It also runs the Manpower Data Centre, an archive of computerised records on the structure and composition of the labour-force, which the
COM and individual mines can draw on for a fee. Teba also hopes, through log-
ging its computer network into that of individual mines, to take over some of the
administrative functions of personnel management[3]. This would guarantee Teba's
continued existence by making its services indispensable. Teba is also investigating other new and possible areas of work in the development field. The search
for a secure role suggests that it is looking for other ways of surviving because its
days as a recruiter of labour are numbered.

By signing on men at the gate, individual mine managers will have more
control over who they hire – a control they are already trying to exercise. Their
telex "orders" for labour stipulate (sometimes in great detail) what kind of men
they are prepared to accept. For example, a telex from Western Areas gold mine
to Wenela Mozambique in September 1987 requesting 50 Mozambicans for underground work stipulated that they should be former Western Areas employees; have previous mine experience; be married; be between the ages of 30 and
40; not be former employees of Anglo American or Randfontein mines; and not
be matriculants. These men were to be hired for a "one-off" contract only[4]. Clearly
the requirements were related to the 1987 mineworkers strike and the mine's
desire not to hire anyone associated with it. However, detailed orders of this
type continued to be sent long after the strike was over.

As an extra safeguard, and as the telex "order" above indicates, at Western
Areas gold mine men are initially hired on a 12-month one-off contract, "where-
after he can be laid off. It gives us a chance to look at the guy, if he's a loafer or
sick every Monday we don't have to re-employ him. We can use it as a sifting
mechanism"[5].

The growing trend among mine managers of hiring men directly at the mine
will result in considerable savings for mine managers. For example, the Western
Areas gold mine will have to pay in the region of an extra R200 000 a year in
service fees for workers recruited through Teba when proposed new fees are
introduced. These increased fees have been forced on Teba through the requirement that it become financially independent. The proposed new fee structure is
shown in the table below.

Men from foreign countries will now cost three times more than men recruited
around the mines. The fee for men recruited in former bantustans will be half
that of foreign workers and one third higher than men recruited in the vicinity of
the mines. Although the fee for existing foreign workers will remain the same
there is an in-built incentive for mines to recruit locally, since the fees for South
African labour will be reduced. There is, moreover, a strong disincentive to hire
foreign novices.

3. *Interview with Mr Moloney, 23 May 1994.*
4. *Wenela offices, Maputo, Telex No 596, Wenela Johannesburg to Wenela Maputo, 7 September 1987.*
5. *Interview with Mr Bellingan, Personnel Manager, Labour Department, Western Areas
gold mine, 13 December 1993.*

TEBA'S PROPOSED NEW FEE STRUCTURE

LABOUR	FIRST YEAR OF CONTRACT	SECOND YEAR OF CONTRACT
FOREIGN	R12 PER MONTH	R6 PER MONTH
BANTUSTAN	R6 PER MONTH	R4 PER MONTH
LOCAL	R4 PER MONTH	R2,50 PER MONTH

Source: Interview with Mr Moloney, Manager of Operations, Teba, 23 May 1994

It seems clear that with the introduction of new fees the already substantial costs of the labour force will become even greater. This burden will be spread across the industry but will particularly hit Anglovaal, Gold Fields and Rand Mines, each with over 50 percent of their labour-force composed of foreign workers.

The proposed fee structure will be only one of the incentives for mining groups to reduce their dependence on foreign labour. The industry is already under pressure to improve migrant workers' accommodation, which is another cost burden. By replacing migrant workers with men hired at the gates of the mine, the industry will no longer need to maintain a housing stock nor provide food for its resident labour force. Nor will it have to pay to transport labour to the mines. This is not an insignificant cost. Transport for migrant labour costs the AAC around R2 million a year at present.

Whether the mining groups will be able to alter the contract conditions of foreign workers already employed is a moot point. This has been done in the past with the gradual introduction of different types of leave and re-employment certificates (Crush et al, 1991: 155-157). Another possibility is a retrenchment policy targeted specifically at foreign workers. Some of these men will be caught in the dragnet of further retrenchments anyway because foreign workers are disproportionately represented in the marginal mines that are very vulnerable to closure. It is possible that employers will also offer attractive packages to encourage them to leave the industry voluntarily.

In mines where cost containment is a major consideration, mine managers are already increasingly using outside contractors. Labour employed by contractors seems to be exclusively Mozambican and Basotho. According to the National Union of Mineworkers (NUM) these contract workers are not only being called on to do highly specialised tasks, but also normal mining operations. "Its happening across the board," commented Teba's Operations Manager[6]. From the

6. *Interviews with Mr Moloney, 14 December 1993 and Mr Ketsise, NUM, 23 May 1994.*

employers' point of view the advantages are obvious. Labourers hired by contractors are not covered by union agreements and are paid less than COM workers. The bargaining position of the union is thus undermined.

Mines may hire experienced former miners on one-off contracts until they have built up a pool of surplus South African workers with similar skills and experience. Hiring men on one-off contracts is already policy at Western Areas gold mine[7]. If this does happen, Mozambique could become a supplier of "supplementary" labour needs.

One obstacle to the phasing out of foreign labour in the recent past was housing. At the moment men recruited from around the mines receive a living-out allowance. Mining houses will probably try to gradually phase out this allowance and pay an all-inclusive wage, the real value of which will be whittled away by inflation. However, if the new government allows foreign migrant workers to own property or live in rented property, mining houses would have to pay them current allowances. This would increase the cost of foreign labour astronomically. Although this is unlikely, it is not impossible, and is an additional reason why the mining industry may phase out foreign migrant labour.

This phasing out is not something that will happen overnight. As the industry argued when the Botha government stopped recruitment from Mozambique and tried to repatriate the labour-force, men with skills cannot be easily replaced. At the same time there would be a political outcry if the industry took dramatic action that flew in the face of South Africa's new policy toward the region.

How then, and at what pace, might this process occur? The figures for the rate of attrition from the industry and the rate of replacement are not available, but we do know that novice recruitment from Mozambique is low and has been steadily declining over the past 30 years – dropping from an average of 12 percent in the period 1961-1970 to 4,2 percent in the period 1981-1993. According to Wenela in Maputo, there is no longer any open novice recruiting. The last order for 40 novices was in 1992. The few novices taken on are recommended by their fathers or uncles already working on the mines to the appropriate mine manager, who then sends a telex to Mozambique requesting the named individual[8]. What this suggests is that the Mozambican labour-force is being phased out by a process of natural attrition. To this should be added the possibility of retrenchments, voluntary or forced, particularly in mines facing difficulties, which are also mines with high concentrations of Mozambican workers.

THE IMPACT OF LABOUR RECRUITMENT

Mine labour is central to the experience of people living in southern Mozambique. Generations of fathers and sons have worked underground, and there is

---

7. *Interview with Mr Bellingan, 13 December 1993.*
8. *Interview with Mr Silveira, Wenela, Maputo, 26 November 1993; interviews with Mr Manhica, Department of Migrant Labour, Ministry of Labour, Mozambique, 24 November 1993 and Mr Bellingan, 13 December 1993.*

hardly a family from which someone has not migrated to the mines (Migueis Lopes Junior, 1980: 92). The introduction and later institutionalisation of migrant labour disrupted both the pattern of peasant production and its social organisation. The absence of men for 12 or 18 months at a time effectively separated them from their normal production tasks. They were not available to mend roofs, build houses and storage bins, to clear land, hunt small game, fish and farm their own fields and cattle. Gradually many of these tasks were taken over by artisans and paid for out of migrant wages (Roesch, 1986: 46).

By 1976 it was clear that migrant labour had become deeply entrenched. For the poor peasantry, who constituted the vast majority, migrant labour, and not the revenue from their farming activities, provided the income they needed to sustain production. Migrant labour was, therefore, also central to the reproduction of the peasantry, although its impact was not uniform.

Richer/middle peasants used the income from mine labour to establish themselves in agriculture. From their earnings they bought agricultural means of production; they engaged in trade; they increased their income by ploughing others' fields for payment; and they produced surpluses for sale in the towns. However, "this stratum within the peasantry was heavily dependent on the dominant process of proletarianisation (within the context of the migrant labour system) as a condition of its formulation and its reproduction" (Wuyts, 1989: 32). Poor peasants continued to rely on migrant labour to sustain their production as well as to buy food (Wuyts, 1986: 32). By the early 1980s Manghezi (1983: 38) notes that mineworkers were investing their earnings in tools, corrugated-iron roofing sheets, sewing machines, bicycles and motorbikes (used in the countryside in trade), and, in bad years, food.

With Mozambique's independence in 1975 the colonial economy entered into crisis. This was precipitated by the massive exodus of settlers from every sector, many of whom engaged in sabotage on an extensive scale as they departed. In the rural areas, they simply abandoned shops and farms, slaughtered cattle, destroyed drainage, irrigation equipment and pumps, and immobilised tractors, combine harvesters and the like. Industrial and agricultural production slumped. To cope with the growing shortages of goods, rationing systems were introduced. In the countryside, peasant production and commercial activities were immediately affected by the disruption of trade. By mid-1977 the effects of the crisis in agriculture and the decline in mine employment could be felt. Living standards started to fall.

The vast majority of peasants never recovered. Frelimo's policy to absorb the surplus rural population and increase the productivity of agriculture through the creation of large state farms and a strong co-operative sector was not successful.

Droughts, floods and cyclones exacerbated the crisis – a major drought in 1991-1992 caused the Limpopo to run dry almost from Beit Bridge to the Indian Ocean (Green, 1992: 1). Crops wilted and died and people went hungry; many died of starvation. The systematic assault on, and destruction of, rural infrastructure, roads and transport and the indiscriminate massacre of many thousands of civilians from 1982 onwards by the South African-backed Renamo contributed to the crisis and fuelled the exodus of thousands of refugees to neighbouring countries.

Not surprisingly these problems were reflected in a massive decline in production, both agricultural and industrial. The Structural Adjustment Programme (SAP) introduced in 1987 did not alleviate the crisis. Industrial production, and hence employment, which grew in 1988 and 1989, has since declined dramatically, and agricultural export production continues to decline. The decline in mine recruitment means that this "traditional" source of income is no longer available to a great many families, but neither are alternative sources of employment. The Economist Intelligence Unit (EIU) estimates that unemployment levels in Mozambique are in excess of 50 percent, and are likely to grow (EIU, 1993: 17). The demobilisation of Frelimo and Renamo soldiers, and the abrupt return of 15-17 000 young skilled and semi-skilled workers after the unification of Germany, will swell the ranks of the unemployed, as will the return of thousands of refugees, many of whom will not be able to make a living from agriculture.

Mozambique's debt of $4.7 billion at the end of 1991 (EIU, 1993 4/4: 39), the international financial institutions' continued commitment to SAPs and the relative youth of the population (over 42 percent of the population of southern Mozambique is under the age of 15) (CNP, 1990: 65) suggest that this crisis of unemployment will get worse. A further reduction of migrant labour to the mines and/or its eventual disappearance will be a catastrophe.

CONCLUSION

If my analysis – that a rather subtle process of reorganisation of the labour supply has been taking place within the mining industry since the mid-1980s – is correct, and we do see the emergence of a South African labour-force hired at the mine gates within the next few years, some important consequences will follow.

The first is that these trends will require careful monitoring by both supplier states and the NUM. Redundancies are probably not too difficult to predict and it is likely that these will be concentrated in marginal mines with a disproportionate complement of foreign workers.

Secondly, it is crucial that the labour-supplying states begin planning ahead. They need to know what the rate of attrition and rate of employment of novices is – industry-wide, within individual mining groups and indeed by individual mines which employ large numbers of foreign workers. They also need to know the profile of the labour-force in terms of age, skill and length of service.

Major efforts must be made to launch employment-generating schemes. The sort of measures being proposed for South Africa under the Reconstruction and Development Programme are appropriate for Mozambique, where housing is in desperately short supply, where road and bridge-building is needed after the long war and where electrification of the countryside and the urban slums is only a dream. The initiatives of non-governmental organisations and international agencies, on whom the burden of employment creation currently falls, are not sufficient to cope with the likely extent of the problem. These projects are important, of course, and vital in the absence of anything else, but are extremely costly and train tens of people for work rather than create the thousands of jobs needed. Clearly, rethinking employment policy is a question for governments, but it is also something that the COM should be pressurised to do. It should not be allowed to get away with making palliative gestures by using Teba/Wenela's infrastructure for small-scale development aid projects. The COM should be making large-scale investments in real economic undertakings, in agriculture, agro-industry and industrial production in the labour reserves from which it has historically recruited workers.

Finally it should be noted that even though formal recruitment of foreign workers through Teba will decline and eventually probably cease, illegal migration will continue and may well increase. However, this will not provide employment for all the men thrown out of work on the mines. These men should not simply be abandoned to the mercy of the "free" labour market. The mining industry must be held accountable for its policies and the consequences of those policies, and make some more effective provisions for its former workers. ◆

REFERENCES

AAC. 1993. Tables of country by age, education, length of service and wage band, 12 January.

Abrahamsson H and A Nilsson. 1994. "Mozambique: macro-economic developments and political challenges in the nineties," The Scandinavian Institute of African Studies, Uppsala, Working Paper No 4.

Bowen, M. 1986. "Let's Build Agricultural Co-operatives." Socialist Agricultural and Development Strategy in Mozambique 1975 - 1983. PhD dissertation, University of Toronto.

CEA. 1979. Problemas de Transformacao Rural na Provincia de Gaza: Um Estudo sobre a Articuacao entre Aldeias Comunais Selecionadas, Cooperativas Agricols e a Unidada de Producao do Baixo Limpopo. Maputo: CEA.

CEA. 1980. Macassane, Estudo de Uma Cooperativa Agraria no Distrito de Matutuine, Provincia de Maputo. Maputo: CEA.

CEA. 1982. Plantacoes de Cha e Economia Camponesa. Maputo: CEA.

CEA. 1983. Organizar os Trabalhadores das Machambas Estatais: O Caso do CAIA. Maputo: CEA.

CEA. 1983. at Familias Camponesas de Angonia no Processo de Socializacao do Campo. Maputo: CEA.

CEA. 1987a (Second Edition). The Mozambican Miner: A Study in the Export of Labour. Maputo: Eduardo Mondlane University.

CEA. 1987b. "The South African mining industry and Mozambican migrant labour in the 1980s: an analysis of recent trends in employment policy," Geneva: ILO, International Migration for Employment Working Paper.

COM. Annual Reports and Statistical Tables, 1990, 1991 and 1992.

COM. 1993. Mining into the Next Century: A Context for Survival and Growth. Johannesburg: COM.

COM. Annual Reports and Statistical Tables, 1990, 1991 and 1992.

Comissao Nacional de Plano. 1990. "Dinamica demografica e processos economicos in sociais e culturais," Maputo, Serie Populacao e Desenvolvimento, Documento No 2.

Crush, J, AH Jeeves and D Yudelman. 1991. South Africa's Labour Empire: A History of Black Migrancy on the Gold Mines. Boulder and Cape Town: Westview Press and David Philip.

Davies, R and J Head. 1994. "The future of mine migrancy: trends in southern Africa," paper presented for the conference on Transforming Mine Migrancy in the 1990s, Cape Town 27-29 June.

De Brito, L. 1980. "Colonial dependence and regional integration," in Mozambican Studies, No 1: 23-32.

De Vletter, F. 1986. "A comparative analysis of skills and other characteristics of foreign mineworkers on the South African gold mines: a case study of the Anglo American mines," report commissioned by the Southern African Team for Employment Promotion for presentation at the Eighth Meeting of the Southern Africa Labour Commission, Blantyre, Malawi, September.

De Vletter, F. 1987. "Foreign labour in the South African gold mines: new insights on an old problem," in International Labour Review, Vol 126, No 2, March-April.

Economist Intelligence Unit. 1993. Country Profile 1993-94, Mozambique, London: EIU.

First, R. 1983. Black Gold: The Mozambican Miner, Proletarian and Peasant. Brighton and New York: Harvester and St Martin's Press.

Godsell, RM. 1986. Address to the Gold 100 Conference on Future Labour Developments, Johannesburg, 16 September.

Green, RH. 1992. "The political economy of drought: southern Africa 1991-1992," London School of Hygiene and Tropical Medicine, Health Policy Unit seminar, 18 November.

Harries, P. 1994. Work, Culture and Identity: Migrant Labourers in Mozambique and South Africa 1860-1910. Johannesburg: Wits University Press (forthcoming).

Harris, M. 1959. "Labour emigration among the Mozambique Thonga: cultural and political factors," in Africa, Vol 29, No 1 January.

Hermele, K. 1986. "Contemporary land struggles on the Limpopo: a case study of Chokwe, Mozambique 1950-1985," University of Uppsala, Working Group for the Study of Development Strategies, Department of Development Studies, AKUT Series No 34.

Manghezi, A. 1980. "The Voice of the Miner," in Mozambican Studies, No 1.

Manghezi, A. 1983. "Ku Thekela: Estrategia de Sobrevivencia Contra a Fome no Sul de Mozambique," in Estudos Mocamicanos, No 4.

Manghezi, A. 1987. "The history and organisation of labour recruitment in southern Mozambique," unpublished paper, Maputo.

Migueis Lopes Junior, A. 1980. "Capital accumulation in South Africa and southern Mozambique," in Mozambican Studies, Vol 1: 89-102.

Mondlane, E. 1969. The Struggle for Mozambique. Harmondsworth: Penguin.

O'Laughlin, B. 1981. "A Questao Agraria em Mozambique," in Estudos Mocambicanos, No 3: 9-32.

O'Laughlin, B. 1992. "Agrarian reform and agricultural revolution: some reflections on the Mozambican experience," Institute of Social Studies, The Hague, unpublished.

Raikes, P. 1984. "Food policy and production in Mozambique since independence," in Review of African Political Economy, No 29, July: 95-107.

Roesch, O. 1986. Socialism and Rural Development in Mozambique: The Case of Aldeia Comunal 24 de Julho. PhD dissertation, University of Toronto.

Roesch, O. 1991. "Migrant labour and forced rice production in southern Mozambique: the colonial peasantry of the lower Limpopo valley," in Journal of Southern African Studies, Vol 17, No 2.

UNICEF. 1988. The State of the World's Children. Oxford: Oxford University Press.

Wuyts, M. 1986 "The political economy of Portuguese colonialism," in Mozambican Studies, No 1: 10-22.

Wuyts, M. 1989. Money and Planning for Socialist Transition: The Mozambican Experience. Aldershot: Gower.

Young, S. 1978. "What have they done with the rain? 20th century transformation in ceremonial practice and belief in southern Mozambique with particular reference to rain prayers," paper presented at the African Studies Association annual conference, 2 November.

Motherless Households, Landless Farms: Employment Patterns Among Lesotho Migrants

Professor David Coplan
Department of Social Anthropology,
University of Cape Town,
South Africa

Dr Thoahlane Thoahlane
Department of Sociology,
University of Stellenbosch,
South Africa

The economic and social destiny of mineworkers from Lesotho is inseparable from that of other migrants, not only those from neighbouring states but also from South Africa's former homelands and other rural areas. Lesotho's extreme degree of involvement in migrant mine labour and lack of plausible employment alternatives may give this country the appearance of being a special case among sending areas, but it seems instead that the very extremity of the situation delineates most clearly the dilemmas facing attempts to transform both the migrant labour system and regional economic and political relations. If economically viable and socially beneficial solutions to the problems of Lesotho migrants could be found, this would certainly augur well for other bilateral agreements on regional labour issues.

The number of Basotho employed in the mines is steadily decreasing through retrenchment, with the loss of more than 14 000 jobs since 1987. Although this decline may soon level off because of the skills and experience Basotho offer, the male population in the 20-54 age group is increasing. Whereas in 1976, 48 percent of Basotho men in this group were mineworkers, the figure had fallen to only 38 percent in 1986 and to 35 percent in 1993. By 2001 the figure may be only 17 percent. Some recruitment does continue and the absolute decline in mine jobs may not be that great, but the number of Basotho between 20 and 54 who lacked such jobs in 1976 was 125 000 and will be 390 000 in 2001 (Sechaba Consultants, 1994: 136).

Within Lesotho there are few employment opportunities that will generate development. Mine retrenchments have an adverse effect that spreads from the migrant and his family through the economic well-springs of all sectors of community and commercial life. Lesotho's Gross Domestic Product (GDP) of R1 669 million in 1992 (after several rounds of massive retrenchments) was still two thirds of its Gross National Product (GNP) of R2 525,8 million (migrant remittances comprising the difference).

Similarly in 1990 exports were only 9,2 percent of imports, and even this was an increase over the 1980s due to expanded clothing and footwear manufacturing (Bureau of Statistics, Lesotho 1993: 126). While higher wages have kept the absolute total of remittances level, an average of six to seven dependents lose their breadwinner each time a migrant loses his job. The number of people remaining in Lesotho for each mineworker outside the country has recently risen to 15 (Cobbe 1992: 2). Lesotho's economy currently has an extremely limited capacity to absorb returning mineworkers or the many aspiring migrants likely to be denied entry into the industry.

Unemployment itself surged from 23 percent in 1986 to 40 percent in 1991 (Setsabi et al 1992: 116). While over 70 percent of those actually in the domestic work-force are engaged in agriculture, this sector contributes only 8 percent of the GNP as against 40 percent from migrant remittances (Sechaba Consultants 1994: 79).

Since agricultural production has long depended on capital inputs, the 55 percent of returned migrants who reported farming as their current occupation (Setsabi et al, 1992: 4) are less productive on the land than were their families during the period when their labour was unavailable. While the harvest varies with the rains, overall Lesotho's agricultural output continues its slow but steady decline.

RETRENCHMENT AS AN INDUSTRY: THE PROFITS OF DOOM

Both the motivations for and logistics of dismissal significantly affect the economic security and quality of life available to workers after they leave the mines. The reasons universally offered by mine management for down-scaling include the former government's internalisation policy, the uncertain and relatively low pricing structure in mineral markets and increasing mechanisation made attractive in part by labour agitation and the failure of productivity to keep pace with negotiated increases in wage scales and benefits.

What is surprising is not that management should offer these rationalisations but the degree to which scholars concerned with monitoring the situation appear, without investigation, to accept them. Almost all writers on employment patterns in the mining industry have criticised the inequity and iniquity of the "rules" of the migrant employment system without questioning further whether mine management, the recruiting agencies or their employees are in actuality playing by them.

Even Seidman (1993), who notes migrants' reports of bribery and favouritism in recruitment, describes her respondents as exhibiting a "rather pathetic failure to understand that even if the gold price rises, the shift to a smaller, more productive work-force means Harmony (mine) is unlikely to return to its former size" (Seidman, 1993: 9). At least as pathetic is the myopia that prevents scholars from recognising in the patterns of retrenchment goals that are not driven by the market, unless it is the market in embezzled retrenchment benefits.

What our respondents complained of, more than the fact of retrenchment itself and without special prompting, was the widespread denial and misappropriation of their severance packages, provident fund and long-service bonuses; systematic attempts to undermine contract provisions negotiated with the National Union of Mineworkers (NUM) and to target unionists for dismissal; and corrupt practices and nepotism in rehiring and recruitment.

The majority of the more than 60 ex-miners we spoke to belong to two broad groups: those dismissed in connection with the massive 1987 NUM strike, and those laid off in the period of heavy labour-force reductions in the early 1990s. Coal and platinum mine workers were well represented, as were those from the gold mines. Those dismissed as a result of the 1987 strike tended to be strong NUM supporters, some even minor officials or shop stewards. Many complained that they had been sent away without severance packages or even their work records and certificates as a punishment for their participation in the strike. Others less involved in union affairs had in many cases been told they were being sacked in this manner because the strike had been illegal (a patent lie). Alternatively they were assured that they were only being sent away until security and peace were re-established, whereupon they would be recalled. Six years later, almost 5 000 of these men are still waiting. Most are still strong supporters of the union, crediting the NUM with having fought, often successfully, against great odds, for the rights of workers, and they rather blamed mine management and the apartheid state for their misfortunes. One notable exception to this view, an embittered ex-shop steward, said: "We protested to the manager but he said, 'Go ask Ramaphosa for a job!'. We did, but they said he was too busy."

The majority of respondents retrenched since 1990 were also members and continuing supporters of the NUM, though not as committed or knowledgeable as the earlier group. Their stories included repeated variations of similar retrenchment experiences.

Those retrenched were given little or no warning, paid the amount outstanding since their last bi-weekly pay slip and told to get taxis at their own expense to Lesotho where their service bonuses and provident fund payouts would be waiting for them at the offices of the recruiting agency, The Employment Bureau of Africa (Teba). Upon reaching Teba they were told that their money was back in South Africa at the mine. Those who managed to return to the mine were told to go back to Lesotho and Teba and wait. The ex-miners' money for transport and patience were by this means exhausted.

Migrants with many years of experience were retrenched in preference to relative novices, violating union and industry agreement on seniority. Inquiring after their service payout many veterans were offered sums far below the approximately R1 000 per year of service to which the NUM informed them they were entitled. Excuses given were that they had changed mines or changed job categories at some point.

Alternatively they were told that if they would not sign for what was offered they could have recourse to the union or a lawyer but in the meantime, and probably for all time, they would be given nothing. Other mines, perhaps more honest, retrenched novices first in order to avoid making large service payouts.

Provident and pension funds (Basotho only qualify for pension schemes if they pay "blue card" taxes – this depends on the way salaries are handled at specific mines) work on the basis of a 50 percent contribution from the employee and 50 percent from the employer. Respondents reported having the 50 percent employer contribution withheld from their provident fund payouts.

Ex-mineworkers who travelled to the mine in search of either their service payouts or their old jobs were told that they would have to see their "old boss"; the white miner who had supervised them at the time of their retrenchment. Such personnel were often, for various reasons, unavailable, and the men waited to see them in vain.

Migrants said that bribery and nepotism at the recruiting offices was common, with a recall requiring a standard payment of R500 or a well-placed relative in the clerkdom of the mine or Teba. Basotho found themselves at a disadvantage in this regard, as under present conditions Teba no longer does much actual recruitment, the mines preferring to hire whoever they choose, whenever they choose, at the mine gates. Limited work-seeker permits and lack of funds for travel, food and accommodation at the mine site all make it especially difficult for repatriated Basotho to attempt to get their service bonuses or their jobs back.

The mines themselves no longer use the term "retrenched" but prefer the euphemism "on leave". This allows them to perpetuate the fiction that the employee is only temporarily unengaged, remains eligible for recall and thus is not (yet) entitled to retrenchment benefits.

Managerial personnel maintain that those placed "on leave" are first offered the choice of other employment or a benefit package. Most respondents, however, said no offers of alternative training or employment had been made. Those who were aware of such offers said these were always for other jobs at lower skills and/or pay levels, that they were regarded as new workers, and that service bonuses accumulated during their previous employment periods were thereby forfeited. Re-employment thus constitutes a means to down-scale labour costs per worker as well as worker numbers.

Mine management is escaping the wage and benefit scales negotiated with the NUM by retrenching workers and then rehiring them through "contract" labour suppliers who serve as the mineworkers' nominal employers. These contractors pay at most half union mandated wages and provide no benefits, employment security, severance packages, disability insurance or next-of-kin compensation in case of death. In real situations, the union has foregone wage increases in order to preserve the jobs of its members, as at Doornfontein mine in 1991, where wage demands were reduced in exchange for restoring the jobs of 6 000 retrenched workers.

The strategies by which the mine industry bureaucracy exploits the insecurity and lack of resources and information available to mineworkers are too varied and convoluted to review here, but let us summarise the prevalent attitude with a singular, but egregious case: Tanki Ranthari, a veteran with 25 years service, contracted tuberculosis underground at Harmony mine in Virginia, Orange Free State. When the condition recurred after initial treatment at the mine he was given a Valid Re-engagement Guarantee (VRG) or "bonus" as the workers call it, and told he should return to Lesotho to recover, and if he did so by 1 March 1995 he would be given his old job back.

Because he was only on "sick leave" he was given no money. Currently he is wasting with the disease and does not have the resources to travel from his village to the hospital in Maseru for regular treatment. Even if he does not die soon it is unlikely he will return in time to claim his job, and it seems perfectly apparent that management anticipated this when they gave him a VRG in lieu of liability compensation.

As a final coda we must report that when a worker does die, either at the mines or at home from work-related conditions, his family may lose a husband and breadwinner but the retrenchment industry does not lose a victim. Ill-informed as to their husband's wage rates or the amount of the benefits due to them, easily intimidated or misled, and without the confidence or resources to pursue legal remedies, widows are often cheated out of a significant portion of their husbands' death benefits by officials at the recruitment agencies.

In reply to inquiries concerning ethnic conflict on the mines and the possible targeting of workers from specific ethnic or national groups for retrenchment, respondents denied that ethnicity was a factor in and of itself. They agreed that there were cases where Basotho and Xhosa were targeted, but argued that this reflected the greater relative involvements of members of those two groups in union activity and leadership. "Faction fights" between Basotho and Xhosa were not attributed to ethnically based ill-feeling but to the unwillingness of Basotho to join Xhosa in unauthorised strikes for higher wages due to the Basotho fear of permanent dismissal and repatriation. Even in this, mine management was implicated, as one of the 1987 cohort testified:

> The bosses stirred up ethnic conflict among the tribes by setting them against one another ... The management went to the jails to bribe a Mosotho convict and a Xhosa convict to come to the compound to cause troubles. By the time we noticed it was too late. After the strike we were all sent off and we were told they are closing down the mine but after some time they took some of the people back but not everybody. Mostly they dismissed the union members. We were sent off because we were told that the strike was illegal.

Others explained that recently Basotho and Xhosa have been retrenched and Zulu migrants, whose co-operativeness is assured by the separate Inkatha-affiliated union to which they belong, are hired in their stead. Conversely, however, in July 1994, 100 Zulu-speaking members of the NUM were dismissed by East Rand Proprietary Mine on the West Rand for engaging in ethnic/political faction fighting with Basotho and Xhosa workers. The NUM took no action on their behalf. Migrants whose mines are located in what up until 28 April 1994 were ethnic homelands, such as the platinum mines in Boputhatswana and Lebowa, also complained that management was bowing to pressure to replace outsiders such as the Basotho with local Batswana and Bapedi.

Many respondents associated the dramatic increase in retrenchments with the rise of the NUM and its ability to secure improved contract provisions for mineworkers. In response to the question of whether they had openly protested the targeting of union members for dismissal either to management or to union officials themselves, we elicited accounts such as the following:

> The union leaders were very worried about the situation because these nations (Basotho and Xhosa) were all union members. But if they tried to speak for people, management bribed them to be quiet. The union did not help, and people who are very strong in the union ended up having good jobs and nice cars, and were paid off by the management ... We were sent away and told to go back to Ramaphosa. Now that we were in Lesotho the union did not help us, and there was no chance to be heard within the union because we were already scattered to our places. But I am still a supporter of the union.

It is true that dismissed Basotho shop stewards found themselves suddenly disenfranchised following the 1987 strike because they were physically unable to be present at union councils in South Africa.

The blanket statement that the NUM did not help is somewhat unfair, however, since their office in Maseru pursues retrenchment, service and benefit claims for individual members, currently operates 13 agricultural and artisans' co-operatives for ex-miners and their wives and is actively pressurising the mining houses to contribute funds for job creation and rural development in Lesotho.

Responding to the sort of bitterness expressed above, unionists simply said they do their best and regard these accounts as more rhetorical cries for help than serious accusations. Union officials, they freely admitted, are often threatened and successfully intimidated by management, and when offered a small portion of a rightful claim they may accept it rather than risk securing nothing. Further, Puseletso Selae, the NUM representative in Maseru, claimed that massive recent retrenchments of Basotho miners have not been a financial necessity and that management representatives have admitted as much[1].

Large-scale retrenchment, we contend, is part of a strategy to undermine the NUM, reduce militancy, avoid the consequences of collective bargaining, reduce labour costs and engage in the "social dumping" of the costs of capital investment and restructuring into the removed environments of employment-hungry labour reserves.

Retrenchment of Basotho workers since 1987 is therefore not so much an unfortunate but necessary process of "structural adjustment" or rationalisation in the mining industry as an industry in itself.

Price fluctuations, low overall averages and technological and organisational innovations have been used as a pretext for excessive retrenchments which serve other objectives beyond the industry's economic viability or even reasonable profitability. For senior management, the goals of the "retrenchment industry" include: 1) the downward restructuring of labour costs in the form of reduced wages, benefits, working conditions and employment security for workers; 2) the undermining of collective bargaining agreements signed with the NUM, and the extension of labour control and labour peace by the systematic retrenchments and victimisation of NUM members. Basotho were frequent targets of such victimisation because they usually are seen to be strong NUM supporters and because their foreign status makes them relatively easy to repatriate permanently to the sending area.

Xhosa migrants were similarly disproportionately victimised but their status as South Africans (former Transkei/Ciskei "independence" notwithstanding) gives them greater ability to defend themselves and makes them more difficult to get rid of in the long term. No migrant with a history of union activity or labour protest, real or imputed, is known to have been recalled to mine employment without personal legal intercession by the NUM.

For junior management, retrenchment provides a steady stream of opportunities to appropriate the compensation packages and service benefits of dismissed

---

1. *Interview with Puseletso Selae, the NUM representative in Maseru, 10 January 1994.*

migrants. The varied strategies used by mine company clerks, Teba officials and other administrative staff to avoid the payment of migrants' benefits or to redirect them into their own pockets range from the brutally simple to the Byzantine, but the amounts involved certainly exceed some millions of rands.

Conversely, those who seek to avoid retrenchment or to be recalled following a period of unemployment commonly must bribe these same officials as well as sign away all claims to benefits previously accrued. Overall, the actual structure and procedures of retrenchment and recruitment are specifically geared to facilitate these abuses.

The status of the Basotho as foreigners and the policies of internalisation, union-busting and repatriation makes them favoured targets of these corrupt practices.

SOCIAL DUMPING: THE IMPACT OF RETRENCHMENT ON LESOTHO

Shifting the discussion from expropriation in the mining industry to the social costs levied on the people of the sending areas may perhaps be most easily accomplished by noting that the Lesotho government, according to the Maseru office of the NUM, is involved in the retrenchment industry and the policy of social dumping. As Puseletso Selae explained[2]:

> The government is opening a new account to hold this retrenchment and benefit money that people are supposed to get, but they are claiming that people are not findable – they are making it so difficult for people to get their money. They say they call their names over the radio, but not everybody has access to one. The recruiting offices have their addresses of course but the government doesn't want to write to them; they are cheating ... The government is not doing anything to help the retrenched men. We took all these problems they and their families are having to the Minister of Employment and Social Welfare but nothing was done. Since Leabua Jonathan, Lekhanya and the Basotho Congress Party today nothing has been done; not even one cent to help.

The consequences of losing a regular salary are unavoidably severe for a Lesotho migrant. A good retrenchment package, well invested, can provide the basis for making a living in Lesotho. In the majority of cases however, even an equitable package is largely spent on immediate needs such as completing a house, buying clothing and paying school fees, assisting close kin and meeting outstanding obligations. Because they have few sources of advice and at best limited entrepreneurial experiences, attempts at investment often fail.

If the migrant is denied contractual benefits upon retrenchment, the results

---

2. *Interview with Puseletso Selae, 10 January 1994.*

may be total disaster. Those hoping to be rehired spend what little money they have travelling to or hanging about at the recruitment offices. In Lesotho, jobs are few, wage scales are dismally low, and apart from building trades, ex-miners rarely have skills that are readily marketable. Efforts to negotiate for jobs at the Lesotho Highlands Water Project where ex-miners could use their drilling, blasting and other skills have not proved fruitful.

Almost two thirds of Lesotho ex-miners have access to fields, but these rarely comprise more than four acres. Many lack draft animals and the cash for seed, fertilizers and other essential inputs. Of those who do farm only 10 percent report that they are able to feed their families on the produce (Setsabi et al 1992: 5). Of course, many of these men have come to regard themselves as miners and resist giving up this identity in favour of that of subsistence farmer. Perhaps the most sorry statistic of all is the finding that whereas 90 percent of recently returned migrants said they were unwilling to participate in the government's food-for-work programmes so popular with rural women, 80 percent of ex-miners who had been at home a year or more said they were now willing to work for the small parcels of staples and the R2 per day that such programmes provide.

In many cases the wives of ex-miners have now gone out to work, are seeking work or have turned to hawking, brewing or selling crafts, but this creates as many problems as it helps to solve. To begin with, there are more unskilled jobs available to women than to men in Lesotho, though the pay for such "women's work" is shockingly low.

Most male respondents said that they readily helped with housework and child-minding, but felt some embarrassment and diminished self-esteem at turning over the role of breadwinner to their wives. Some indeed did not want their wives to work, fearing that granting such independence would lead to the breakup of their marriages. At the very least, they wished for their wives to come home every evening and not live out or take up labour migrancy as they had done. As one ex-miner worried:

> I wouldn't like my wife to go to South Africa to work because I think she will get a rich man and she will forget all about me. I don't like my wife to work as a domestic because the pay is not good and also her employer will make her his lover. If she refuses she gets sacked and so sometimes, because we have so many problems, she will agree. Then this guy will be using my wife. She said to me that was all right, because there is nothing else we can do.

Although we have no reliable statistics, an increasingly prevalent phenomenon is the wife who heads off to South Africa or a border town to find work, promising to send money and to return as soon as she can, never to be heard from again. Others make no such promises but simply inform their husband that now that he has lost his job he is losing his wife and the mother of their children as well. To the farms without land we must add the families without mothers: the increasingly prevalent male-headed single-parent households. Young women are especially likely to leave, since they can most easily find housing and support from other men, and unlike older, long-married women, they rarely have land or livestock (Thoahlane, 1994).

It would be misleading, however, to suggest that the above is the dominant pattern. While our female respondents were by their very availability those who had not abandoned their husbands, they gave love and loyalty as some of the reasons for their constancy.

The willingness of migrants and ex-migrants and their wives to leave Lesotho and live in South Africa varied with their social and material investment in their homesteads. The greater the investment, the greater their commitment to remaining labour migrants and keeping their families on their homesteads in Lesotho.

Without exception all respondents wanted the right to seek and take up employment freely in South Africa. As one of Seidman's (1993: 32) respondents put it, people should be able to flow down into South Africa as freely as water from the Highlands Water Scheme. They varied, however, in the kind of political arrangements they felt should be made to secure this. The majority were willing to exchange their Lesotho passports for South African identification documents as the price of labour mobility, even if it meant returning to Lesotho as a paper visitor, but they were not in favour of the political incorporation of Lesotho into South Africa.

"That would mean the end of Sesotho," they protested, by which they mean a personal as well as communal, genealogical and national history, an identity and its entitlements, reciprocities and their resources, investments of the self and substance and, most materially, a land tenure system in which land is not a factor in the market. As it stands, no one, citizen or foreigner, can buy or sell land in Lesotho: it can only be leased or allocated. This, as one veteran migrant explained, prevents "the white man from owning everything, as he does in South Africa". Clearly Basotho ex-mineworkers, who see foreign labourers rather than themselves employed on the Highlands Water Scheme, want the "water" to flow only from Lesotho to South Africa, and not in the opposite direction.

SOME IMPLICATIONS FOR POLICY

The story of mine labour retrenchment is by extension a cautionary one regarding the hardships that already hard-pressed migrants would face if the social ideal of ending labour migrancy were rapidly achieved. Certainly one area in which the new ANC government, in partnership with the NUM, should and can intervene is the unfair labour practices and corruption within the mining sector's "retrenchment industry". In view of the down-scaling proceeding in the industry, the NUM has been encouraging retrenched Basotho not to think of themselves as unemployed but as permanent ex-miners, and to look to other forms of income generation. To this end the union has sponsored the creation of trade, craft and horticultural co-operatives and is negotiating with external donors and the mining houses to get into the business of rural development in Lesotho. A very large majority of migrants and ex-migrants, however, prefer to carry on or resume migrating. The NUM recently had to re-examine its official support for the policy of labour stabilisation, for example, in recognition of the suffering its implementation would cause those already most exploited. A recent survey found that only 47 percent of South African married migrants living in single-sex compounds would prefer to move with their families to the worksite. For foreign migrants, the figure is only 30 percent (Crush et al 1991: 162, 173-174).

Of course, Basotho and other non-South African migrants have particular reason to be wary of schemes promoting stabilisation through the subsidisation of permanent family housing in proximity to the mines. To begin with, since management responds to costly contract agreements by cutting labour, the idea of creating "company towns" around the mines will encourage further reductions that are likely to disproportionately affect non-South African workers (Thoahlane, 1994). Currently, mineworkers who are not South African citizens need formal permission from the municipality to live in a township rather than in a compound hostel (Seidman 1993: 17). Standing immigration restrictions forbid foreign miners from living in married quarters or acquiring land and property in South Africa. The government, if not mine management itself, is bound to push for the provision of permanent housing for citizens in preference to foreign migrants and policies of stabilisation and internalisation appear to Basotho as opposite sides of the same coin.

Conversely, the fear of retrenchment leads Basotho workers to avoid even minimal investment in family housing schemes at the worksite, since the loss of a job would then involve the loss of one's house as well (Seidman 1993: 17). In Lesotho a stand can be obtained for the price of a "Form C" permit from the chief, and a house, once built, remains the family homestead regardless of where its members are or are not working. Extending this consideration to migrants as a category, South African as well as foreign, the restructuring and apparently permanent down-scaling of the mine labour-force appears to operate at cross-purposes with announced intentions to improve workers' quality of life through stabilisation.

What then, at a minimum, should be done? The principle of mobility of labour seems to us paramount in the end. The mining houses are likely to continue to employ whoever they want, wherever they want, with even less restriction than they do now. What can a future South Africa offer workers who have financed the country's development and struggled to free it from destructive racial domination at their cost, if not the basic right to sell their labour on an open regional market without discriminatory, artificial legal hindrance? Because if pushed to it Basotho will not stay in Lesotho. Nowadays the border at the Caledon River (which the Basotho call *Mohokare*, "a border amidst our land)" is as porous as it was before the imposition of strict influx control in the early 1960s. It would be an uncharacteristic wickedness for Mandela's government to place troops and electric fences around Lesotho just to keep a few thousand Basotho workers out. At least some South African Basotho, who outnumber the population of Lesotho, would certainly act to undermine such a policy. As Cobbe (1992: 7) recognises, there will be Basotho migration and emigration no matter who tries to prevent it. The issue is the conditions under which it takes place, its volume, and the ability to move between Lesotho and the worksite. Illegal migration exacerbates class conflict, ethnic divisiveness, worker factionalism, illegal settlement, undocumented employment, employer abuse and exploitation and disrespect for the law. It also undercuts legal wages, unionisation, solidarity, collective bargaining and the rights of all workers. It is not just migrants who are better off when they are legal: so are their industries and their fellow workers.

When migrants are asked what they think, their responses are remarkably varied: how can these variations be accommodated within the framework of what clearly has to be a negotiated regional labour policy agreement? Without such a policy, enshrining the regional mobility of labour, all workers will remain to some degree vulnerable and dependent. Unless the union uses its political and organisational resources to secure rights for all workers, stabilised and migrant, local and foreign, employed and retrenched, to pursue their varied strategies and goals, then the rights and benefits for which they have fought so long, and even the NUM itself, may not effectively endure. ◆

REFERENCES

Bureau of Statistics. 1993. Lesotho Statistical Yearbook, 1992. Lesotho government.

Cobbe, J. 1992. "Lesotho and the new South Africa: economic trends and possible futures," paper presented to the 35th annual meeting of the African Studies Association, Seattle, November.

Coplan, D. 1993. "Dammed if we know: public policy, labour law and the future of the migrant labour system," paper presented to the Department of Social Anthropology, University of Cape Town, August 1993.

Crush, J, AH Jeeves and D Yudelman. 1991. South Africa's Labour Empire: A History of Black Migrancy to the Gold Mines. Boulder and Cape Town: Westview Press and David Philip.

Sechaba Consultants. 1994. Lesotho: Looking Back ... Moving Forward. Maseru.

Seidman, G. 1993. "If Harmony closes, will the last one to leave turn out the lights? Down-scaling in the Free State goldfields," Unpublished manuscript.

Setsabi, AM, MA Lesaoana and JJ Molefi. 1992. A Study of the Socio-Economic Situation of the Basotho Miners. Roma: National University of Lesotho.

MACROECONOMIC STATISTICAL EVIDENCE FROM LESOTHO

PROFESSOR JAMES COBBE
Department of Economics,
Florida State University,
Tallahasee, USA

It has been a feature of the economy of southern Africa for well over a century that some of the demand for relatively unskilled wage labour has been met by temporary, oscillating migration. For almost as long, there have been disputes about the economic impact of such migration on the sending areas, particularly when the incidence of temporary outmigration is high. This chapter examines some statistical evidence relevant to these debates drawn from Lesotho, but does not review in detail the theoretical debates about the economic impact of outmigration on sending areas, nor the other forms of evidence relevant to the debate. It is important to note that the statistical evidence presented here is in no sense conclusive; it is suggestive, no more.

Throughout the period for which national income account estimates for Lesotho are available, net factor income from abroad has varied between about half of the Gross Domestic Product (GDP) to as much as GDP or more. The Gross National Product (GNP) has therefore been between 50 percent and 100 percent more than GDP. Net factor income from abroad is overwhelmingly, in most years, accounted for by the earnings of temporary migrants working in South Africa, and for much of this period these earnings were growing quite rapidly. Published World Bank data suggest that real GNP per capita grew at 4,9 percent per annum over the 1965 to 1990 period, the fastest rate in low-income sub-Saharan Africa and the sixth fastest rate in the world. The same source suggests, however, that Lesotho's GNP per capita fell at a rate of 0,5 percent per annum from 1980 to 1991. Estimates based directly on data from Lesotho suggest a growth rate of under 3 percent per annum from 1965 to 1990, but still about 2,8 percent per annum on average and much better than most countries in Africa (Cobbe, 1992). Real GDP per head probably grew at about 2,7 percent per annum on average between 1968 and 1990, also a much better record than in most of Africa, even though most of the positive growth had occurred by 1980.

Throughout this period, the role played by migrant labour in Lesotho's economy, and particularly in its growth and development, has been controversial. In proportion to the total male labour force, migration in some periods has been massive. Early estimates often suggested that as much as half the adult male labour force were absent in South Africa at any given time, and in the first decade of independence migrants outnumbered wage employees within the country by at least five to one.

More recently, as South Africa has reduced the number of foreign migrants employed in its mining industry, the total number of migrants from Lesotho has stabilised or declined. The number of people in Lesotho per migrant worker has therefore grown from a low of fewer than 10 in 1977 to over 16 in 1992. In these circumstances, where the total earnings of migrants have in many years been the same as GDP, current earnings of migrants are a crucial component of current family incomes and overall income and facilitate current consumption and imports.

THE ISSUES

The impact of such massive migration on domestic output, growth and the style of development is controversial. Several social anthropologists, supported by some agriculturalists, have argued forcefully on the basis of household-level data that access to current remittances is, for many households, a necessary prerequisite for successful agricultural production (Murray, 1981; Spiegel, 1981). For agricultural production to be successful, they say, certain purchases have to be made. Without access to current migrant remittances, most rural households are unable to finance such purchases[1]. The implication is that migration should increase domestic output via the improved ability of rural households to plough, buy

---

1. *This is a slight simplification because in many cases the crucial binding constraint is draught-power for ploughing, which is often not purchased for cash even when households do not provide it fully themselves (co-operative reciprocal arrangements are common – it takes more cattle to pull the plough than most households own). Land tenure in Lesotho is based on customary law, with the result that land is relatively equitably distributed (although there are rapidly growing numbers of landless households), and in principle monetary transactions involving agricultural land (either sale or rental) are illegal, ie there is no market in*

fertiliser, etc. An implicit assumption here is that the constraint on agricultural production is not male labour but purchased inputs.

The conclusion that migration has a positive impact on current production is consistent with a variety of interpretations of simple Keynesian notions of the multiplier (the total expenditure generated in the home country for every one rand remitted by migrant labour), and on typical interpretations of regional analysis using notions of exogenous and endogenous income and multipliers.

The argument is basically that the bulk of migrant earnings are remitted to Lesotho and spent in Lesotho; although the country has a very high propensity to import (imports have exceeded GDP since the mid-1970s), extra spending in Lesotho will generate greater domestic output because spending generates greater activity in the services sector (commerce, transport, government) and construction industries, as well as in at least the small-scale and micro-enterprise manufacturing sectors aimed at the domestic market (large-scale manufacturing almost solely serves export markets).

Government output may also be influenced because under the Southern African Customs Union Agreement each additional Loti (the Lesotho currency, plural Maloti [M]) generates an additional 20 cents of government revenue, and current government expenditure is believed to be strongly influenced by current government revenue. Thus it is reasonable to expect that some current migrant earnings, in addition to adding to GNP directly, should be spent on goods produced in Lesotho, thus producing a multiplier effect on both GNP and GDP.

Given the openness (to foreign trade) of the economy, one might expect this multiplier effect to be quite small, but overall the GNP multiplier should be greater than one. Using imperfect data from the 1970s, I made a crude estimate that the overall GNP multiplier for migrant earnings was probably in the range of 1,25 to 1,85, implying that 20 to 45 percent of migrant earnings were actually spent on output produced in Lesotho (Bardill and Cobbe, 1985: 65).

However, there is a counter argument to the one which concludes with positive impact. The men who migrate do so from an economy which has absolutely no provision of state assistance for income maintenance. Unemployment compensation or insurance does not exist, and migrant miners do not normally qualify for payments from the South African Unemployment Insurance Fund.

Although in the past some relatively secure miners could afford to spend fairly long leave periods at home in Lesotho without having to generate income, those days are now long gone. For many years the mines have been "stabilising" their labour forces, and now they are also reducing them. As a result migrants are now essentially professional miners who get limited home leave, and if they do not return on their recall date they no longer have a job. Recruitment of novice miners has almost ceased and in many cases the mines are now retrenching

---

agricultural land. Sharecropping in various forms, mostly involving households with low wealth and low current income contributing land, and higher income and wealth households being the actual cultivators, is fairly widespread. The assertion here is that sharecropping does not sufficiently substitute for access to remittances for the purchase of inputs to maintain agricultural output at the level the land makes potentially possible with the technology in use.

workers. Potential migrants can no longer obtain a contract by just showing up and demonstrating that they are able-bodied.

Thus a migrant who does not return to the mines each year after a short period has no income except what he can generate himself from his own assets, enterprise and labour. The consequence is that clearly now, and probably for much of the past 20 years, most Basotho cannot afford to be idle while at home in Lesotho. They may well be very much less productive than they would be as miners, but unless they earn something they would have no income. The scarcity of co-operating factors and employment opportunities means the income they can generate is probably very limited, but because most have few assets, some income is essential for survival (extended families and communities may support individuals without income for a while, but after a relatively short period of time generally will expect work of some kind in return).

It follows that whenever a migrant leaves the country there is a negative impact on domestic output in the form of reduced production corresponding to the income that the migrant would have earned if he had remained within the country.

Of course, it is possible that while at home in Lesotho a worker could enter a field of self employment with low entry barriers in which the addition of his labour adds nothing to total output. Instead, a fixed amount of total income is now shared with one extra worker with the initial workers receiving lower incomes as a result.

If this were to happen in all cases, migration would produce no negative impact on domestic production. In fact, the individual incomes of those left behind would increase, although this would not show in the national income accounts. However, it seems unlikely that this would be so for all potential and actual migrants, because at least some of them are likely to engage in agriculture or commodity production, and because greater entry to low entry barrier activities is likely to have an impact on output prices and therefore total output in some cases[2].

However, the question is not what might happen, but what evidence suggests has happened. An obvious difficulty with investigating this kind of issue empirically is the availability of this data.

NAIVE REGRESSIONS

National income accounts from Lesotho do not have a long history, are subject to large errors, are somewhat murky with respect to the methodology used to produce some of the estimates and have had numerous changes of approach and

---

2. *Of course, one can question the extent to which output in the micro-enterprise, informal sector in Lesotho is accurately measured by the national income accounts, and therefore the extent to which either of these possibilities can be detected. However, the qualitative, as opposed to quantitative, impact (ie the sign of the effect) should reach the national income accounts because earnings in the informal sector are, in part, spent in the formal sector.*

basis. This has, in the past, made it impossible to construct a consistent series of figures over a specific time period. However, recently (Kingdom of Lesotho, 1992) a set of consistent annual national income account estimates for Lesotho for the period 1980 to 1991 became available. These obviously do not allow any very complex modelling, but they do permit some statistical investigation of these competing hypotheses concerning the effects of current migrant earnings on current output[3].

Basically, what I will report are the results of some very naive regressions on the Lesotho Bureau of Statistics national income accounts data in fixed 1980 prices, supplemented by some additional data on numbers and earnings of migrants (Cobbe, 1992) (Appendix).

I will report on three different sets of naive simple ordinary least squares (OLS) regressions. The first set concerns attempts to "backcast" – in other words to find the best fitting equation to explain dependent variables. The second set are specific attempts to fit simple multiplier formulations, with the independent variables chosen partly on the basis of the variables that show up with high significance in the first set, and partly on a priori considerations. The third set is based on an approach from the regional economics literature and simply estimates a multiplier on the basis of an assumed relationship between two aggregates ("autonomous" and "dependent" product) derived from the national income accounts.

In the data set, there are three series that approximate the earnings of migrants. One is labelled RNFIFA, and is simply net factor income from abroad deflated to 1980 prices in the source. For current purposes there are some problems with this series. First, by definition, it is one of the components of GNP, and this makes for statistical difficulties. Second, it includes net capital earnings payments in addition to labour earnings, and in some years the net interest and profit outflow is quite substantial. Third, the labour component of RNFIFA, as specified in earlier national accounts publications, is somewhat mysterious, because it bears no consistent relationship to migrant earnings as estimated independently (Cobbe, 1991a).

Accordingly, two alternative series have been calculated. The first is labelled REARN, and is an estimate of migrant labour earnings derived from published data on the numbers of migrant mineworkers, the average earnings of black mineworkers in South Africa and the implicit GNP deflator. This series is not ideal either, since the earnings data are not Lesotho-specific but refer to the average earnings of all black mineworkers, whereas the skill-mix and experience, and therefore average earnings, of Basotho miners are believed to be superior to that of all black mineworkers. In addition, there is no good reason to suppose that the proportion of cash earnings that find their way back to Lesotho should

---

3. *The results presented here are essentially the same as those in the earlier SEA paper, although the presentation and interpretation is slightly different in places. I had hoped by now to have been able to construct a usable data set extending over a longer period, perhaps allowing some stronger inferences, but unfortunately I have so far been unable to resolve some fundamental inconsistencies between the 1980-1991 national income accounts data and estimates for earlier years and the early 1980s published previously.*

necessarily be constant from year to year.

The second alternative series is labelled RLABINC, and is derived from the "labour income" series in current prices from the foreign transactions accounts in the Bureau of Statistics national accounts data, deflated by the implicit GNP deflator. As suggested above, the ratio of REARN to RLABINC appears to fluctuate somewhat randomly, and there is no information available on the basis of which the current price labour income series is estimated. In what follows, all three series have been used wherever appropriate, and results are reported for all three.

The "backcasting" approach was implemented by specifying regressions with all potential explanatory variables from the data set that could be accommodated given the short series, and then using a stepwise remove procedure. Where necessary, this was done with alternative possible subsets (eg alternating REARN, RLABINC and RNFIFA).

The first exercise was to see if migrant earnings helped explain agricultural output (RAGRIC). The short answer is a foreshadowing of the other results of this paper: the picture is confused. This is not very surprising because the weather is the most important determinant of agricultural output. Weather is highly variable across geographic regions within the country[4], and no good proxy for the weather was available. However, it turned out that the one variable that did have some explanatory power in all formulations was the number of mine migrants, NoMINERS, which was retained in the regression with a significant coefficient[5], whatever other variables were present. The coefficient on NoMINERS was positive and surprisingly large, suggesting that an additional migrant was associated with an increase in agricultural output of the order of M900 to M1,900. However, REARN also stayed in some regressions in which it was entered with NoMINERS, with a significant and negative coefficient; RLABINC also remained if a level of significance of 10 percent was used, also with a negative coefficient.

One possible interpretation consistent with micro/anthropological evidence would be that although migration of an extra miner in at least some cases allows the miner's household to cultivate when it would otherwise not have, at the margin additional migrant earnings reduce agricultural output because the miner's remittances substitute to some extent for agricultural income[6].

This seems plausible. The effort made by those at home to generate greater

---

4. *Some parts of the country can be experiencing drought while others have adequate rainfall; as a result no single rainfall measure works well as a predictor of agricultural output.*

5. *Unless otherwise specified, the word "significant" means "statistically significant at the 5 percent level", ie the probability is less than one in 20 that the result has occurred by chance.*

6. *The coefficients on REARN and RLABINC, although consistently negative, were also consistently quite small – in the range of -0.06 to -0.16. RNFIFA never had a significant coefficient. Without a proxy for weather, it was not possible to get a good fit at all, but interestingly some variables that did enter some regressions with coefficients significant at better than 5 percent were population (possibly proxying for labour) and real government consumption expenditure. The latter had a negative coefficient, and the direction of causation is probably reversed – drought results in low agricultural production and increased government spending for drought relief. In some cases, real imports also had a small positive coefficient that was significant.*

income from agriculture, once they are cultivating, is relatively large. As a result, extra migrant earnings may reduce agricultural output (it is not worth making the extra effort if current consumption can be financed from migrant earnings), even though an extra migrant does increase agricultural output (because as the number of migrants increases, the number of households receiving remittances and therefore able to finance the purchased inputs needed to cultivate also increases).

In the backcasting exercise for RGDP, real GDP, the interesting point is that none of REARN, RLABINC, or RNFIFA survived as explanatory variables. The most powerful explanatory variable turned out to be RGFCF, Real Gross Fixed Capital Formation, which invariably survived with highly significant positive coefficients; closely followed by population, perhaps proxying for labour[7]. RM, real imports, also showed up consistently, with a coefficient of the order of 0,2, which is not unreasonable economically if output is partly dependent on imported intermediates, as it is in Lesotho.

In the regression with RGNP, real GNP as the dependent variable, REARN also did not survive as an explanatory variable. However, in this case both RLABINC and RNFIFA did, with coefficients that were significantly less than one, at about 0,68; for RNFIFA, slightly larger than one[8]. Whether this reflects causation, or is just an artefact because net factor income from abroad is part of GNP, is unclear, although other evidence tends to suggest the latter. As with RGDP, RGFC and RM remained in the regression with positive and significant coefficients.

In the second naive exercise, on the basis of a notion of investment and migrant earnings as being exogenous expenditures, and then backcasting results, simple OLS regressions were run for RGNP and RGDP on RLABINC/REARN/RNFIFA and RGFCF as dependent variables. Results were as follows (statistics in parentheses below coefficients):

RGNP=222+1,06 RLABINC+0,518 RGFCF Adj. R2 = 0,839 F=29,63 DW=1,10
(3,28)   (4,04)   (4,27)
RGNP=297+0,759 REARN+0,439 RGFCF
(3,66)   (2,41)   (2,37)
Adj. R2=0,724 F=15,47 DW=1,29

RGNP=206+0,970 RNFIFA+0,913 RGFCF
(3,20)   (4,48)   (8,20)
Adj. R2 = 0,860 F=34,68 DW=1,33
RGDP = 126+0,331 RLABINC+0,795 RGFCF
(2,32)   (1,57)   (8,16)

---

7. Population is not a proxy for a time trend, even though the growth rate of population is not greatly different from linear; year f entered into regressions never had a significant coefficient.

8. 1,06 to be precise, with a statistic of 10,86 in the "best" regression.

Adj. R2 = 0,896 F=48,18 DW=0,87
RGDP= 79,6+0,521 REARN+0,665 RGFCF
(2,33)   (3,93)   (8,51)
Adj. R(2) = 0.951 F=107.8 DW=2.02

RGDP=149+0,207 RNFIFA+0,899 RGFCF
(2,51)   (1,04)   (8,79)
Adj R2 = 0,88 F=41,8 DW=1,04

All coefficients are significant at the 5 percent level except the coefficients on RLABINC and RNFIFA in the RGDP regressions. Note that in the RGNP regressions, the coefficient on REARN is significantly less than one. Note also that several of the Durbin-Watson statistics are not satisfactory. A standard naive response to that is to run the regression over in terms of first differences. Doing that, in the RGNP regressions the coefficients on REARN and RLABINC became insignificant, whereas with RNFIFA in the regression, the coefficient on RNFIFA was highly significant and the Durbin-Watson statistic improved substantially:

RGNP1D=11,2+0,705 RNFIFA1D+0,367 RGFCF1D
(2,56)   (6,05)   (3,19)
Adj. R2=0,82 F=23,8 DW=2,20

However, when the RGDP regressions were run in first difference terms, neither REARN nor RLABINC nor RNFIFA had significant coefficients, and the results were worse that those of the regressions on the variables in levels in terms of both the adjusted R2, the F statistics, and the Durbin-Watson statistic.

The third approach was to follow the simplistic regional economics approach, and separate GDP into autonomous and dependent components (Black et al, 1991). The available data do not allow ideal division of GDP into these two components, and a variety of definitions were tried. Happily, the variant that worked best was also a variant that makes reasonably good sense theoretically. A, the autonomous component of GDP, is defined as real net factor income from abroad, plus real foreign aid, plus real gross fixed capital formation, plus real exports; D, the dependent component of GDP, is real GDP minus (A plus the real change in stocks). The regression in terms of levels yields (t statistics in parentheses below coefficients)[9].

D = 65,9 - 0,523A
(1,77) (-8,19)
Adj. R2=0,857 F=67,1 DW=0,515

---

9. *Several alternative definitions of A were used (with appropriate modifications to D), for example substituting REARN for RNFIFA and omitting exports from A (for several years in this period the bulk of exports were generated by an enclave-style diamond mine). In all formulations, both in levels and in first differences, the regressions generated negative coefficients on A that were highly significant.*

In first difference terms, the result is,
D1d =6,32 - 0,742A1d
(1,24) (-9,48)
Adj. R2 =0,899 F=89,9 DW=1,11

In both cases, the coefficient on the autonomous component of GDP, A, is negative and highly significant. This implies that an increase in autonomous GDP reduces the dependent component of GDP, which is consistent with increased migrant earnings reducing current output, presumably because the migrants are no longer producing what they would have done if they had not migrated.

DISCUSSION

The relatively short series available, and the inherent weaknesses in the data, make it impossible to draw quantitative conclusions about the multiplier effects of current migrant earnings on the Lesotho economy with any confidence. However, most of the approaches used when trying to fix the value of the multiplier result in an estimate that the GNP multiplier is less than one, and that thus the effect of additional migrant earnings is to raise GNP but lower GDP. The exception is the equation in levels for RGDP regressed on real earnings and RGFCF alone, where the coefficient on REARN is positive and significant (0,521). This has to cast some doubt on any strong conclusion, but the fact that when the regression was rerun in first difference terms the coefficient on REARN was found to be negative and no longer significant suggests that too much weight should not be placed on that one result.

Overall, the above naive regression exercises are consistent with the view that migration does reduce current output (because of the loss of labour that would not have been idle if the workers had remained at home). This is despite the widespread view that there are comparatively few opportunities for productive activity in the domestic economy. The statistical evidence also seems to be consistent with the micro-based assertions that more migration (at least in terms of numbers of migrants) increases agricultural output (presumably by increasing area cultivated and purchased inputs), although more migrant income at the margin may reduce agricultural output by reducing effort expended on it (for those households already cultivating).

However, the overall implication of the evidence is that the GNP multiplier is less than one (and autonomous GDP multiplier negative), suggesting that although a positive effect on agriculture from migrant numbers may be present, it is more than offset by output falls, in agriculture from the income effect, and elsewhere in the economy (presumably services and commodity production) from the absence of male labour. This evidence gives very little comfort to those who believe that migration results in an increase in contemporaneous domestic output. However, it does have the positive implication that fears about the consequences of reduction of migrant numbers for domestic output may be somewhat overblown. This is not to suggest that reductions in migrant numbers will not have disastrous consequences for Lesotho's consumption and well-being, only that such reductions are not, in themselves, necessarily likely to reduce domestic output in Lesotho, at least on the basis of this evidence. ◆

REFERENCES

Bardill, JE and JH Cobbe. 1985. Lesotho: Dilemmas of Dependence in Southern Africa. Boulder: Westview Press.

Black, PA, FK Siebrits and DH van Papendorp. 1991. "Homeland multipliers and the decentralisation policy," in South African Journal of Economics, Vol 59, No 1: 36-44.

Bureau of Statistics. 1992. "National Accounts 1980 to 1991," in Statistical Reports. No 13, August. Kingdom of Lesotho.

Cobbe, J. 1982. "Emigration and development in southern Africa, with special reference to Lesotho," in International Migration Review, Vol 16, No 4: 837-868.

Cobbe, J. 1983. "The changing nature of dependence: economic problems in Lesotho," in Journal of Modern African Studies, Vol 21, No 2: 293-310.

Cobbe, J. 1986. "Consequences for Lesotho of changing South African labour demand," in African Affairs, Vol 85, No 338: 23-48.

Cobbe, J. 1988. "Economic aspects of Lesotho's relations with South Africa," in Journal of Modern African Studies, Vol 26, No 1: 71-89.

Cobbe, J. 1991a. "Lesotho: what will happen after apartheid goes?" in Africa Today, Vol 38, No 1: 18-32.

Cobbe, J. 1991b. "Homeland multipliers and the decentralisation policy: comment," in South African Journal of Economics, Vol 59, No 4: 493-499.

Cobbe, J. 1992. "Lesotho and the new South Africa: economic trends and possible futures," Florida State University, Department of Economics Working Paper No 92-11-01.

Murray, Colin. 1981. Families Divided: The Impact of Migrant Labour in Lesotho. Cambridge: Cambridge University Press.

Spiegel, AD. 1981. "Changing patterns of migrant labour and rural differentiation in Lesotho," in Social Dynamics, Vol 6, No 2: 1-13.

DATA APPENDIX (DEFINITIONS OF VARIABLES):

RGDP Gross Domestic Product at 1980 market prices, in millions of Maloti

RGNP Gross National Product at 1980 market prices, in millions of Maloti

Pop Population, in millions

RX Exports of goods and services, constant 1980 prices, in millions of Maloti

RM Imports off goods and services, constant 1980 prices, in millions of Maloti

RGFCF Gross Fixed Capital Formation, constant 1980 prices, in millions of Maloti

RGC Government Final Consumption Expenditure, constant 1980 prices in millions of Maloti

RCHSTKS Changes in Stocks, constant 1980 prices, in millions of Maloti

RNFIFA Net Factor Income from Abroad, constant 1980 prices, in millions of Maloti

RAGRIC GDP by kind of activity, agricultural total, constant 1980 prices, in millions of Maloti

MGNP Gross National Product at current market prices, in millions of Maloti

IGNPDEF Index of GNP implicit price deflator, 1980 index equals 100

M'AID' Receipts of unrequited transfers from foreign countries, in millions of current Maloti

R'AID' M'AID' deflated by IGNPDEF, ie in millions of Maloti

NoMINERS Average annual number of miners

MWAGE Average annual cash earnings per black mineworker in South Africa, actual Rand

MEARN MWAGE times NoMINERS, in millions of current Maloti

REARN MEARN deflated by IGNPDEF, ie in millions of 1980 Maloti

LABINC Labour income from abroad, in millions of current Maloti

RLABINC LABINC deflated by IGNPDEF, ie. in millions of 1980 Maloti

DATA APPENDIX (TABLE)

Lesotho Data Set, 1980 – 1991

Year	RGDP	RGNP	POP	RX	RM	RGFCF	RGC
1980	287	492	1.33	70.2	350.2	115.8	74
1981	289.8	519.3	1.37	63.7	375.5	116.5	74.3
1982	300.2	577.6	1.4	79.4	396.5	141.6	78.4
1983	274.4	558.8	1.43	68.6	387.5	84.3	76.7
1984	297.6	584.8	1.46	54.9	398.2	101.2	79.7
1985	308	571.5	1.5	40.8	388.4	132.4	84.5
1986	314.1	563.6	1.59	38.9	353.7	105.9	93.2
1987	330.1	594.7	1.62	38	378.5	111.2	94.5
1988	372.6	654.1	1.66	35	465.7	148.5	97
1989	416.5	668.5	1.7	50.2	469.9	220.7	91.3
1990	437.5	695.1	1.75	49.7	443.2	277.3	92.7
1991	445.5	657.3	1.8	58	466.5	281.5	89.2

RCHSTKS	RNFIFA	RAGRIC	MGNP	IGNPDEF	M'AID'	R'AID'	NoMINERS
6.3	205	59.2	492	100.0	81.9	81.9	120733
6.5	227.3	62.3	583.2	112.3	71.0	63.2	123538
-1.6	284.9	49.9	745.8	129.1	47.8	37.0	117641
0.4	285.1	48.5	813.7	145.6	88.1	60.5	115327
2.8	289.1	54	942.6	161.2	137.3	85.2	114041
-0.5	265.8	52.2	1065.4	186.4	172.9	92.7	116223
6.8	254.8	56.4	1214.6	215.5	165.9	77.0	121450
2.4	271.7	52.5	1459.1	245.4	157.1	64.0	125934
0.8	285.3	67.3	1856.5	283.8	225.1	79.3	124781
1.5	264.9	72	2227.2	333.2	472.5	141.8	126264
-2.5	266.1	73.8	2611.9	375.8	603.9	160.7	127385
-1.5	178.8	54.6	2525.8	384.3	1265.2	329.2	122188

MWAGE	MEARN	REARN	LABINC	RLABINC
2037	245.9	245.9	205.0	205.0
2520	311.3	277.2	255.0	227.1
2986	351.3	272.1	378.0	292.7
3436	396.3	272.1	421.0	289.1
3927	447.8	277.8	475.9	295.3
4452	517.4	277.6	499.0	267.7
5136	623.8	289.4	583.6	270.8
7160	901.7	367.5	718.5	292.8
7598	948.1	334.0	844.3	297.5
8679	1095.8	328.9	956.8	287.2
10069	1282.6	341.3	1106.2	294.4
11327	1384.0	360.2	1206.2	313.9

Sources : Kingdom of Lesotho, Bureau of Statistics, 1992; Cobbe, 1992.

RESPONSE

DR TESSA MARCUS
Department of Sociology,
University of Natal,
Pietermaritzburg,
South Africa

These papers, collectively, contribute significantly to theory, social understanding and policy.

What is striking to me about the Aids debate is the way that global capitalism operates. It likes to free itself up to enter economies and countries unhampered, but it systematically creates barriers of various kinds for labour's movement into and between economies. In other words, it closes down options for working people while all the time opening up options for itself.

In this context the question of Aids and Malawian workers is illustrative. Aids becomes an issue, like ethnicity or being foreign, which is used to divide the work-force within the industry. Saying that Malawians are the source of Aids in South Africa – which would surprise most of us – is like saying foreigners are the source of the lack of jobs in this economy. The Aids issue shows how divisive the industry can be.

What the paper on Aids also reveals is that the community bears the costs. This raises a major question about the mining industry in this country. Who should be bearing the cost of Aids? How are we going to face it? Should this national pandemic not be challenged by a national effort which engages everybody? Ironically, Aids seems to be being sidelined by the industry although its effects will not bypass mining in this country. It is going to touch every single sector and every single economy in this region. Yet we don't seem to be dealing with it seriously.

These papers all allude to regional barriers of various kinds. This is all about incorporation into South Africa at a political level or about being subsumed by South African domination, which has been one of the major fears of southern African countries. Regional integration and barriers also raise questions about workers and their rights, within civil society in their nation states as well as within the region.

We are faced with a major problem of many people who have engaged in this economy physically, daily and directly, people who have borne the brunt of the effects of migrant labour, yet who will experience no real benefit from the changes that are supposed to be coming.

There is also the question of the impact of migrant labour on the rural economies, on "petty commodity production". There is every evidence to indicate the significance of migrant labourers' incomes to agricultural production for peasants and petty commodity producers. But what is also very clear is how very fragile and unsustainable this relationship is. Migrants who have been working for 20 years or more, who at the end of their working lives in the industry take home their retrenchment packages, have very little capacity to sustain agricultural production in the way that they were able to whilst earning a wage. In the rural areas throughout the region there are workers who have laboured on the mines for most of their lives and who today are without work or the means to continue producing on the land.

The reality in this region is such that we may erect political borders, but these will be crushed by the weight of unemployment and people's desire and need to work. This raises the debate around employment levels and wage rates. We have heard the argument that workers cannot be better paid because they would then lose their jobs or reduce the number of employment opportunities. In response, let me say from my research on farm workers, that people work because they are desperately poor and they are so desperately poor because they work. You can't justify poor working conditions by levels of employment. This is as clear in the mining industry as it is in agriculture. You will not protect jobs by keeping wages low and you will not secure decent livelihoods for people by insisting that you are giving them jobs by keeping wages low. The knock-on effect for rural development of a living wage for farm workers far outweighs any claim that at least some people have jobs. The depth and extent of farm worker poverty over generations bears loud testimony to the negative consequences of not working towards decent conditions and standards of living.

So the debate about what to do about migration in the region is a debate about the structural crisis that we face. It is a debate about how people will fight for jobs and how they will migrate illegally to look for jobs. These are the problems that have to be placed before the policy makers. We have to ask them whether they are going to erect new barriers to entrance into the economy and to jobs, which is probably the strongest tendency and the easiest option. Or are they going to open up the region and create a whole new dynamic? The consequences of the former could be devastating and counter-productive to democracy and the national interest. The challenge of the latter requires vision, co-operation and serious regional engagement. ◆

ECONOMIC AND SOCIAL ISSUES

South African Gold Mining: the 1980s and Beyond

Dr Nicoli Nattrass
School of Economics,
University of Cape Town,
South Africa

Gold mining has long been the backbone of South Africa's migrant labour system. However, since 1987 there has been a steady haemorrhaging of labour from the gold mines and this has raised doubts about the long-term demand for labour in this industry. This chapter explores the major economic dynamics behind the profit squeeze in gold mining during the 1980s.

Key Trends in the Mining Sector from 1981 to 1992

The South African gold-mining sector has come under severe pressure over the past decade from falling ore grades, rising costs and the declining real gold price. Although the last decade started on a high note with the gold price averaging $613 in 1980, these favourable conditions did not last. Sentiment and the market fundamentals which had supported gold in the 1970s turned out to be very different in the 1980s. As a result it can be argued that the prospects are slight for any dramatic, sustained increase in the gold price – and thus also in the demand for labour[1].

In contrast to trends in the dollar price of gold, the Rand gold price actually rose for most of the 1980s owing to a strong depreciation of the Rand. This was especially evident in 1984 and 1985 when the economy was rocked by the State of Emergency and the debt crisis. However, in real terms (that is, with inflation factored in) the Rand gold price started falling from 1987 onwards. This exercised a major squeeze on the South African gold-mining industry. Between 1988 and 1992 vast numbers of jobs were lost. On gold mines belonging to the Chamber of Mines (COM), employment fell at 6,3 percent a year during that period.

This was bad news for the South African economy which remained trapped in recessionary conditions for most of the 1980s. Gold mining is at the heart of the South African minerals sector and has been an important provider of foreign exchange. It was thus a major blow to the economy when gold's contribution to total exports fell from 46,2 percent in 1982 to 27,2 percent in 1992. As a percentage of Gross Domestic Product (GDP), the contribution of gold mining more than halved, falling from 9,5 percent in 1981 to 4,4 percent in 1992. These negative developments were mirrored in trends in profitability: from a high of 40,3 percent in 1981, the net profit rate in the total mining sector dropped to a mere 7,7 percent.

A major economic consequence of the decline in profitability in gold mining was the sharp drop in contributions to the fiscus. The proportion of tax revenue collected from the gold-mining industry dropped from 26,4 percent in 1981 to 2,0 percent in 1992.

Although South Africa remained an important depository of gold and retained its position as the world's largest producer of gold, the country's share of world production dropped from 52,1 percent to 27,7 percent over the same period. Part of the reason for this was the decline in South African ore grades. But the major factor was the seven-fold increase in United States production (largely from Nevada), the 10-fold increase in Australian production (mainly from western Australia) and the doubling of Canadian production (Gold Fields, 1993: 16).

TRENDS IN PROFITABILITY IN THE MINING SECTOR: 1981 TO 1988

The crisis of profitability in gold mining is often portrayed in terms of rising costs. However, a closer examination of the data reveals that the fall in revenue (due to the depressed gold price and falling ore grades) was the major culprit (Nattrass, 1993).

---

1. *Looking more closely at the 1980s, the only exception to the decline in the gold price during this period was a recovery in the mid-1980s encouraged by crashes on major stock markets. From 1987 to 1992 the gold price declined steadily, despite a brief upsurge to over $400 during the Gulf War. The only positive development was the underlying strength of jewellery demand.*

In fact gold mines were able to contain working costs to a remarkable degree even though they suffered from increases in the costs of water and electricity (COM, 1993: 3) and despite having to mine at ever-increasing depths. It is interesting to note that real labour costs *fell* between 1981 and 1988 whereas other real costs remained stagnant. In commenting on the fall in real working costs for every ton milled, the COM (1993: 11) noted:

> Without a doubt this has been the major achievement of gold mine managements ... an achievement that would not have been possible had the unions representing mining industry employees not recognised the realities currently facing the industry.

Attempts to reduce working costs and to boost profitability can conflict with concerns relating to mine safety. Mining is a dangerous occupation and miners regularly pay with injuries and death. Between 1981 and 1992, an average of one miner died for every ton of gold mined. Although the mining companies are concerned with safety, the search for profits appears to have interfered with this goal. The worst example of corporate neglect in the 1980s was the 1986 Kinross mining disaster in which 177 miners were killed. It was described by the Mining Engineer as the "most serious accident in the history of this country" (RP 46/1987: 19). But, the "accident" – an underground polyurethane foam fire – was entirely preventable.

Polyurethane foam was introduced into Gencor's Kinross mine in 1980 for insulation and as a means of preventing minor rock falls on the main tramming line. When the foam caught fire in 1986 during a welding incident, the flames spread rapidly through the mine, releasing deadly toxic gases. Gencor claimed ignorance of these dangerous properties of polyurethane foam. However, considering that the substance had been banned in the United Kingdom since 1967 after a fire killed nine miners in Scotland, and in the United States after a similar incident killed 91 miners in Idaho, such claims to ignorance lack credibility. Extensive reports on both overseas incidents were sent to the COM and circulated to its members (Flynn, 1992: 258-9). Furthermore, it is worth noting that Gencor installed the foam at Kinross – even after it had been removed from its own collieries because of the dangers (Flynn, 1992: 259). For these reasons, Flynn (1992: 259-260) argues that Gencor made the decision to save money and ended up costing 177 miners their lives.

GOLD-MINING EMPLOYMENT AND WAGES

Both white and black employment rose from 1983 to 1987 and then declined steadily thereafter. The only time that white employment grew at a time when black employment was falling was in 1982. According to the Government Mining Engineer, the increase in white employment "can be attributed to the fact that the mining industry was able to fill vacancies as a result of the levelling off in other sectors of the economy" (RP 25/1983: 16). The mining industry thus provided a buffer for skilled and semi-skilled whites which shielded them from recessionary conditions. However, from 1988 onwards, the chronic skills shortage disappeared and white workers were shed alongside black workers.

Migrant workers as a percentage of total COM employment fell from 88,1 percent in 1981 to 82,7 percent in 1992. Most of the decline took place from 1988, that is, at the same time as the gold mines started shedding labour dramatically. It is clear that migrant workers bore the brunt of the lay-offs – particularly those from the former homeland areas. A more detailed analysis of the data reveals that workers from Transkei were affected most severely. Between 1982 and 1992, they dropped as a percentage of migrant workers from 28,6 percent to 23,8 percent.

The COM obviously took the opportunity during the late 1980s to lay off proportionally more unskilled workers. As noted above, an indication of this is the decline in the percentage of migrant workers in the work-force. Another indication is the large increase of 13,6 percent in the real average Category 1-8 (black, unskilled) wage in 1988 – at a time when Category 1-8 employment was reduced by 5,4 percent. Given that the bargained real increase in unskilled gold-mining wages was about 3 percent in 1988, the rise in the average real wage reflects the changing composition of the unskilled category towards the more experienced, and hence better paid, workers. This also reflects the effect of closures of non-profitable mines – and hence the reduction in the proportion of lower paid workers.

RACIAL DISCRIMINATION ON GOLD MINES

Through fighting a strong rear-guard action in support of job reservation on the mines, the white miners' union was able to block the removal of racial discrimination on the mines until July 1988. But from then onwards black workers were able to obtain blasting certificates, winding drivers' certificates and other certificates of competency which had until then been denied them. But it is ironic that blacks were welcomed into the ranks of skilled workers at precisely the time when the mining industry started laying off workers.

Since 5 December 1988, the day the first black man with a blasting certificate started work, the power of white miners has been declining strongly. According to Ungerer, the general secretary of the white Mine Workers' Union, the mines started "bending over blackwards (sic)" to train black workers "so that in the not too distant future there will be a surplus of these skills which will put the Chamber in a stronger position when it comes to the wage negotiation table" (quoted in *Mining World*, 1989.) While black workers are indeed moving into more skilled positions, this has been limited by the economic crisis and by restrictions on entry into skilled positions such as the requirement to have passed Std 8.

Although the Chamber has consistently opposed racially based job reservation, the role of mine management has been ambiguous when it comes to racism on the mines. For example, training documents produced by Gold Fields (which were still in use at least as late as 1986) for white recruits contained the following advice about black workers:

> Keep off larking with him. His father would never do that and you are in
> the place of his father ... repetitive jobs do not bore him. He will make up a
> song to go along with them ... The black, when wanting to discuss any-
> thing of importance, cannot just raise the subject and get to the point. Being
> emotionally inclined, the black will go for anything that will make people
> admire him (Quoted in Flynn, 1992: 126).

Given such reinforcement of racist beliefs, it is not surprising that research
conducted by the Chamber concluded that attitudes to employee participation
in job-related problem-solving were least favourable among lower-level (white)
skilled workers (COM Research Organisation, Annual Report, 1988: 34). Rather
belatedly, the Chamber's research into the improvement of industrial relations
targeted "the role of the supervisor in dealing with problematic conditions before they become causes of generalised complaint" and recommended that management "achieves an authentic sense of industrial leadership by demonstrating
a willingness to solve industrial problems and handle grievances" (Research Organisation, Annual Report, 1988: 30, 33).

THE NUM AND PROFIT-SHARING AGREEMENTS

This sudden concern about industrial relations on the part of the COM was largely
a response to the rise of the National Union of Mineworkers (NUM) and subsequent strike activity (James, 1992). From small beginnings in 1982, the NUM
grew from a verified membership of 6 000 members to 187 000 in 1987 on mines
belonging to the COM (COM, 1988).

In August 1987, the NUM embarked on a three-week strike after wage negotiations with the COM broke down. Eighteen gold mines were affected by the
strike involving 230 000 workers. The COM adopted an uncompromising stance.
The NUM was forced to accept the original pay offer at the end of the strike
which cost 43 000 miners their jobs and in which R105 million in wages was
forfeited (COM, 1988).

In 1988 verified NUM membership was down to 140 000 as a result of the
strike (COM, 1989). Despite this blow to the trade union, an important result of
the strike was the apparent increased commitment on the part of the COM to
avoid debilitating industrial conflict.

It is tragic that the NUM became a powerful voice for black mineworkers at
precisely the time when the mining industry started coming under the most economic pressure. From 1987 onwards, the NUM could do little other than preside
over the severe contraction of employment in the gold-mining industry. Keeping
jobs became the priority for the union. For this reason, the NUM entered a series
of path-breaking agreements with the COM which tied wages to the economic
performance of the gold-mining industry.

This process was aided by the formation of the Mining Summit (which included representatives from labour, the mines and government) in June 1991 to

address the crisis in the industry. According to the chief executive of the COM, Tom Main (1991: 4):

> An immediate benefit flowing from the summit was that the annual wage talks between employers and the unions were characterised by a new sense of economic realism, reflected in the lower basic wage increases agreed on, with certain mines agreeing to pay bonuses depending on movements in the gold price and in productivity at mine level.

The first of these was the gold performance bonus agreement between the NUM and the COM in 1991 which comprised an average 6 percent wage increase supplemented by a gold price bonus and performance bonus scheme. In addition, the NUM made significant gains on non-wage issues such as stop-order payments of membership fees, better facilities for shop stewards, improved access to workers, a death and funeral benefit scheme, and so on. As Marcel Golding, the acting general secretary of the NUM, noted:

> The choice we had to make was whether to drive a higher wage increase with less employment in the industry as a real prospect – or whether we try to achieve maximum employment, and at the same time augment wages and win social rights (interviewed in *South African Labour Bulletin*, Vol 16, No 2, 1991: 19).

This scheme, although innovative, was complex, varied significantly from mine to mine and proved confusing and complicated to administer. The performance bonus scheme related to indices of collective performance. The agreement stipulated that the actual criteria of collective performance would be fully discussed at mine level with the union, and be as simple as possible. It was this reliance on local-level solutions that proved problematic. Suspicions arose on the part of the NUM that certain mines were not disclosing relevant information and the agreement eventually disintegrated.

The second agreement was a great deal more transparent. In December 1992, the NUM signed an agreement with the COM which included wage increases of between 5 and 6 percent (that is, real wage cuts) and an "in-principle agreement on a profit-sharing scheme at certain gold mines owned by Anglo American, Genmin and Rand Mines" (*Business Day*, 14 July 1992). According to the NUM, the agreement was in response to the "extraordinarily difficult circumstances of the gold industry at present and the efforts of the NUM to preserve jobs and protect standards" (*Business Day*, 14 July 1992).

The move to profit sharing as opposed to a gold price related bonus was a vast improvement. The principles provided for profit sharing of up to 20 percent of the profit pool available for distribution (with the pool varying across the industry). The agreements still differ from mine to mine – with some mines only paying 5c out of every Rand profit until a trigger point is reached after which 20c is paid out – however the scheme was clearer and more simple to apply.

The 1993 agreement shares many of the same principles as the 1992 agreement. Increases of between 8 and 10 percent (that is, slight real wage declines) were agreed on with bonus schemes agreed for certain mines and groups. The commitment to keep wage increases in line with profitability on the part of the union has helped limit job losses and points the way forward for other profit sharing breakthroughs in the South African economy.

RECENT TRENDS

Between 1988 and 1991, gold output fell at 3,3 percent a year as a result of mine closures (for example, Stilfontein in 1991) and major rationalisations (Gold Fields, 1991: 16). However, what is remarkable about the performance of the gold-mining industry in the early 1990s is its tenacity and ability to keep production going. Despite widespread predictions of further falls in output, South Africa's production of 614 tons in 1992 was 2 percent higher than in 1991 (Gold Fields, 1993: 19). Any production that was lost due to rationalisation and the handful of mine closures was more than compensated for by higher output from the rest of the industry's mines (Gold Fields, 1993).

Many of the high cost mines were able to continue operating through a combination of cost-cutting, innovative rationalisations, increasing the grade of ore mined and successful forward selling. A recent COM study concluded that upwards of 60 000 additional jobs would have been at risk in the past five years had the industry not dealt with rising working costs as vigorously as it has done (*Chamber of Mines Newsletter*, 4 June 1992: 1).

Future productivity improvements flowing out of the better utilisation of black labour following the demise of the colour bar are also a positive sign. But because of the weak gold price, prospects for future growth remain bleak. According to the COM, an average gold price of $443 an ounce would be needed before the gold-mining industry attained a level of profitability in which there were no marginal producers (*Chamber of Mines Newsletter*, 2 March and 3 June 1993). Given that the gold price averaged only $339 for the first five months of 1993, the prospects do not look good for South Africa's marginal mines. Although some expansionary projects (such as Moab) are going ahead, "elsewhere, projects have either been put on hold pending a more favourable gold price or abandoned" (Finch, 1992b: 6). The atmosphere of political uncertainty has contributed to this. The fact that the production of gold in the first two quarters of 1993 was less than that in the first two quarters of 1992 is a further sobering sign.

Despite the rise in ore grade in the early 1990s, most analysts believe that the long-run prospects for South African gold mining are poor: "The South African gold-mining industry is in a mature phase and despite any changes in the gold price, production is set to decline" (Finch, 1992a). The fact that the grade of ore mined declined from 5,34 to 5,27 grams per ton during the course of 1992 – despite attempts to mine richer ores – suggests "that at least some of the mines have reached the point where they are being constrained by geological limitations and associated grade inflexibility" (*Chamber of Mines Newsletter*, 4 June 1992: 10). Currently, 40 percent of South Africa's gold ore reserves are "sterile" because they cannot yield sufficient gold per ton of ore milled at the current gold price to produce revenues equal to, or exceeding, average working cost (*Chamber of Mines Newsletter*, 4 June 1993: 1). According to Bulmer (1990: 19), gold mining has a life expectancy of between 11 and 22 more years depending on whether a pessimistic or optimistic gold price scenario is assumed.

This raises the question of what is likely to happen to the gold price. Anyone who can answer this question with certainty would be rich indeed! Trends in the gold price are notorious for being strongly influenced by unpredictable, fickle and faddish changes in sentiment. For example, the gold market in 1993 appears to have been strongly influenced by investors responding like herd animals to billionaire George Soros. In April, Soros sparked a mini boom in the gold price when he purchased 10 percent of the Newmont Mining Corporation. The subsequent wave of speculation (fuelled also by fears of renewed inflation as the Western economies picked up momentum) sent gold to a three-year high of $414 in early August. But the rally fizzled out shortly thereafter on rumours that Soros was shifting out of gold and into bonds as inflation worries subsided. The $8,80 increase in early November appears also to have been fuelled by talk that Soros was changing his portfolio to reflect greater gold assets and less bonds.

But gold appears to be losing a lot of its appeal as a good investment and safe haven in a time of uncertainty. The Gulf War, for example, did not boost the gold price anywhere as strongly as it may have done 10 years earlier. Even the partial breakdown of the European Exchange Rate Mechanism in September 1992 did not attract investors and speculators into gold. It appears that investors are relying more on the growing range of financial instruments to hedge and protect their investments.

The influence of Soros aside, it is unlikely that the gold price will increasingly reflect market fundamentals – and thus start acting more like any other commodity. This implies that jewellery demand (which absorbed two-thirds of newly mined gold in the 1980s) will continue to operate as the cornerstone of the gold market. Interestingly, market conditions could be seen to be favouring a rise in the gold price over the next few years given that the demand for gold from jewellers and industry has been outstripping the supply of new gold production by a wider and wider margin since 1989. Furthermore, the liberalisation of major emerging gold markets such as India and China is widely considered to have a huge potential for gold offtake. The increases in the gold price during 1993 appear to be the result of such dynamics.

However, the downside of this strong demand for gold from jewellers (primarily from the fast growing markets of China and South East Asia) is the huge overhang of gold in the world's central banks. In 1992, the stock of gold in world central banks was over 10 times the supply of gold onto the market that year. Bearish sentiment about gold and persistent rumours of central bank sales had a depressing effect on the gold price in the 1990s. By mid-1992, the price premium available for gold forward sales had all but evaporated. In the first quarter of

1993, producers were only able to secure a 0,7 percent revenue gain through forward sale transactions.

Unfortunately, if gold loses its characteristic as an investment good, this may also affect the demand for jewellery. According to research carried out by the World Gold Council in 1985, the demand for gold jewellery in the developing markets of the Far and Middle East is in large part an investment demand – whereas in the developed Western markets, the demand is largely for adornment. Thus whereas fashion and changes in cultural values are more likely to influence the demand for gold in Western markets, the fall in the gold price may (seemingly perversely) result in the dampening of jewellery demand in the Far and Middle East.

It is interesting to note that South African jewellers have been very slow to respond to the jewellery boom which followed the fall in the gold price. Whereas Taiwanese gold jewellery production rose from three tons in 1984 to 90 tons in 1988, and South Korean from one ton to 65 tons respectively, South African production only rose from one to two tons over the same period (Edwards, 1990: 58).

Given this poor showing, and in the light of the fact that South Africa produces 0,1 percent of world jewellery production, Edwards (1990: 59) recommended greater government support (such as tax incentives) for South African jewellers. But according to the COM, the limiting factors to the development of a significant internationally competitive South African jewellery industry are "the difficulty and expense of establishing export sales outlets abroad; the very high costs of South African labour ... and the risk of political and social instability" (*Chamber of Mines Newsletter*, 2-3 June 1993).

Clearly, it makes a great deal of sense from the point of view of minerals beneficiation (and of increasing exports) to develop a stronger South African jewellery sector. Once the political transition has occurred, the future South African government should investigate ways of helping South African jewellers establish export markets. If jewellery demand is to grow in importance as the cornerstone of the gold market, such efforts will pay off for the gold-mining industry and the South African economy.

Even so, it is worth bearing in mind that gold mining in South Africa is not likely ever again to play the central economic role it did in the past. As manufacturing grows in importance, the economic incentives supporting the continuation of the migrant labour system will decline. Even though the mines themselves are reducing the proportion of migrant workers in their work-force, structural economic change away from mining will be the greatest factor affecting the demand for migrant labour in South Africa. ◆

REFERENCES

Boyle, G. 1982. The Theory of Wasting Assets with Reference to the Regulation and Pricing of Gold in the South African Gold-Mining Industry. MA dissertation, University of Cape Town.

Bulmer, D. 1990. "The effect of escalating working costs on South Africa's economic gold reserves," in Minerals Bureau Report. R5/90, Johannesburg.

Chamber of Mines. 1988. 1987/88 Review. Johannesburg: Chamber of Mines of South Africa.

Chamber of Mines. 1989. 1989 Review. Johannesburg: Chamber of Mines of South Africa.

Chamber of Mines. 1993. Mining into the Next Century: A Context for Survival and Growth. Johannesburg: Chamber of Mines of South Africa.

Edwards, A. 1990. "South Africa's gold jewellery: a scenario for the future," in Mining World, Vol 8, No 12.

Finch, A. 1992a. "South Africa's gold production: the next five years," Frankel Max Pollak Vinderine Briefing.

Finch, A. 1992b. "Outlook for gold," Frankel Max Pollak Vinderine Briefing.

Flynn, L. 1992. Studded with Diamonds and Paved with Gold. London: Bloomsbury.

Gold Fields (Mineral Services Ltd). 1991. Gold 1991. London: Gold Fields.

Gold Fields (Mineral Services Ltd). 1993. Gold 1993. London: Gold Fields.

Greyling, M and N Odendaal. 1992. Guidelines for Investments in South Africa's Mineral Industry. Johannesburg: Minerals Bureau.

James, W. 1992. Our Precious Metal: African Labour in South Africa's Gold Industry 1970-1990. Cape Town and London: David Philip and James Curry.

Maas, W. 1989. "Profitability of South Africa's gold mines and the factors influencing it," in Minerals Bureau Bulletin. B18/89, Johannesburg.

Main, T. 1991. "Gold production in South Africa," address to the 4th Nikkei gold conference, Tokyo.

Marais Committee. 1988. Report of the Committee of Inquiry into the Position of Marginal Profit Mines. Pretoria: Government Printer.

Marais Committee. 1990. Report of the Committee of Inquiry into the Position of Marginal Profit Mines. Pretoria: Ministry of Finance.

Melament, D. Report of the Commission of Inquiry into State Assistance to the East Rand Proprietary Mines Ltd. RP/99/1990. Pretoria: Government Printer.

Minerals Bureau. 1992. South Africa's Mineral Industry 1991/92. Johannesburg: Minerals Bureau.

Moll, T. 1992. "Accounting for gold: the South African case," in Review of Income and Wealth, Vol 38, No 2.

Nattrass, N. 1993. "The South African mining industry from the Second World War to 1981," Working Paper No 4, Migrant Labour Project, Department of Sociology, University of Cape Town and African Studies Unit, Queen's University.

RP/25/1983. Report of the Department of Mineral and Energy Affairs for the year 1982.

RP/46/1987. Report of the Department of Mineral and Energy Affairs for the year 1987.

Shafted: The Social Impact of Down-scaling in the OFS Goldfields

Professor Gay W Seidman
Department of Sociology,
University of Wisconsin-Madison,
Madison, USA

During the past five years, lowered gold prices combined with increased worker militancy have prompted a dramatic change in the labour policies of most South African mining houses. This has entailed a shift away from the large, relatively unskilled African work-forces that have been an historical feature of the industry to smaller, more stable work-forces whose higher wages would be offset by higher productivity.

Changes in the international economic context, coupled with those in the domestic political context, have left the mine companies with little choice but to reconceptualise their approach to labour, replacing the repressive patterns of the past with a more co-operative relationship in which workers have some stake in the mine's survival (Crush et al, 1991; James, 1992; Leger and Nicol, 1993).

What have these changes meant for the communities and households that have sprung up around the mines? This study, focusing on the community around Harmony mine in the Orange Free State town of Virginia, examines an extreme case of down-scaling and changing labour relations.

As one of South Africa's largest mines, opened shortly after the National Party came to power in 1948, Harmony could once have been described as a quintessential apartheid product: a large migrant work-force, housed in compounds, mined low-grade ores for low wages. In 1992 most of the mine's African workers came from outside South Africa's border: half from nearby Lesotho and 10 percent from Mozambique.

Yet in the 1990s Harmony could serve as a prime illustration of changing labour processes and labour relations. In 1993 it cut its work-force by half and instituted a series of labour process changes, including productivity bonuses, which raised productivity from 27,5 tons of rock per worker per month in 1990 to an estimated 35,4 tons in 1993 (NUM, 1992a: 43). By early 1993 Harmony seemed on its way to developing the kind of co-operative, productive labour relationship that management analysts seemed to consider the gold-mining industry's best survival strategy.

This study explores the ways in which people in mining communities have experienced this shifting policy. It uses a three-pronged research strategy: unstructured interviews with local business people in Virginia, current mine personnel and leaders of local civic associations (both black and white); a semi-structured survey of a random sample of township residents; and semi-structured interviews with retrenched Harmony workers in Maseru.

The study hints at the complexities of the changes in mine labour policy. Firstly, although Harmony has made concerted efforts to create a smaller, more productive work-force, the persistence of pre-existing social policies makes this process problematic. An entrenched racial order – entailing strict segregation, repressive labour relations and persistent discrimination – will not disappear overnight; the social institutions of the mine and the community are more resistant to change than the mine's Johannesburg head office might have expected. Secondly, and perhaps more importantly, the study shows the extent to which apartheid's legacies are unequally distributed: while stabilisation may improve the situation of some workers, the burden of down-scaling falls hardest on those with the least resources to bear it. Paradoxically, in a context where rural African households have become dependent on remittances, the medium-term effects of the shift to a more humane labour policy may be to create a deepening crisis for the very people who suffered the most from the migrant labour system.

VIRGINIA'S LOCAL ECONOMY

Virginia and its associated township, Meloding, grew up when Harmony was opened and the town's fate has been inextricably linked with that of the mine. Today, Virginia/Meloding includes roughly 15 400 whites and 30 000 blacks, with another 14 500 African workers housed in migrant hostels. Harmony is the town's major employer, ratepayer and home-owner. It pays out about R25 million a month in wages, about R6 million for electricity to Eskom and about R17 million for stores and materials, largely in the Orange Free State. It pays about 17 percent of Virginia's rates – about R1 million a month – and owns 32 percent of the town's houses.

Businesses which serve the mine directly, such as those which supply the mine with timber, have been relatively unaffected by down-scaling; presumably, they will survive as long as the mine produces gold. But those businesses which do not have mine contracts have been devastated by the reduction in Harmony's work-force: directly or indirectly, nearly all of these businesses serviced mine employees. Some businesses have reported a drop in turnover of about 80 per-cent in the last five years and the vacant shop windows in Virginia town centre stand as testimony to the recession. It seems likely that Harmony will close in the next few years, particularly because of the lawsuits that will follow a disaster early in 1994 in which cyanide-laced mud swept through Virginia after a slime dam burst its banks.

Most business people interviewed plan to leave Virginia if the town's economy does not improve. There is little evidence that they are trying to find new strate-gies to survive changed circumstances. Frequent complaints about the mine's failure to buy goods locally – along with constant references to future improve-ments in the gold price – reveal persistent dependence on the mine.

Moreover, white business people seemed unwilling to consider efforts to ex-pand their businesses among the town's black population, despite repeated de-nials of racism. Residential segregation persists, reinforced by occasional attacks on blacks in town, and schools remain essentially segregated. Undoubtedly, the failure to integrate reinforces the sense that if the mine closes, businesses which once catered to the white centre will have no choice but to pack up and leave.

The persistence of racial attitudes also has an official side. In 1990 a consumer boycott prompted town officials to negotiate with the township's civic associa-tion. The negotiations resulted in the establishment of a new clinic in the town-ship and in the resolution of conflicts over water and electricity rates. But the forum collapsed shortly after the boycott ended and in early 1993 administrators seemed to have reverted to a sense that strong-arm tactics work best: the local authorities had already cut off nightsoil collection to the squatter area and were threatening to cut off water to force rent payments.

MINE HOSTELS AND MELODING TOWNSHIP

Probably the most striking trend revealed in the unstructured interviews with officials from the black civic association and the union was the degree of distrust of the mine's management. Most evident in the hostels, where several residents refused to be interviewed for fear they would be singled out in the next round of retrenchments, this distrust was based on a sense that the mine would continue to shirk what interviewees considered to be its responsibilities to the community which had grown up around Harmony.

Many respondents, referring to the mine's refusal to negotiate with the National Union of Mineworkers (NUM) before 1989, viewed the current retrench-ments as an attempt to remove union militants. Others described the failure of the mine to follow through on promises for community assistance in the provision of cheap housing materials, education for mine employees and, in particular, in enforcing affirmative action for mine personnel.

Among hostel residents, levels of distrust towards mine management seemed even higher than in the township, largely because Category 1 to 8 miners, who make up the bulk of hostel residents, are so vulnerable to retrenchment. But this distrust also seemed to reflect the fact that the mine's patterns of social organisation continue to assume that black mineworkers are single male migrants. Thus, for example, despite the rhetorical shift towards a stabilised work-force, living-out allowances remain based on the costs of maintaining a miner in the hostel, not on actual living costs. Similarly, respondents mentioned the lack of adequate visiting facilities for miners' families, the mine hospital's refusal to treat mineworkers' families and the mine's decision to rent subsidised family housing only to workers in higher skill grades as evidence that the mine persisted in viewing African workers as temporary, single migrants.

The hostel residents' emphasis on the mine's failure to cater for families underscored the extent to which most miners viewed themselves as "career" miners. Many had been at Harmony most of their working lives, in some cases since the first shafts were opened. They viewed retrenchment with real fear: they have no transferable skills and no jobs to go to outside mining and are aware that down-scaling poses a real threat to their future on the mine. The fear of retrenchment probably keeps workers living in the hostels, since they expressed reluctance to invest in a house if they could not be sure of a job in the area.

For residents of the local township, Meloding, the mine also remains at the centre of economic life. Yet in contrast to respondents from the white business community, most expected to stay on in the region if the mine were to close. Township residents clearly viewed the future with concern, recognising that the mine's closure would have severe repercussions. But few respondents viewed leaving as a real option.

One respondent said if Virginia closed down he would simply have to acquire his provisions in nearby Welkom. He was "here to stay because it is the same everywhere. The community will get used to new problems and to changing times".

MANDELA PARK

This almost fatalistic commitment to the town was echoed, often magnified, in the more systematic survey of the squatter area, Mandela Park. Since 1989 an informal settlement of about 1 750 shacks has grown up just across the railway tracks from the mine. In the study, semi-structured interviews were conducted with a random sample of 80 households. The mine is central to life in the settlement. More than half of the households in the informal settlement contain a present or former mineworker; 35 percent of households contain current mineworkers; and another 32,5 percent include retrenched miners.

About half of the residents of Mandela Park were born outside the Orange

Free State and their birthplaces – Transkei (21 percent), Lesotho (10 percent) and Mozambique (7,5 percent) – show the impact of the migrant labour system on individuals' lives. Among the other half, most came to the area looking for jobs – from overcrowded peri-urban areas such as the QwaQwa homeland or the resettlement township of Botshabelo or as former farmworkers forced to leave white-owned farms in the region.

About 85 percent of respondents said they viewed Mandela Park as their permanent home. Their reasons for choosing Virginia/Meloding over their birthplaces often reflected the depth of crisis in rural southern Africa – the lack of jobs, land and social services. In a fairly typical response, a 39-year-old Harmony retrenchee said he would only choose to live in Transkei "if there was work there and the living conditions were not so bad. There in Transkei clinics are inadequate and hospitals are too far away".

On the other hand, about half of respondents said they had dependents living elsewhere. Generally, the reasons given for living apart from family reflected a rational effort to make use of whatever services and resources were available: children were attending school or wives had jobs elsewhere. Only three respondents appeared to prefer migrancy, giving reasons that seemed to reflect an effort to retain links with a rural community.

Perhaps the most striking characteristic of households was their poverty. Ten households reported earning no income; half of households earned less than R233 a month. These incomes reflect the lack of job opportunities in the area: just under half of respondents were unemployed. Households which included a working miner, especially if he earned high production bonuses, were by far the best off, while households without current miners clearly battled to survive.

Among former miners a sharp division emerged between those with sizeable retrenchment packages who had managed to invest them and those who had not. Eight retrenched miners were doing relatively well at the time of the study, having used their packages to open tuck-shops in the informal settlement, to buy a taxi or to buy a van with which to deliver coal in the settlement. Most retrenched miners, however, were unable to invest their packages, either because these were too small or because the men did not know what to do with the money. Most got no advice on how to use their packages and spent the money on fixing houses, paying debts or on family maintenance. One said, "I saved my money in the bank and kept withdrawing it until it was finished".

About half of the households in the settlement rely on relatively unprofitable informal sector activities to scrape by, such as buying vegetables in town to sell in the location, selling prepared foods or selling cleaned bones and bottles taken from the mine hostel's garbage bins. A few rely on social services, such as food parcels or the Meloding soup kitchen, while others live off a single pension. These survival strategies underscore the problems that would face any development strategy seeking to rely on informal sector activities: although most respondents described retail selling as the activity they would engage in if they could get a bank loan, most had neither the experience nor the skills to run a business. Of respondents for whom data is available, 43,2 percent had left school by Std 3 and

80 percent had left before Std 7.

Nevertheless, despite the lack of visible opportunities, nearly all respondents said they planned to stay on at Mandela Park if the mine were to close. Their comments reveal a fatalistic sense of the region's prospects and of their own. If the mine closes, a 45-year-old retrenched miner said, "I foresee problems because everybody, including private businesses, depend on the mines. But I will stay on; I have nowhere else to go." Or a 29-year-old woman married to a miner: "We will all starve to death but will stay on. Where else can we go? Some will die, others will survive." Most respondents displayed a realistic sense of their chances of finding work elsewhere. A 33-year-old retrenched miner from the Transkei said: "There is a shortage of work everywhere. There's no point in moving." A 39-year-old retrenched miner noted: "Life will go on. Yes, some will go but others ... will stay. I will not go except when I get employment somewhere else."

Visions of the future were not much more optimistic and expectations seemed meagre. A 50-year-old man whose wife is a domestic worker in a nearby town said there had been real changes since 1990: "Life is more comfortable; we are not asked to produce passes by the police and I am not charged with trespassing when visiting my wife where she works." But even he added, "I have no expectations at all". Another man, who had been retrenched from Harmony twice, in 1989 and again in 1992, said: "Harassment by the police has stopped. One works wherever one wants and there is less beating up by whites in Virginia." Perhaps the most hopeful comment was that of a 28-year-old man who said he would like to see "changes in the economy so that everyone can have a job and can afford to own a house of his own".

LESOTHO

If expectations were bleak in Mandela Park, they were even grimmer for ex-Harmony workers in Lesotho. Our interviews suggest that while mine-owners may think they have shifted only recently to a policy of employing "career miners", many migrants already think of their work as a career. The men we interviewed have done little else during their working lives. They have few skills that make them employable outside the mine and expect to continue as miners for the rest of their lives. For these men and their families, the effects of down-scaling are devastating.

Using a snowball sample, we interviewed 10 former Harmony employees in Maseru; all were NUM members and most were in town to visit the offices of The Employment Bureau of Africa (Teba) on a daily basis in case mining jobs were to open up. Although we cannot ascertain the extent to which these cases are typical of Harmony workers, they are certainly representative of a large number of ex-miners in Lesotho who are finding it extremely difficult to earn a living now that the mines are shrinking.

The ages of our respondents, which ranged from 25 to 42, are telling. One began mining at Harmony in 1974 but most were hired in the 1980s. None were old men who had mined all their lives and could not change; rather, they were younger men who grew up in a society dependent on migrant workers' remittances and who had expected this pattern to continue. When they worked at Harmony they sent home between R300 and R600 a month; today their incomes are far lower. Half the households surveyed report no cash income of any kind – not even the unemployment incomes available for several months to most South African citizens. Four reported incomes from R120 to R160 a month earned by wives who brewed traditional beer or worked as childminders or sold sheep or vegetables – in nearly all cases, purchased or grown on land paid for with mining wages.

As in Mandela Park, most respondents have used up their retrenchment packages on family maintenance or house repairs. One man had invested his package in a liquor business which failed – ironically, perhaps, since liquor businesses were widely viewed by respondents in both Maseru and Mandela Park as the kind of retail business they would choose to enter into.

In the entire study only one former miner, living in Maseru, managed to use a skill learned on the mines to earn a living at home: he does welding, using borrowed equipment and earns about R400 a month. He was also the only miner in the study with a clearly expressed view of what he would do with a small business development loan: he would buy welding equipment and make burglar bars.

What prospects do these men have? Again, they expressed few ideas other than entering retail trade for alternative employment. They go daily to the Teba office, hoping for employment but knowing that as ex-workers from Harmony their chances are slim. Teba now has a policy of directing workers back to the mines they worked at before and Harmony's new labour strategy leaves them with little hope. "At Teba, Harmony ex-workers are told to stand aside and wait for the Harmony management to fetch us". "We always come to Teba but we former Harmony workers are not considered."

Several respondents said they "do not go to Harmony because we are threatened with police dogs". Since Harmony management categorically denies police dogs have ever been used on retrenched miners seeking work, we conclude that the pervasiveness of this view probably reflects the extent to which former miners in Lesotho feel excluded from the jobs on which their families depended. Although most respondents insisted proudly on their national identity, all the men we interviewed said they would move to South Africa with their families if they could because they believed the chances of employment would be higher.

Sociologists have long argued that South Africa's migrant labour system has externalised the costs of mine labour: neither the South African state nor the mining companies have paid for the schools, hospitals, pensions or other services needed for miners' families. In the same way, the international border seems to allow South Africa to externalise some of the costs of down-scaling: the situation of our Lesotho respondents, and undoubtedly of former miners' households in rural Lesotho, is even more extreme than the situation of retrenched miners in

Mandela Park.

In the long run, however, the effects of down-scaling are likely to leak across the border, either in the form of illegal immigration or, as in a case reported by a family of former farmworkers in Mandela Park, in the form of raids by "men in blankets" on homesteads near the Lesotho border. The gold mines' changing labour relations policies may ultimately create a more humane set of work relations but in the absence of any alternatives the shift leaves people who have become dependent on migrant remittances with few resources and fewer prospects.

CONCLUSION

Over the last century South Africa's entire economy has become dependent on the mining industry. Areas like the Orange Free State goldfields have depended on the mines for economic growth and rural areas have become dependent on remittances. What will happen to these areas and these households as a result of down-scaling?

At the regional level, the need for economic diversification in the goldfields area is obvious. The infrastructure is there, as is a potential work-force; what is lacking is any vision of a possible alternative strategy on the part of the mine, the business community or former workers.

This study suggests, however, that leaving the area to its own devices spells disaster for most of the people who worked in the mines. Lacking education or skills that can be used outside the world of mining, few mineworkers have been able to discover the strategies that would allow them to do much more than survive. By themselves, retraining programmes, while certainly beneficial, are probably inadequate; portable skills, except of the most basic sort such as literacy, will not help if workers have no jobs to which to take those skills. The people of Mandela Park seem fairly realistic in their assessment of their future: lacking in skills, capital and job possibilities. If the mine closes, "people can die of hunger".

To help former mineworkers, any policy for the region's economic diversification must include large-scale job creation rather than reliance on informal sector or small businesses alone. That conclusion points to the need for planned down-scaling rather than the kind of ad hoc process currently taking place. There is an alternative to expecting the people who depended on the mine to find individual solutions. More can be done than simply giving individual workers retrenchment packages and allowing, almost encouraging, businesses to leave the area. This study suggests that only a more gradual process, almost certainly involving subsidies to keep marginal mines open while diversification and retraining can take place, could prevent widespread hardship.

Planned down-scaling would allow the state, mining companies, unions and political actors to jointly plan some alternative economic strategy for the region, while allowing the region's population to survive the interim period. This study thus seems to support the argument that has been made by the NUM: "The scale and intensity of the suffering of the people that has been brought on by the crisis in the mining industry call out for state intervention" (NUM, 1992b).

In a society divided by apartheid, it comes as no surprise that down-scaling affects different groups in different ways. Inevitably, those with the least resources – African mineworkers and their families – have less to cushion them during hard times and are least able to adjust to the change. The white business people of Virginia will leave the area if the mine closes; the black population feels itself stuck there; while those in Lesotho are shut out entirely. This may be one of the last of the many grim ironies produced by apartheid: the final legacy of the gold-mining industry could be that former mineworkers, long forced to live in single-sex hostels far from their homes, may only be able to bring their families to live near the mine, just as Virginia becomes a ghost town. ◆

This paper is drawn from an earlier version which appeared in the <u>South African Socio-logical Review</u>, Vol 5, No 2, 1993. The study was conducted in 1992 and 1993 under the auspices of the Sociology of Work Programme at the University of the Witwatersrand. It was funded by the social responsibility programme of Rand Mines. Most of the interviews for the study were conducted by Gloria Mzondeki, Jabulani Sibeko and Erika Jankowitz.

REFERENCES

Crush, J, AH Jeeves and D Yudelman, 1991. <u>South Africa's Labour Empire: A History of Black Migrancy to the Gold Mines</u>. Boulder and Cape Town: Westview Press and David Philip.

Leger, J and M Nicol, 1992. "South Africa's gold mining crisis: challenges for restructuring," in <u>Transformation</u>, Vol 20: 17-36.

James, W, 1992. <u>Our Precious Metal: African Labour in South Africa's Gold Industry, 1970 – 1990</u>. Cape Town: David Philip.

National Union of Mineworkers, 1992a. "Marginal mines: documents on the summit discussions on state assistance to marginal mines," December.

National Union of Mineworkers, 1992b. "Means for managing down-scaling of mine operations, or lessening the impact of mine closures," paper prepared for the Mining Industry Summit task group on marginal mines, 9 October.

Seidman, G, 1993. "Shafted: The social impact of down-scaling in the Orange Free State goldfields region," in <u>South African Sociological Review</u>, Vol 5, No 2.

THE NUM JOB CREATION AND DEVELOPMENT PROGRAMME

MS KATE PHILIP

Co-ordinator of the Development Unit,
National Union of Mineworkers,
Johannesburg, South Africa

Massive retrenchments are gripping the mining industry and impacting on the lives of thousands of workers. The scale of retrenchments has had significant organisational implications for the National Union of Mineworkers (NUM), and the union has had to face the question of how to respond.

When 40 000 workers were dismissed during the 1987 strike the NUM was a mere five years old. The effect of these dismissals was devastating since among those dismissed were most of the union's national executive, its president and most of its regional committees, branch committees and shop stewards. The NUM did not at the time choose to draw attention to the crippling effect of the dismissals on union structures, precisely because the aim of the Chamber of Mines (COM) and the mining industry was to devastate the union. Instead, it put on a brave public face to mask the fact that it had to rebuild the structures and retrain the leadership of what was still a very young organisation.

At that stage the NUM was the fastest growing union in the world: founded in 1982 it expanded in its first five years to 280 000 paid-up members. Over the next five years it lost 180 000 workers through retrenchments but nevertheless managed to increase its membership to the current level of 320 000.

Despite the principle of "last in, first out," NUM militants are invariably targeted for retrenchment. This was clearly illustrated, for example, at the De Beers-owned Finsch mine in 1992. Altogether 93 out of 95 elected shop stewards were retrenched at Finsch. Also significant was the way in which these retrenchments took place. Workers coming off their shifts were met by managers who handed out letters to workers informing them that they were being retrenched. The men were immediately sent to the hostels to pack and were put on buses bound for home. Workers were given a month's pay in lieu of notice, which meant that although the legal requirement for a notice period was met, workers had no "psychological" notice. And those workers left behind found that overnight they had lost almost all of their elected representatives on the mines – and much of the collective skills and experience those representatives had accumulated as shaft stewards. By the time the NUM discovered it had lost almost all of its elected representatives on the mine, most of the men were already on a bus making their way home.

The point is that massive organisational devastation has gone hand-in-hand with retrenchments – and this must be borne in mind when examining the effectiveness of the NUM's response to lay-offs.

The NUM is the only union in South Africa with a fully-fledged development unit dealing solely with issues of job creation and support strategies for people who have left the industry and are no longer members. The NUM does not claim that it can create jobs for 180 000 retrenched workers but it can try to find development strategies, models and pointers which offer hope in a context of devastation. NUM strategy has taken place in two phases – a co-operative development strategy from 1987 and a micro-enterprise strategy from 1992.

THE CO-OPERATIVE MOVEMENT

During the first phase the union set up some 30 producer co-operatives, thereby creating about 500 jobs at the height of the programme. Though the incomes involved are low and have increased very slowly, 25 of the co-operatives are still functioning and are largely financially self-sufficient – a development achievement in itself.

However, as valuable as those 500 jobs were, they still left 179 500 retrenched mineworkers who did not benefit from the programme. This was the main reason why the NUM opted for a substantial shift in strategy in 1992. Another problem with the co-operative option was that enormous resources were needed for training and support of former mineworkers to develop their self-management skills. This is understandable if one looks at the steps entailed, for example, in setting up an NUM agricultural co-operative.

Firstly, workers conducted a comprehensive marketing survey. For example, Noluthando Co-operative in Tsomo district, Transkei surveyed six supermarkets, two schools, four churches, three hotels, one jail, 20 shops and 50 villages.

Once local demand had been assessed, an agricultural technical support team helped former mineworkers design a planting plan that would stagger planting and harvesting. The aim was to reap as regular an income as possible. A six-month work plan was then drawn up, followed by a six-week work plan and then a daily work plan which included allocation of labour. The projected income from crops for each crop plan was then examined. Finally, projected expenditure and cash flow were scrutinised to provide the basis of a financing proposal.

The NUM learned the hard way about the problems involved in setting up self-managed enterprises. Among these is the vast amount of time and resources required to develop the skills needed by members to reach this level of planning, a level that precedes any implementation. The resources and time required also impact upon the productivity and output of the co-operative. Given that in most of the co-operatives the majority of members are neither literate nor numerate, there are considerable difficulties in embarking upon a programme of development of self-managed enterprises. To make matters even more difficult, such attempts at developing enterprises take place in areas where any form of business is marginal and will struggle to survive.

The NUM, faced with a flood of retrenchments and aware of these problems, therefore opted for a more inclusive strategy accessible to *all* former miners. The result was a shift to micro-enterprises as a possible solution.

THE MICRO-ENTERPRISE PROGRAMME

The NUM faces extensive logistical problems with each wave of retrenchments. The practise of paying notice pay in lieu of a served notice period means that the names of retrenchees are often released days, if not 24 hours, before the men are expected to leave the mine. So although the union may have been involved in negotiations about the terms of the retrenchment, and although workers may therefore be aware of the impending retrenchment, the names of the individuals affected are not known until the retrenchment is actually implemented. This limits the potential for effective planning, counselling or training before the workers leave the mine. The NUM then faces a further challenge: after retrenchment, workers are often dispersed throughout southern Africa and the union must somehow service and reach them.

In response to this, when retrenchments now take place, the NUM tries to organise retrenchees into district contact groups so that a network is established with those workers *before* they leave the mine. Where possible, the union includes in retrenchment negotiations time off for workers while they are still on the mine to undergo micro-enterprise training. Increasingly we are trying to negotiate to use the notice period as a training period.

The NUM has 40 enterprise training options which are mainly applicable to rural areas. It has a mobile unit consisting of a 20-ton truck carrying a selection of supplies for these options, which include the manufacture of candles, paving slabs, grave stones and roof tiles as well as bread baking, battery charging, key cutting, leather goods production, maize meal processing and T-shirt printing.

The new strategy was developed with workers retrenched from Arnot Colliery who organised themselves and other members of the community into a district contact group in Gazankulu. Since this model involves both former miners and members of the community, it is inclusive and results in loose groupings of people who associate in whatever ways they choose.

Retail trade is often the starting point for NUM-initiated businesses and the Gazankulu group has opted for buying and selling poultry. The mobile unit was not yet in existence when this group was retrenched with the result that the NUM was unable to reach the workers before they left the mine. Because the workers had already spent their retrenchment packages the NUM piloted a micro-lending scheme starting with loans of R300 – amounts large enough for workers to start buying and selling live chickens. In March 1994, R91 000 worth of micro-loans had been made. On the basis of the pilot scheme, the union has managed to get backing from De Beers and Amcoal to provide security for an expanded scheme.

While the eventual aim would be to break out of pure retail, it is the easiest place to start. Whereas each co-operative consists of only 15 to 20 people, earning low incomes, the village-based groups in Mhala have about 70 self employed members who are able to earn an average of R600 a month from buying and selling live chickens. Low as this may seem, it is more than the 1994/95 minimum wage of R448 negotiated with the COM, and is three times as much as any co-operative members are able to earn. It is clear that the impact of the micro-enterprises is far greater than that of the co-operatives since after only a year the micro-enterprises have engaged as many people in productive activities as the co-operatives.

In addition, co-operatives take months to start production; in the poultry businesses people were earning incomes within three months. The poultry concerns also require far lower levels of skill and far less skilled input and support.

In the Gazankulu case the NUM also set up a development centre and a poultry supply unit. This unit is supplying 2 000 live birds each week to the group at R5 below the going rate for each bird. They sell these at the going rate, which means a gross income of an extra R40 000 a month is being injected into this rural economy.

The union's next task has been to work out how to service micro-enterprise groups country-wide. A rural development strategy was needed which would specifically address what could be called "intermediate institutions" for rural development – transport services and the bulk supply of raw materials and equipment, for example. Marketing was also an issue: an agricultural co-operative in Transkei was uprooting wild gooseberries, oblivious to the fact that in the cities these fetch a high price. Members of the co-operative also lacked the skills to access this urban market. Another example is that of goats' milk products such as feta cheese: while there are many goats in the rural areas there is no culture of milking them and processing the milk.

The critical issue here is the need for an intermediate institution capable of identifying local resources and marketing them in the formal economy.

When people are still developing skills it is acceptable to start at the lowest value-added end of the market, but ideally one is aiming at higher value-added products that can be exported out of rural areas and bring in money from urban areas. This is the aim of the NUM's research and development as well as the intermediate processes.

The union's strategy has been to set up development centres that are to an extent self-financing. Appropriate technology for rural development – including equipment and training elements – is located at the centre. Workers may come for training on the equipment and can buy equipment and raw materials there. Most importantly, they can actually produce at the centre. Thus a person wanting to make roof tiles, for example, can do so without having to buy the equipment. This means people do not have to invest in capital equipment before they start testing what works on the market and how they can get a decent return.

The question of the supply of raw materials is a critical constraint in terms of rural production activities. The NUM has worked with non-governmental organisations in setting up a central buying office that will provide professional services to a network of rural bulk supply outlets. This means individuals can gain from the economies of scale of a national buying office. This system started functioning in mid-1994 with the bulk supply unit in Gazankulu as the first depot to be serviced through the central buying office.

Another example of the potential usefulness of supply units are seedling nurseries. The NUM's agricultural co-operatives in Lesotho buy their seedlings in South Africa. It is ludicrous that in many areas there is no access to appropriate seedlings or appropriate inputs for agricultural production.

The first development centre was launched in May 1994 in Transkei and the second in July in Gazankulu. The next centre is scheduled for Maseru, then Swaziland, Namaqualand and Thabong in the Orange Free State. NUM organisers have recently been conducting business training for retrenched De Beers workers in the Northern Cape towns of Koffiefontein and Springbok.

Funds were obtained from several mining houses during retrenchment negotiations and the NUM has proposed that these be used to finance a core programme involving self-employment training by the union's mobile unit, access to business education and credit and the establishment of development centres in key sending areas. This has been agreed in principle.

Logically, these NUM operations should link up with the government's Reconstruction and Development Programme. The centres should be a base for the community as a whole, not only for former miners. Because of costs, former miners can only be effectively served via services that are widely accessible.

The co-operatives are currently viewed as the graduate school of the development process. At this stage the NUM would not assist former miners to start co-operatives if they were "first-time" entrepeneurs, or had not graduated through the micro-enterprises stage of the process.

In addition to the projects already mentioned, the NUM has set up a Section

21 company called Mineworkers Enterprises to start and control beer halls, such as the Lapologa Chris Hani beer hall at Premier mine. The name means Rest in Peace Chris Hani. If the project at Chris Hani works well, as seems to be the case, the aim will be to take over the beer halls and mine shops throughout the industry. These are currently owned by worker structures on the mines and are more like consumer co-operatives than producer co-operatives. There may be a way of linking both NUM strategies: the Chris Hani beer hall is progressing well and there are plans for it to stock a unique product of marula beer produced at the Gazankulu development centre.

With the retrenchment of key unionists and former miners scattered across the rural landscape, the NUM has had major problems to contend with. But with its job creation and development programme, the union is responding to the challenge. ◆

Migrant Workers' Co-operatives in Lesotho

Mr Motlatsi Thabane
Department of History,
National University of Lesotho,
Roma, Lesotho

For more than a decade the number of Basotho men able to find employment on South African mines has been declining. The reasons for this are many, but chief among them are the policies of stabilisation, internalisation, mechanisation and retrenchments.

After the protracted mineworkers' strike in August 1987, close to 10 000 Basotho workers were dismissed. This marked a watershed in the way the National Union of Mineworkers (NUM) approached the problems facing migrant workers. Even though the union was able to secure the reinstatement of some of the workers, many did not get their jobs back and returned home to joblessness and bleak survival prospects. Since the strike, over 20 000 more workers have been retrenched. The NUM decided to tackle the resultant problem by involving retrenched workers in labour-intensive income-generating projects.

POSSIBLE SOLUTIONS

The rural areas, home to 85 percent of the population in 1986, offer few employment opportunities. Industries and factories are concentrated mainly in the urban areas and agriculture does not provide an economically viable option. Economists and others have therefore proposed other solutions to the problem of rural unemployment.

Foulo (1991), for example, suggests that government action in initiating and managing fiscal policies could stimulate the economy as a whole, leading to the creation of jobs. Cobbe (1986: 45) proposes the promotion of small business as a way out of rural unemployment. The small-scale enterprises advocated could be run either by individuals or groups of people working, for example, as co-operatives. The recommended economic activities are labour intensive ones such as horticulture and poultry farming. A final proposal is that the government of Lesotho and organisations representing the migrant workers' interests should appeal to the South African government and, in particular, the mining industry's goodwill to ensure continued employment of Basotho migrants.

However, the likely consequences of these solutions are difficult to assess, given the unpredictability of the market. For example, Lesotho has very little control over its fiscal policy as it is largely dictated by fiscal policy in South Africa.

THE CO-OPERATIVE MOVEMENT

Rather than discuss the speculative solutions to Lesotho's unemployment problem, this study looks at one of the concrete results of Basotho retrenchments, the Basotho Mine Labour Co-operative (BMLC) movement. The BMLC is an umbrella organisation for a number of co-operatives in Lesotho. The co-operatives are assisted financially by the NUM, with the BMLC acting as a channel for these funds as well as providing legal and other counsel. This study concentrates on the Botha-Bothe Poultry Co-operative, the Leribe Blockmaking Co-operative and the Kolo Diamond Digging Co-operative in an attempt to establish their effectiveness as a solution to unemployment and retrenchments.

The Botha-Bothe Poultry Co-operative, with 19 members (not all ex-migrants), was formed in 1991. On seven hectares of land bought from the local chief for 16 000 Maloti (about R16 000) provided by the NUM, the co-operative farms poultry as well as some vegetables.

The Leribe Blockmaking Co-operative was formed in August 1989 and currently has 14 members, not all of whom are ex-migrants. The site of the co-operative is the same size as a residential site.

The Kolo Diamond Digging Co-operative mines a kimberlite pipe (a volcanic intrusion in which diamonds could be found) which covers an area of 60 by 32 square metres. This co-operative was formed in August 1992 and has 15 members, two of whom are not ex-migrants.

The leaders of all three co-operatives believe that their co-operatives are growing. All are expanding and producing more now than when first formed. The Botha-Bothe and Leribe co-operatives, for example, have expanded beyond their original economic activities. The former now grows maize, sugar beans and cabbage, while the Leribe co-operative is considering moving into agriculture. The Kolo co-operative has grown as a result of installing machinery to help in the digging and recovery processes.

The members of the three co-operatives do not earn much from their work. The average monthly income at the Botha-Bothe co-operative is 300 Maloti, at the Leribe co-operative members earn on average 125 Maloti a month, and at the Kolo co-operative 150 Maloti. However, these average earnings do not reflect the total income of the co-operatives. The total costs of each co-operative include not only overheads but also a contingency fund, pension contributions, an education fund and other expenses.

The potential of these co-operatives to improve the lives of the people in rural Lesotho should not be measured only in material and quantitative terms. Ex-migrants who now work in co-operatives feel that the quality of their lives has improved as a result of earning an income in their home country. Wages were higher in the mines, but the work was oppressive, bureaucratic and stifled initiative. Co-operative workers feel that they are in control of their lives, are able to fulfil their various responsibilities, can share domestic responsibilities with their wives and, above all, can live at home with their families while their children are growing up.

These points could also be made by others who are gainfully employed in Lesotho, but members of co-operatives are part of teams which together decide on issues affecting the allocation of work and the distribution of profits between various needs – wages, pension, education and contingency funds.

Because all the co-operatives on which this study is based have been formed within the last five years, it is difficult to assess their impact on the communities within which they operate. However, the leaders of the co-operatives were able to offer some ideas about the changes they had brought about in the daily lives of the rural communities. The leader of the Botha-Bothe co-operative, for example, said that local people were happy that they no longer had to go to town to buy their vegetables. As a result of the presence of the Kolo co-operative the villagers now have a passable road and piped water and are able to use the co-operative's electricity generator.

PROBLEMS

The real challenge, however, is to overcome the difficulties experienced by these co-operatives. These problems can be divided into two types – organisational problems which can be solved by the co-operatives themselves and more serious obstacles which can only be overcome in the medium or long term.

An example of an organisational problem is the supply of work materials. The leader of the Leribe Blockmaking Co-operative complained that there have been times when broken machinery or vehicles and the lack of cement has caused long work stoppages. Leaders of the Kolo Diamond Digging Co-operative spoke of long delays in getting fuel supplies for the machinery.

Some workers find that they are unwittingly engaging in a number of work practices that they resisted as miners in South Africa; living away from their families[1], working without protective clothing, risking tuberculosis, lacking basic provisions:

> The other problems that we have here I think which are the biggest are those like safety ... that is, we do not have first aid here. We have already had many accidents here ... we do not have bandages ... there is a lot of dust and we keep remembering in the mines that people contracted TB and all other things like that. They are some of the (diseases) which will affect our people here, maybe if we are still here after five years we will have people suffering from TB[2].

The lack of skills and training also presents difficulties. On the whole none of the jobs held by ex-migrants in the mines prepared them for work in co-operatives. The leader of the Botha-Bothe Poultry Co-operative, for example, was a boring-machine operator, while the leader of the Leribe Blockmaking Co-operative was a boiler maker. The situation in the Kolo Diamond Digging Co-operative is an exception, where the skills required are similar to those learned on the South African mines. The leader of the co-operative said he had carefully observed the tasks of mine administration while in South Africa and was finding this useful in his present occupation. Although the NUM organised some managerial training courses before the establishment of the co-operatives, members felt that they would benefit from further training as well as regular refresher courses. Workers on the ore processing plant at the Kolo co-operative, for example, felt that their training had been inadequate:

> The training that we were given was just a way of making regulations of administration ... (and) not so much training which is connected to the work that we are doing ... we are using machines .. we have not gone for training on machines or anything (of that kind)[3].

Although the problems outlined above can severely affect the smooth running and success of the co-operatives, they are all resolvable in the short term. All that is required is the maintenance of regular contact between the co-operatives or their representatives on the one hand, and government, suppliers and sponsors on the other. More serious problems can only be addressed in the medium or long term. These are problems which are connected to the nature of the economy of Lesotho. If the co-operative movement is to succeed in Lesotho, these problems have to be systematically analysed and addressed.

All three co-operatives complained about the lack of a market for their pro-

---

1. *Most of the members of the co-operative come from areas in Lesotho other than Kolo itself. Although some of them have rented houses in the nearby village, there are others who live in corrugated iron shacks.*
2. *Kolo co-operative, interview with chairperson, May 1994.*
3. *Kolo co-operative, interview with member, May 1994.*

duce. The market in Lesotho is very small, and the Southern African Customs Union Agreement between Botswana, Lesotho, Swaziland and Namibia compels Lesotho to give South African goods unrestricted access to its markets (Cobbe, 1986: 45-46). This means that producers in Lesotho have to compete with those in South Africa. The leader of the Botha-Bothe Poultry Co-operative described the predicament:

> I find that this country of ours has allowed produce from South Africa in large quantities ... but what ought to be happening (is) that Lesotho itself should be vigilant that, when the co-operatives here in Lesotho have a commodity, these commodities should be bought until they are finished, and then when they are finished they should open for South Africa to bring in commodities which we no longer have[4].

The competition between South Africa and Lesotho is unequal. South African goods are cheaper and consumers in Lesotho often prefer goods from South Africa to those made locally. Wallman (1972: 256) suggests that Basothos' exposure to life in South Africa has helped them develop tastes for South African goods. Commodities bought in South Africa, she says, "have, whatever their quality, a certain cachet". Cobbe (1986) argues that consumers in Lesotho are more used to goods manufactured by the more experienced South African producers, who have supplied goods to them for decades. South African manufacturers are able not only to supply better quality and cheaper products, but they are also able to offer better terms of payment. Unlike a large company, the small producers cannot wait for six months to be paid in full.

Marketing presents a particular problem for the Kolo co-operative. Here the difficulty is not of competition with South African producers or the size of the market in Lesotho; rather, the members of the co-operative have very little knowledge of the commodity they produce. It is the buyers who weigh, evaluate and determine the price of their diamonds. As one member pointed out:

> We do not have the ability to know that when a diamond is this big it can give us this much and do this and do that ... they are things which come from the buyer, a buyer just tells you that "your diamond I shall take it for this much ... I see the problem [with it] being this and this here on it"[5].

The solution is not necessarily to train members of the co-operative in the specialised diamond business but rather for the government to provide them with expertise on evaluating diamonds and in testing the quality of the different grades of ore deposit. Without this assistance, the diggers are ignoring the less productive areas and concentrating on the more productive part of the deposit, which will result in the life of the mine being shortened. Poorer parts of the

---

4. *Botha-Bothe co-operative, interview with chairperson, May 1994.*
5. *Kolo co-operative, interview with member, May 1994.*

deposit will remain unmined and will be uneconomical to mine on their own.

Clearly government intervention is required in a number of areas if co-operatives are to successfully address the unemployment problem in Lesotho, yet government support has been virtually non-existent. The only hint of government assistance was the provision of spades and pick-axes to the Kolo co-operative. Even then, this was not an innocent gesture of goodwill; the co-operative has been forced to sell through the government's department of mines and this arrangement makes it possible for the government to collect some sales tax on diamonds sold. Ventures such as the Botha-Bothe and Leribe co-operatives, which offer no direct benefit to government, have received no assistance at all. Although lack of government resources is part of the reason, members of all the co-operatives agree that the government's lack of interest in the emerging co-operative movement is also political. They believe that the government would rather control than support an independent co-operative movement.

Lesotho residents still find it difficult to get used to the concept of self employment and the insecurity this often brings. Some simply want to work as employees receiving monthly salaries from their employers. As the leader of the Botha-Bothe Poultry Co-operative put it, some local people would not join his co-operative, refusing to "work where (they) do not get paid".

The leaders of the three co-operatives imply that individualism and the lack of a co-operative spirit adversely affect the smooth running of these operations. People are used to a hierarchical order at the workplace, and when production processes and decision-making are based on equality and participation, it becomes difficult to assign tasks to different members of the co-operative. The leader of the Kolo co-operative said that some members simply refuse to take assignments from other members on the grounds that all members are equal and none has the authority to allocate tasks to others. The tendency at the Leribe co-operative, according to a member, is for the group to shirk their work. The problem seems to be the perception members have of co-operative work – some think they have the same authority over the co-operative as they have in their families, and others think they can leave the work to the rest.

Finally, there is a worrying development in the Leribe and Kolo co-operatives. The NUM's original idea was that work in all co-operatives should be labour intensive, but there is a growing movement towards and wish for mechanisation. For example, faced with problems of irresponsibility among members, the leader of the Leribe Blockmaking Co-operative spoke strongly against a labour-intensive venture; he would prefer what he described as "work that does not require hard work". This tendency to mechanise is even more glaring at the Kolo co-operative. At present almost all aspects of the labour process have been mechanised – digging is done by bulldozer, loading by a power shovel and the ore is carted to the processing plant by a truck. Hopefully this tendency is only a temporary phenomenon, for if it is not it will inhibit the expansion of the co-operatives and their ability to help resolve Lesotho's unemployment crisis. ◆

REFERENCES

Cobbe, J. 1986. "Consequences for Lesotho of changing South African labour demand," in <u>African Affairs</u>, Vol 85: 338.

Foulo, T. 1991. "Migrant workers' retrenchments: implications for Lesotho's economy," in Central Bank of Lesotho staff occasional paper No 6.

Wallman, S. 1972. "Conditions of non-development: the case of Lesotho," in <u>Journal of Development Studies</u>, Vol 8, No 2.

RESPONSE

DR PAUL JOURDAN
Department of Mineral and Energy Affairs,
ANC, Johannesburg,
South Africa

The problem of the gold price has recently re-emerged as one of the key issues for the mining industry. I have watched the different crystal ball-gazers knocking and insulting each other and it has become clear to me that it is pretty much an imprecise science – it has been called voodoo many times. Some points within this voodoo need to be brought out.

Nicoli Nattrass's paper focuses on demand which was also touched on in several other analyses. The surprise factor is also very important, especially since the late 1970s when the big change in technology in heap leach came in. Heap leach operations now probably supply about half the world's gold supply. The advantages, in terms of a future higher gold price, are very short term. They just scoop off the top of an old mine, normally with a viability of between three and 10 years compared with tabular reef mines like those on the Witwatersrand which have had lives of up to 50 years. Thus, we have had a lot of people predicting a higher gold price because this heap leach phenomenon is going to run out. On the other side there is an argument which I have been putting forward: "Why did heap leach happen only in Australia, Canada and America?" It is because they had the technology and infrastructure. So while they are short-term there are many of them – especially in north-east Russia – that will come into operation. The conclusion is that much more research is needed in this area and that it is very unclear where the price will go. The demand side is very strong, mainly from the Far East, as Nattrass pointed out.

A very important aspect that demands emphasis is Nattrass's illustration that the crisis of profitability is caused mainly by a fall in real revenue rather than rising costs, as the industry always argues. Both real wages and real inputs have fallen, yet the industry gets away with this argument all the time. They constantly raise this as a way of further pushing down their costs.

Productivity is another important point. The National Union of Mineworkers (NUM) has indicated that productivity in ore has increased two and a half fold since 1970. In the case of gold it has been stagnant because of the fall in grade, meaning that the same quantity of ore has been producing less and less gold.

Profit sharing is problematic. One aspect is its bias towards the mining companies whom employees basically have no choice but to believe. NUM, as far as I know, only proposes profit-sharing schemes at mines in crisis. There is also the problem of a top-down management style in our mines which has often been called "plantation management". It is unlike Swedish mines, for example, where the workers on the face effectively have control over productivity. Profit sharing is important, but when one doesn't have control it really does not make any difference. You can only move more ore, but you do not have control over the decisions on how you blast, save holes and increase overall productivity. Thus, it has been argued that profit-sharing schemes will only really work when the management structure on our mines has been changed.

Gay Seidman's paper gives very real evidence of the enormous scale of suffering brought about by retrenchments. Those outside mining tend to experience retrenchment just as numbers in the newspaper. The industry constantly attempts to convey it as a sterile process where people are given packages and there is nothing they can do.

I grew up in Bloemfontein and Kroonstad and remember very clearly when those mines were opening up in the boom era of the late 1950s. Everyone said the Welkom mines were going to last only 20 years – at the fixed gold price then of $34. They planned to establish secondary industries to avoid ghost towns developing. The mines have lasted 20 years longer than anticipated and there are still no secondary industries. I believe this is a criminal indictment.

Another problem is whether we give a subsidy to a dying mine. We need to be able to justify this because a range of industries are going under in this country and the loss of jobs in manufacturing, in fact, has been higher proportionately than in mining. The subsidy should be generic.

What we are losing in mining then are employment and foreign exchange (forex). The forex is important in terms of its role in maintaining employment in other areas. Thus, what would have more chance of succeeding in government would be a policy that had limited funds to subsidise any industry that maintained large employment and also had large forex implications.

Concerning Kate Philip's paper, the move from co-operatives to this kind of micro-enterprise focus is extremely interesting. My only comment would be that this again appears to be something that should be generic and not just for ex-miners. It sounds like the core of a national rural development strategy that should be co-ordinated with other initiatives. ◆

Towards a
New Policy

THE FUTURE OF MINE MIGRANCY: TRENDS IN SOUTHERN AFRICA

DR ROBERT DAVIES
Member of Parliament,
Cape Town, South Africa

DR JUDITH HEAD
Department of Sociology,
University of Cape Town,
South Africa

The issue of migration has been seen as relevant to the discussion about future regional economic co-operation in two main ways. Firstly, the new democratic government's attitude to legal migration, particularly but not only to the mining industry, is viewed as a litmus test of real commitment to "reconstructing regional relations on new lines" (ANC, 1992). Secondly, the prospect of escalating clandestine migration is interpreted as a real or potential threat which underscores the need for an equitable and mutually beneficial programme of regional economic co-operation (Davies et al, 1993).

The future of legal migration to South Africa and the attitude of a democratic South Africa to the employment of migrant workers from other southern African countries is clearly a matter of great concern to neighbouring countries and could therefore be expected to feature as an item in future bilateral or multilateral negotiations between the new government and its neighbours. The possibility that economic stagnation in neighbouring countries or a highly uneven process of regional interaction may fuel further clandestine migration to South Africa has also been cited in support of calls for a democratic South Africa to commit itself to acting to promote equitable, balanced growth in the region.

Legal movement to the mines is, in fact, no longer the main form of migration to South Africa. Many more people are now involved in clandestine and illegal migration. Much of the latter remains largely undocumented. We do not know precisely how many people are involved or where they go. The only reliable figures available are for deportations. Although these cover only the tip of the iceberg, they are telling enough. They indicate that half as many citizens of neighbouring countries were deported from South Africa in 1992 as there were working legally in the mining industry (83 000 against 165 000). In the case of Mozambicans, there were more deportees than legal workers on the mines.

While migrant labour to the mines may no longer be the most significant form of migration, it is still, nevertheless, very important in terms of the income it generates for the labour supplying states and as a source of employment for their citizens.

Under such circumstances there is clearly a need for more reflection on the implications of recent trends in both legal and clandestine migration in southern Africa. The relationship and dynamic between the two forms of migration, changes in the patterns of migration and their potential impact on both employment policies within South Africa itself and a future South African regional programme need to be understood.

This chapter hopes to contribute to the discussion in two ways. Firstly, it will examine current and possible future mine labour recruitment and employment trends. Secondly, it will consider the strategic choices, and hence policy options, facing employers, unions and the new government. This discussion will take place in the context of an analysis of the broader trends in migration in the region.

CHANGING PATTERNS OF LEGAL MIGRATION TO THE MINES

South Africa is the industrial centre of a regional economy which has entwined neighbouring states in a web of relations for more than 100 years. Crucial among these relationships has been the demand for and supply of migrant labour (Legassick and De Clerq, 1978).

In 1975, member countries of the Southern African Development Coordination Conference (SADCC) provided 73,8 percent of the black workers employed in the gold and coal mines owned by the Chamber of Mines (COM), the largest employer of migrant workers from neighbouring states. Within seven years – by

1982 – this proportion had fallen to 42,8 percent, with a total of 58 710 jobs lost, nearly a quarter of the 1975 total (Crush et al, 1991).

While the proportion and absolute number of workers recruited from other southern African supplier states began to decline in the mid-1970s, the total number of black workers employed in the industry continued to increase until 1986. However, since 1987, and particularly after the August 1987 strike, the mines have shed nearly 200 000 jobs.

The context within which these changes have taken place is a depressed world gold price and the fact that most mines in South Africa have passed their peak. In the aftermath of the 1987 strike, and with a number of marginal mines in the industry facing closure, mining companies began to develop new policies aimed at reducing costs (COM, 1993). Among other things, the COM began a programme of retrenchments accompanied, in some cases, by the introduction of new technologies.

Hamstrung by a fluctuating gold price, mine management has started to re-think the organisation and planning of underground work, introduce new concepts of team work and improve management of resources[1]. The drive is to increase the productivity of labour using existing technology, despite current technical constraints. At Western Areas mine this strategy has paid off. According to the personnel officer, "we are producing much more now than in 1990 with less labour"[2].

The 1980s policy of "heterogeneous sourcing" ensured that the industry did not become too dependent on any one source. This policy remained in place after 1987 and partly arrested the earlier trend towards reducing the proportion of "foreign workers". The proportion of non-South African workers on the mines has, accordingly, risen from 41,5 percent in 1986 to 48,0 in 1993. But this masks the fundamental fact that workers from neighbouring states have been laid off in large numbers. The average number of SADCC citizens employed on COM-affiliated gold and coal mines fell by 56 796 between 1986 and 1991 (over a quarter of the total number employed in 1986). In terms of absolute numbers, the average number of SADCC citizens employed in 1991 was 165 825 compared to 222 621 in 1986 (COM, 1991).

Up to 1987, employment from more SADCC supplying states remained stable or increased, but since then the totals of all foreign suppliers (with the exception of Swaziland and Mozambique which has hovered at around 42 000 men) have been steadily declining.

The average number of men employed from Lesotho on the gold mines reached an all-time high of 105 506 in 1987. In 1993 the figure stood at 79 530. The reduction of Basotho labour on Chamber-affiliated coal mines is even more dramatic. In 1981 an average of 12 314 men were employed, by 1992 the figure stood at less than half – 5 037 (Crush et al, 1991: 234; COM, 1991: 60).

---

1. *Interview with Mr Bellingan, Personnel Manager, Labour Department, Western Areas gold mine, 13 December 1993.*
2. *Interview with Mr Bellingan.*

These changes have both prompted and been reflected in the changed role of the mine labour recruiting organisation, The Employment Bureau of Africa (Teba). Twenty years ago Teba ran approximately 130 recruiting stations across southern Africa and its officials were engaged in actively seeking out men to sign contracts to work on the mines. Today, Teba has 70 stations in southern Africa (including South Africa) and it no longer actively recruits labour. Its function has become a bureaucratic one of processing the contracts of foreign workers, dealing with telex requests for labour outside and beyond the normal quotas, processing payments, liaising with governments and passing on messages between mines, miners and miners' families.

Within South Africa it no longer recruits on any significant scale. With the repeal of repressive legislation in the mid-1980s, workers from the homelands did not need to sign a contract. They could simply sign on at the gate of the mine. This change is reflected in the discrepancy between mine strength and the numbers that have actually passed through Teba offices. According to Teba's operations manager there were 330 000 men on strength in 1992 compared to the 280 000 men Teba actually handled[3]. However, the mining companies continued to pay the monthly capitation fee of R6 per man, meaning that the industry paid at least R3 million to Teba for men who had not in fact passed through its depots. Changes in legislation in South Africa, the decline in recruiting and the restructuring of the labour force have deprived Teba of its traditional role. This has put its future on the line. For the past few years, therefore, Teba has been in a process of restructuring.

CHANGING PATTERNS OF CLANDESTINE MIGRATION

While the employment of legal migrant workers in the mining industry has declined, clandestine or illegal migration has escalated. The war in Mozambique was responsible for the movement of large numbers of refugees across the subcontinent. At its height, there were a million and a half Mozambican refugees in six SADCC-member countries, and a further 300 000 in South Africa (only some receiving limited protection from the authorities in Gazankulu and KaNgwane).

The fact that war refugees are now beginning to return to Mozambique does not mean that migration has disappeared as an issue. The phenomenon has clearly reached well beyond a movement of war refugees.

Clandestine economic migration to South Africa continues, driven by poverty and unemployment in home countries and fuelled by expectations that political change in South Africa might create a more accommodating environment. This situation is recognised by the United Nations High Commission for Refugees (UNHCR) which is charged with the repatriation of Mozambican refugees

---

3. *Interview with Mr Moloney, Manager of Operations, Teba, 14 December 1993 and 23 May 1994.*

from South Africa. It identifies a category of Mozambicans resident in South Africa who have migrated essentially in search of work. This group consists almost exclusively of young men who have crossed the border from Mozambique in 1992 and early 1993. "They are of relatively young age (20-30) and unmarried." They transit through the refugee camps (often forming almost exclusive settlements of young men) on their way to the cities (UNHCR, 1993)[4].

By virtue of its illegal nature, it is difficult to obtain reliable information on this movement. However, it is a movement that goes back over 100 years and it is obvious that it is relatively easy to cross the border. People with family ties on both sides of the border and those who speak the common language slip across most easily. Others pay a runner to guide them across. The going rate, for example, for a guide through the Kruger Park, is R300[5]. Some men cross the frontier, make their way to the mine where they wish to work or have been told to go to, and "buy a telex" – confirmation that they have a job – from a corrupt mine official. Another method is through the practice, common in the Eastern Transvaal, of registering illegal migrants with the authorities once they have found a job. Teba also facilitates the legalisation of labour for contractors to the mines. Although it represents only about 2 percent of Teba's business at present, it seems that this is a growing trend.

No reliable data on clandestine migration is available, except figures for deportations of "illegal immigrants". This is confusing, however, because it includes genuine refugees and some people who have been living illegally in South Africa for years, and are effectively domiciled there. In addition, the fragmentary accounts that exist suggest that some men cross the border illegally, look for work or work illegally on the farms in the Eastern Transvaal, get picked up and deported and turn round and come back again. According to figures from the Department of Home Affairs, 82 575 illegal immigrants were deported from South Africa in 1992 – a sixfold increase over the number deported in 1988. Seventy-four percent of these came from Mozambique and 14,5 percent from Zimbabwe. The figures for the first nine months of 1993 (the latest available at the time of writing) are even more telling. They point to an increase in clandestine migration, despite the ceasefire in Mozambique in 1993 and the breaking of the drought there. Between January and September 1993, there were 63 191 deportations, representing an increase of 140 per month compared to 1992. Unofficial estimates have suggested that the total number of illegal immigrants in the Witwatersrand area alone has reached more than a million, while the deputy director general of the Department of Home Affairs has spoken of an estimated 2,2 million Mozambicans living in South Africa.

---

4. *Interview with Ms Elizabeth Mpyisi, Legal Protection Officer, UNHCR, Maputo, 25 November 1993.*
5. *Interview with Mr David Kapya, Deputy Representative of Operations, UNHCR, Maputo, 29 November 1993.*

TABLE 1: AVERAGE ANNUAL GROWTH RATES, REAL GROSS DOMESTIC PRODUCT & POPULATION (PERCENT) — SOUTH AFRICA & SADCC COUNTRIES

| | GDP | | POPULATION | |
	1965-80	1980-90	1965-80	1980-90
SOUTH AFRICA	3,7	1,3	2,4	2,4
SADCC COUNTRIES				
ANGOLA	-	0,5	2,8	2,6
BOTSWANA	13,9	11,3	3,6	3,3
LESOTHO	6,8	3,1	2,3	2,7
MALAWI	5,5	2,9	2,9	3,4
MOZAMBIQUE	-	-0,7	2,5	2,6
NAMIBIA	-	0,4	2,4	3,0
TANZANIA	3,9	2,8	2,9	3,1
ZAMBIA	2,0	0,8	3,0	3,7
ZIMBABWE	5,0	2,9	3,1	3,4
(SWAZILAND - FIGURES NOT GIVEN)				

Source: World Bank, World Development Report 1992, Oxford University Press, 1992, Tables 2 and 26.

THE REGIONAL ECONOMIC CONTEXT

The overall context within which these trends need to be examined is, firstly, the continuing economic stagnation characterising South Africa and most neighbouring countries and, secondly, the increasing polarisation in the southern African regional economy. The table above shows that during the 1980s, rates of growth of real Gross Domestic Product (GDP) fell to levels below population growth in South Africa and eight of the 10 SADCC member countries.

Several factors clearly underlie the poor economic performance reflected in such figures. Changes in the world economy since the mid-1970s had a major impact on all countries dependent on primary product exports, including those in southern Africa. The socio-economic crisis confronting the region in the 1990s was a product, too, of violent conflict derived from South African policies in the 1980s. This has been dealt with extensively elsewhere (Hanlon, 1987; Martin and Johnson, 1986). In addition to the horrendous loss of life and substantial economic damage to the region caused by apartheid aggression and destabilisation, the 1980s also saw South Africa disengaging from a number of service relationships where it had historically been a buyer and, thus, a provider of revenue to other countries. This pattern continues in southern African regional economic relations today. South Africa sells five times as much to the region as it imports. Historically this was partly financed by income received by neighbouring countries through the provision of services to South Africa. But with these invisible earnings having declined the acute polarisation characterising visible trade has been exacerbated.

All of this has had a major impact on domestic formal sector employment in several neighbouring states. So too have the first generation International Monetary Fund (IMF)/World Bank-sponsored Structural Adjustment Programmes (SAPs) which most of the SADCC member countries have been obliged to implement since the mid-1980s. These have sought to promote macro-stability through a standard package of sharp currency devaluations, state budget cuts and the withdrawal of subsidies. They have also sought to reduce the role of the state in the economy, to "free" markets from what have been seen as distortions created by policy interventions and to enlarge the space for private sector entrepreneurship. In some cases these policies seem to have resulted in some measure of economic growth. However, this has been at the cost of living standards, particularly of the urban poor, and resulted in drastic cuts in social expenditure and major reductions in public sector employment. They have also resulted in a dramatic increase in social inequality.

The Final Report of the United Nations Programme for African Economic Recovery and Development (UN-PAAERD, 1991) is instructive in this regard. It concluded that Africa was in a worse state in 1991 than it had been five years earlier, despite the provision of some $128 billion to support SAPs. Gaps between the working age population and formal sector employment in most SADCC supplier states have remained enormous – and indeed in some cases have widened.

A survey carried out in Lesotho in the mid-1980s for example found that of the economically active population of 755 388, 270 000 (or 36 percent) were wage or salary earners, but that 59 percent or 159 000 of these were migrants working outside Lesotho. This meant that only 15 percent of the working age population of Lesotho were in wage or salary employment in the country. This was less than the 143 000 (53 percent) described as not employed but seeking and/or available for work. Of the latter, 63 000 (or 8 percent of the working age population) had never been employed (Lesotho Bureau of Statistics, 1990).

In the case of Mozambique, a sample survey found that there had, in fact, been an absolute decline in employment in 590 key productive enterprises – from 149 000 in 1991 to 137 000 in 1992 (Comissao Nacional do Plano, 1993: 91). The 41 000 Mozambican miners employed in the South African mining industry was thus equivalent to nearly a third of the total number of people employed in the 590 key firms. Cuts in state expenditure have also led to a reduction of employment in the state sector. Reduced employment opportunities inside the country have occurred at a time when the numbers seeking work have been boosted by political events. The Organisation of Mozambican Workers estimates that 17 000 young people have been repatriated from Germany following the collapse of the German Democratic Republic[6]. Many of these are skilled workers, others have industrial experience, yet few can find jobs in Mozambique. Both the Frelimo and Renamo armies are involved in a process of demobilising several thousand men. In the past they would probably have sought work in South Africa but now, at least legally, this option is no longer open.

In spite of the fall in numbers employed on the mines, migrant labour remittances remain a critically important source of income and foreign exchange for labour supplying states. In the case of Lesotho, for example, a recent survey found that migrant wage remittances accounted for 39 percent of the rural household income in the mid-1980s (Lesotho Bureau of Statistics, 1990: 22). Teba payments to Lesotho totalled R284 million in 1992 – an amount equal to 65 percent of the country's 1990 GDP. The country's Gross National Product (GNP), which measures transfers as well as domestic production, was greater than its GDP (measuring domestic production) by an amount equivalent to 60 percent of GDP in 1990. The transfers reflected in this gap were more than one and a half times the country's exports (Chipeta and Davies, 1992: 106-108). In the case of Mozambique, migrant labour remittances provided 15,8 percent of the country's total visible and invisible foreign earnings in 1992. The amount of $58 million was equal to 42 percent of the country's total visible export earnings (Comissao Nacional do Plano, 1993: 97).

POTENTIAL IMPLICATIONS OF FURTHER REDUCTIONS

The employment of citizens of neighbouring states in South Africa is one of the longest established and most enduring relations between South Africa and the rest of the region. The migrant labour system has long been criticised as both exploitative and an impediment to growth and development in "labour reserve" areas. Individual countries have repeatedly expressed their desire to disengage from it, but this has proved impossible because of the continuing high level of dependence of many households on miners' remittances.

In the period since the mid-1970s, supplier states have found themselves sub-

---

6. *Interview with Mr Macuacua, Gabinete de Estudos e Planificagao, Organiszacao dos Trabalhadores Mocambicanos, Maputo, 26 November 1993.*

jected to policies, imposed unilaterally by employers, which have rendered impractical any strategy of phased withdrawal from the migrant labour system. Instead of being able progressively to disengage at a pace determined by the development of alternative income and employment opportunities at home, levels of recruitment from SADCC-member supplier states have been cut at a rate far in excess of the capacity to create new employment opportunities. This has meant that unemployment has, in effect, been exported to neighbouring states in a context where the scope for domestic survival strategies has become increasingly restricted. All of this has created a powerful incentive to clandestine migration.

Southern Africa seems poised on the brink of what could be another major reduction in the employment of migrant workers in South Africa. Most attention in this regard has been focused on the potential attitude of a democratic government. Fears have been expressed that a democratic government may adopt populist policies which, explicitly or implicitly, aim to reduce the employment of migrant labour in the hope of increasing employment opportunities for South African nationals. What this focus has obscured, however, is the fact that structural changes within the mining industry, resulting largely from the breakdown of apartheid, from the mid-1980s, have led to a restructuring of the labour-force. Over the next decade, contract migrant labour is likely to become a thing of the past.

A number of factors have facilitated the mining industry's quiet reorganisation of its labour supply and labour process. Sources of labour already existed in the vicinity of the mines before the repeal of apartheid legislation. The literature variously suggests that these were not drawn on because local labour was not prepared to work underground for uncompetitive wages and/or because South African urban workers were too militant and spelt trouble for mine management. Alternatively, or related to these factors, was South Africa's wider political project which involved using economic relationships as a lever in its southern African regional policy. Finally, mine managers, mindful of the problems they had in the past, were anxious not to put all their eggs in one basket but rather to draw on diverse sources of labour.

The existence of the National Union of Mineworkers (NUM) and the unionisation of a significant number of workers have meant that the wage gap has narrowed between mining and industry. Deregulation and the previous government's implicit approval of a laissez-faire market-driven industrial relations system within mining and other industries, coupled with escalating unemployment inside South Africa, means that the prospect of drawing on local labour is no longer as problematic as it might have seemed some years ago. Moreover, the repeal of the job colour bar which has made possible the promotion of a small but significant number of African and coloured workers, and the opening up of apprenticeship schemes to South Africans other than whites, presumably makes the prospect of mining more attractive to local men seeking jobs. On the part of management, there is a growing demand for well-educated English-speaking workers, who are more likely to be local men. Secondly, there would be no need to provide local workers with housing and, thirdly, the free movement of labour, the good and fast road network with the proliferation of easy and relatively cheap taxi transport and the existence of very high levels of unemployment mean that mine management no longer has to concern itself with labour recruitment. It can draw on a growing reserve army of labour within the borders of South Africa itself, at no cost.

What we are suggesting then is that a stable labour-force – in the usual sense – seems likely to emerge in South Africa's mines as a result of a combination of economic and political factors related to the abolition of apartheid. This will occur independent of the new government's thinking on the question. These processes were already under way by the mid-1980s and there is every reason to believe that they will now be accelerated. It is likely that as the present generation of foreign workers retires they will largely be replaced by men from South Africa who already constitute the majority of novice workers. Teba will probably maintain a skeleton presence in the four foreign supplying areas but other foreign workers will continue to arrive illegally at the mines or join contractors' teams. Nevertheless, the numbers of men involved will probably diminish.

If these or other factors do result in a sharp and disproportionate reduction of employment from neighbouring states, this will not, under existing conditions, be without consequences either for the countries concerned or for South Africa.

The COM has estimated that the half a million employees on all its mines support families and dependants totalling 3,1 million people (COM, 1992: 23). This would give a ratio of worker to dependants of 1:16. Other estimates put the figure a little lower (eg 1:11 by the NUM), but all agree that there are large numbers of family members supported by mine wages. What this means is that each job lost potentially affects the livelihood of up to 16 people. With limited opportunities in the domestic economies of supplier states the loss of mine jobs will push more than one person in a family or community to move clandestinely to South Africa. In other words there could be a multiplier relationship between loss of mine employment and clandestine migration.

IMPLICATIONS FOR A PROGRAMME OF REGIONAL CO-OPERATION

Closer regional co-operation has been widely defended as potentially holding out benefits for all the countries of southern Africa. Increased trade with the rest of the region could be of considerable significance for South Africa's manufacturing industries. Although that country's exports to African countries, other than members of the Southern African Customs Union (Sacu), made up only 8,8 percent of its total exports in 1992, over 70 percent of these exports were manufactured goods. In some cases, exports to non-Sacu African countries made up a sizeable portion of the total exports in the category concerned – 26,8 percent of foodstuffs and beverages; 25,5 percent of chemical products; 45,7 percent of plastics and rubber products, 10,8 percent of products of base minerals; and 43 percent of miscellaneous manufactures (Davies et al, 1993). An increase in this trade could thus provide an important boost to South African manufactured exports.

Other countries, too, could benefit from expanding their exports to South Africa. At present, only Zimbabwe, Namibia and the BLS countries, primarily Swaziland, have more than a token presence in the South African market. Zimbabwean exports have, moreover, declined sharply in recent months – by over 20 percent, from R586 million in the four months between January and April 1992 to R436 million in the corresponding period of 1993. This is at least partly due to the delay in reaching agreement on a new bilateral trade agreement, itself a reflection of a strong underlying protectionist stance towards potential imports from the region. If this were to change, however, agricultural and industrial producers in several neighbouring countries could receive an important boost.

Co-operation in regional construction, infrastructural and resource development projects, as well as in virtually every sector and area, could also be of considerable benefit. Projects would be of immediate benefit to the countries in which they are located, and the construction process could offer important business to contracting firms. In several cases, notably that of potential water and hydropower projects in several SADCC member states, these will not be economically viable unless they can count on exports to South Africa. At the same time, South Africa would benefit in environmental terms by importing hydropower and could well become absolutely dependent on water imports from other countries in the years ahead (Davies et al, 1993).

Beyond this, closer regional economic co-operation could lay a firmer basis for more effective participation in the world economy. Southern Africa remains an extremely small player in global terms. The combined GDP of South Africa and SADCC member countries is a little over half a percent of world GDP – roughly equal to that of a country like Finland. All of the individual countries of southern Africa need to restructure their economies in the face of a changing global economy, and in particular to reduce their dependence on primary product exports by becoming more significant exporters of manufactured goods. They face the challenge, moreover, of having to do this in a global situation characterised not only by huge disparities of economic power but also by the existence of structured disadvantages for less developed countries.

It has been argued that, under these circumstances, a more integrated southern African regional economy would benefit all the countries and peoples of southern Africa in at least the following ways:

◆ By allowing certain economies of scale which will facilitate restructuring at a higher level of productivity;
◆ By creating a climate conducive to raising levels of investment and encouraging investment in new forms of production;
◆ By helping to create the kind of competitive environment likely to facilitate innovation;
◆ By encouraging a rationalisation of investments in infrastructure and creating economies of scale which make infrastructural projects more

economically viable;

◆ By helping to strengthen the bargaining position of the countries of the region in an asymmetrical world;

◆ By promoting the freer movement of human resources and thereby increasing output and productivity (SADCC, 1992).

These benefits, however, will not be realised unless the disparities, structured inequalities and potential unsuitability of many existing regional relations are taken into account. In particular, if the strongest and most advanced country was seen to be benefiting disproportionately from a programme of regional economic co-operation, tensions would rise. If growth were to occur in some parts of the region while others experienced continuing stagnation, pressures towards continuing large-scale mass migration would intensify. If official trade continued to remain highly skewed, incentives for unofficial trade in arms and drugs will remain.

CONCLUSION

Recent reports have pointed to possible counter-tendencies to the trends described in this paper. On the one hand, there have been suggestions that after years of "downsizing", employment in the mining industry may begin to increase. COM economists have spoken of capital projects to the value of R2,7 billion announced at the end of 1993 probably leading to the "creation of new mine employment opportunities" (*Cape Times*, 3 January 1994). At the same time, repatriation of Mozambican war refugees from South Africa and other neighbouring states has begun.

It is our view that neither of these counter-tendencies fundamentally alters the argument developed above. Even the Chamber's own announcement of possible new jobs in the industry was hedged with qualifications about the "fragile outlook" for new recruitment and the need for a continued focus on cost containment and productivity. Moreover, clandestine migration has now moved well beyond a movement of war refugees as highlighted by the fact that the rate of deportations increased in 1993 despite the ending of the war in Mozambique.

A democratic South Africa needs to remain sensitive to the needs and interests of neighbouring countries. In a context where every job lost on the mines fuels a several-fold increase in clandestine migration, this would be as much in South Africa's own interests as that of neighbouring countries. While quotas or other guarantees about numbers seem improbable under current circumstances, firm guarantees against discrimination and the avoidance of any actions which may, intentionally or unintentionally, result in a disproportionate unloading of the burden of retrenchments on supplier states would be essential.

The whole question of deregulation and the concomitant undercutting of union rates is one that needs to be revisited by the labour movement with the new and more sympathetic government. Mine management should not be permitted to call in contractors to undercut union rates. The political implications of foreigners being employed by these contractors must be taken very seriously. Rather, minimum wages and conditions should prevail across the industry and mine management should be pressured to take on its historic responsibility towards the supplier states and invest significantly in large scale job-creation schemes. Programmes of employment creation should seek to encourage involvement in cross-border trade, various projects and co-operation schemes in small and medium-sized enterprises as well as larger established ones. The South African mining industry, which has for decades prospered through the contribution of migrant workers from southern as well as South Africa, needs also to make an appropriate contribution to employment generating programmes throughout the region. ◆

REFERENCES

Chamber of Mines, 1991. Annual Report 1991. Johannesburg: COM.

Chamber of Mines, 1992. Annual Report 1992. Johannesburg: COM.

Chamber of Mines, 1993. Mining in the next Century: A Context for Survival and Growth. Johannesburg: COM.

Chipeta, C and R Davies, 1992. Regional Relations and Co-Operation Post-Apartheid: a Macro-Framework Study. Gaborone: Consultancy report for SADCC Secretariat.

Comissao Nacional do Plano. 1993. Direccao Nacional de Estatistica. Anuario Estatistico, 1992. Maputo.

Crush, J, AH Jeeves and D Yudelman, 1991. South Africa's Labour Empire: A History of Black Migrancy to the Gold Mines. Boulder and Cape Town: Westveiw Press and David Philip.

Davies, R, D Keet and M Nkuhlu, 1993. "Reconstructing economic relations within the southern African region: issues and options for a democratic South Africa," document prepared for Macro-Economic Research Group (Merg) workshop.

Hanlon, J, 1987. Beggar Your Neighbours: Apartheid Power in Southern Africa. London: James Currey.

Legassick, M and F de Clerq, 1978. "The origins and nature of the migrant labour system in southern Africa," in United Nations Economic Commission for Africa: Migratory Labour in Southern Africa. 1985.

Lesotho Bureau of Statistics, 1990. "The labour force of Lesotho: a statistical report," based on The Labour Force Survey 1985/6, Maseru.

Martin, D and P Johnson, (eds,) 1986. Destructive Engagement. Harare: Zimbabwe Publishing House.

SADCC, 1992. "Towards Economic Integration", theme document for 1992 consultative meeting, Maputo, January 29-31.

UNHCR Maputo, 1993. "Mission report," Johannesburg, South Africa, November, unpublished report.

UN-PAAERD, 1991. "Economic crisis in Africa: final review of the implementation of UN-PAAERD," extracts reproduced as Backgrounder No 5, Centre for Southern African Studies, University of the Western Cape.

World Bank, 1992. World Development Report. Oxford: Oxford University Press.

THE ROLE OF TEBA:

CHANGES AND POTENTIAL

MR ROGER ROWETT
General Manager,
The Employment Bureau of Africa,
Johannesburg, South Africa

Recruitment of mine labour by The Employment Bureau of Africa (Teba) has decreased from a total of 490 000 in 1988 to about 340 000 in 1994 – and this decline is expected to continue steadily until the year 2000[1]. While recruitment will continue to be an important part of the service the organisation has to offer, its function is, by necessity, extending beyond that of a simple recruitment agency for the mines.

Teba has identified five core functions for the organisation:
◆ facilitation of employment;
◆ provision of payments;
◆ liaison with families of absent mineworkers;
◆ regular contact with disabled and injured miners;
◆ identification and co-ordination of community projects.

The first four of these core functions are historically rooted, while the fifth can be seen as a new initiative to facilitate development in areas where the mining industry has traditionally sourced its labour.

Although Teba became a stand-alone company in November 1993, it remains dependent to a large degree on income generated by labour processing for its

---

1. *Teba does not do much recruiting for the coal mines, and the statistics given represent figures for mainly gold and platinum mines.*

member mines. However, this dependency on the industry is steadily declining, from 100 percent in 1988 to 66 percent in 1994.

Teba's management has taken a policy decision to resist the reduction in the number of recruiting stations (down from 130 to 70 in the last two decades) because we believe that these offices can perform critical development functions in South Africa and the sending countries. We do not believe it would be sensible to shut rural offices and retrench staff when they could continue to be engaged productively. To this end, our policy since the early 1990s has been to effect cutbacks at head office rather than to reduce our rural operations.

The development potential of the rural infrastructure is evident if we consider the following: 60 of the 70 offices throughout the southern African region have been "localised" ie managed by members of the local communities. These local representatives have credibility in the community and they are responsible for injecting considerable sums of money into those communities.

These offices are very often situated in places where there are no banks, post offices, telephones or fax machines. They also often have the only computer in the area. We are working gradually towards computerising our whole operation and this also creates definite potential for development. Far from reducing our operations, the cuts in total numbers recruited have opened the way for a more extensive alternative role. Our current vision is to provide these core services and to facilitate employment.

Teba provides a range of financial services, the most important of which is the shepherding of deferred pay, particularly to Lesotho and Mozambique. Our 70 offices paid out R776 million in 1993 on behalf of mineworkers and their families throughout southern Africa. Clearly there is scope for money to be fraudulently syphoned off, but our auditors go into the rural areas to interview widows and payees to check receipts. As a result of these investigations we recently terminated the services of the entire staff of an office in Lesotho for that kind of activity. We also regularly make payments on behalf of the mineworkers' provident fund, the Rand Mutual Assurance company and several other pension and provident funds.

Contact with families also constitutes a major activity and during the last year we processed more than 300 000 messages between absent mineworkers and their families.

As part of our support programme we visit the mineworkers who have been injured at work at least once every three months. Our representatives are not medically qualified but they have had some rudimentary training which enables them to recognise the start of a bedsore, to help fix a wheelchair and advise the family on matters like fixing ramps instead of steps and broadening doorways to accommodate wheelchairs. We already regularly visit almost 600 people but there are many more on the Rand Mutual Assurance database and we are in the process of following these up. A number of them are in Mozambique where previously we could not visit because of the war.

In a major shift of direction for the organisation, Teba has had to recognise a wider customer base than we had in the past. Historically we viewed member mines as our only customers because they are the people who pay us but the customer base has now been extended to the mineworker and his family.

We are not a profit-making company; Teba's overall running costs amounted to R48 million in 1994 and we set out to cover our costs. Our two major expenses are labour and buildings and we are looking at new ways of labour and building utilisation. One possibility could be to use our buildings after hours for extra-mural activities such as adult education. Very often rural centres in the region lack the infrastructure for these activities. The infrastructure Teba brings to these areas is one of the organisation's strengths, and will improve its chances of survival.

In Mozambique, we are looking at a kind of reverse migration initiative where we are providing entrepreneurial training from certain offices to retrenched miners. In the Ingwavuma area in KwaZulu/Natal, we have become involved with certain donor agencies in building clinics. Elsewhere, communities have approached us to use our buildings for schools and creches. We believe that we can play a significant role in primary health care, adult basic education, job creation in the rural areas; in this way we see Teba making a contribution to the Reconstruction and Development Programme. In terms of community development, Teba sees its role as that of a facilitator bringing together community organisations and donor agencies.

We also believe that our Manpower Data Centre could play an important role in keeping a record of migrants engaged in the mining industry. Prior to the general elections, for example, there was some panic about voting rights for migrant workers when the qualification date was changed from 1978 to 1986. We were able to produce a data base within 24 hours showing that, on this basis, 170 000 people in the mining industry qualified to vote. The Department of Home Affairs has not kept these records and we are well placed to continue this function. As shifts in migration and migratory labour policy continue, the importance of maintaining a rigorous database of this kind will increase. ◆

THE POLITICS OF NORMALISATION: MINE MIGRANCY IN A DEMOCRATIC SOUTH AFRICA

PROFESSOR JONATHAN CRUSH
Department of Geography,
Queen's University,
Kingston, Ontario,
Canada

PROFESSOR WILMOT JAMES
Executive Director,
Institute for Democracy in South Africa,
Cape Town, South Africa

PW Botha, President of South Africa until 1989, made every effort during his years in power to resist domestic and international pressure to dismantle apartheid. For years he made repeated imperious gestures designed to show the world that he, and his white constituency, were still very much in charge. One of these was a blunt announcement in 1986 that all foreign workers, and Mozambicans in particular, would be expelled from the country; repayment, so he said, for Mozambique's support for the ANC's armed struggle (Centro de Estudos Africanos, 1987). The announcement was greeted with consternation by the Mozambican government, Mozambican workers and their major employer in South Africa – the gold-mining industry. High-level delegations and behind-the-scenes negotiations convinced Botha that he was shooting himself in the foot and the expulsion order was soon quietly shelved (Leger, 1987: 29-32).

Nevertheless, this move shook regional actors and even today, although a democratically elected government is in place, concern persists about the future of regional migration to South Africa. Recent interviews with migrant workers and their families in countries such as Mozambique and Lesotho reveal a deep sense of foreboding that, in the words of one miner, "Mandela will do what Botha could not".

The ANC has yet to declare itself on the question of the position of foreign workers in the country but, with domestic unemployment running at up to 60 percent in many parts of South Africa, and a new government committed to massive and rapid economic and social upliftment, many migrants from the former frontline states fear that their official days in South Africa are numbered.

This chapter addresses the fundamental question of whether these fears are justified. It considers the stark alternatives that are framing much of the discussion of the issue of foreign workers in a post-apartheid South Africa, presenting instead several alternative scenarios. Maintenance of the status quo or the summary expulsion of foreign workers are only two of the available options and neither are particularly desirable for anyone. This contribution reviews and briefly critiques these options as well as examining several other viable alternatives, arguing a case for the "normalisation option". At this point the discussion moves from analysis to advocacy.

This paper is based on research conducted over the last three years by the International Development Research Centre (IDRC) Migrant Labour Project on the future of cross-border labour migration in southern Africa[1]. In March 1994, the project advised the ANC's Department of Economic Planning on the alternatives to the migrant labour system and the place of foreign miners in particular. The argument of this paper for the normalisation of labour migration is an abbreviated version of the analysis presented to the ANC (Crush and James, 1994).

POST-APARTHEID SCENARIOS

It seems likely that the mines will present the same arguments for foreign workers in the late 1990s as they did in the 1980s. Just as certainly the supplier states

---

1. *The Migrant Labour Project, of which the authors are co-directors, is a co-operative research venture between Canadian and South African researchers, funded by the Canadian International Development Research Centre. Copies of the project's working papers are available from Wilmot James, Idasa, PO Box 575, Rondebosch 7700, South Africa.*

will want to see their citizens continuing to migrate to the mines, provided that they remit and return. The mining industry and the supplier states therefore share a common interest in the maintenance of the status quo after apartheid. Foreign miners also want continued access to mine jobs in South Africa though they also have strong views about how the migrant labour system might be re-formed and humanised. Foreign miners may want to actually settle in South Africa and there is evidence that some, anticipating that they may be excluded from the mines by the ANC, are already moving clandestinely into South Africa. Given the option, however, the majority would prefer to retain their home base in their country of origin.

Should the ANC try to put the needs and demands of its domestic constitu-ency ahead of the interests of non-South Africans? The basic dilemma which confronts the ANC is not all that different from the one that confronted the old apartheid state. Should mining employment be used to address South Africa's own chronic unemployment problem or are regional relationships with the sup-plier states more important? There are five possible scenarios which adequately capture the range of policy options open to the new government. Whichever one is adopted will obviously have different effects on cross-border labour migration in the region.

THE STATUS QUO OPTION

Under this scenario, the current conditions and constraints governing the hiring of foreign workers would continue without interruption. The case for a continu-ation of the status quo with minimal state intervention in the sourcing policies of the industry will be strongly pushed by the Chamber of Mines (COM) and the mining houses. The mining companies would continue to enjoy "special status" in their ability to recruit, employ and dismiss foreign labour outside the condi-tions that govern other employers. They would also be free, as in the past, to make their own unilateral agreements with foreign governments on labour flows and conditions of service. All decisions about labour sourcing and work-force composition would remain exclusively in the hands of the mining companies and be governed purely by their interests. Monopsonistic hiring practices would remain in place with all hiring in foreign countries being orchestrated by a COM monopoly through Teba. Foreign miners would continue to be treated as single contract workers, hired on annual agreements, forced to return home at the end of a contract and prevented from bringing their dependents with them to South Africa. Unable to participate in low-cost housing and home-ownership schemes, most would continue to reside in hostels, though some might use their living-out allowances to take up residence in townships and squatter camps (Crush and James, 1991; Moodie and Ndatshe, 1992). In exchange for all this, supplier gov-ernments would insist that compulsory deferred pay schemes remain in place and the COM might well agree.

The new South African government would be reduced to the role of passive endorser of mining industry policy. Mine management has rarely been held ac-countable for its decisions about the hiring and firing of labour and this would continue to be the case. The mining industry would be viewed as a major contributor to state revenue (and social reconstruction) through taxation, but the state would allow the employers free reign in the regional labour market to source labour where they wished.

Under these circumstances, it is likely that the proportion of foreign workers on the mines would remain relatively stable or even continue to increase. In effect, the state would be rejecting the argument that the mining industry should play its part in directly addressing South Africa's chronic unemployment problem. The state would also abdicate any responsibility for improving the work and living conditions of miners (domestic and foreign) in a fundamentally labour-repressive system. The degrading and humiliating aspects of the system would remain in place or at best be relegated to issues for collective bargaining between the National Union of Mineworkers (NUM) and the employers. Foreign workers would continue to be the vulnerable, exploitable and disposable set of labour units that they were under apartheid.

THE NIGERIAN OPTION

Under this scenario the new government would summarily do what Botha threatened to do in the 1980s, which is to expel all foreign miners from the country. This strategy would parallel the Nigerian governments's decision to deport three million foreign workers in the mid-1980s. As in the Nigerian case, international criticism would probably be muted and manageable (Gravil, 1985; Aluko, 1985; Brydon, 1985). The scenario would be fiercely opposed by the mining industry (which would mobilise the old arguments about skill and experience), supplier governments and foreign miners.

There would, of course, be enormous ironies if the ANC were to expel foreign miners, punishing former friends and allies who were once threatened by Botha for helping the ANC.

The Nigerian option would mean the immediate suspension of recruiting and hiring in areas outside South Africa. All existing labour agreements with supplier states, including compulsory deferred pay clauses, would be cancelled. A massive recruiting effort within South Africa would be necessary to replace foreign workers leaving the country. But with Teba's recruiting network and computerised waiting list, the infrastructure would already be in place for such an effort (Crush, 1992).

Since 1986, 95 000 South African miners have been laid-off. There are now only just over 150 000 foreign miners on the mines. Simply replacing the foreigners with unemployed South African miners would go a long way towards mitigating any disruption to production and productivity. In the higher, more skilled job grades replacement might be slower but again not impossible. For South Africa, the benefits would be dramatic and sudden. Many retrenched South African miners would be re-employed with an immediate improvement in rural livelihoods in the areas affected. Wages earned in South Africa would remain in the country with considerable local spin-off effects. The appeal of this strategy as a short-term fix is apparent provided the new government is willing to ride out the opprobrium (and possible labour unrest) that would attach to the kind of action all too reminiscent of its predecessor.

But the Nigerian option would also have dramatic negative political conse-quences for South Africa's fledgeling relations with its neighbours, undermining efforts at regional integration and a new regional dispensation. Economically, the impact on supplier states such as Mozambique and Lesotho would be severe. Households and communities that are heavily dependent on mine wages for survival would be devastated. But how, if at all, would this rebound on South Africa itself?

Over the last decade, South Africa's chronic clandestine migration problem has reached epidemic proportions. The South African government has deported over 300 000 illegal migrants to the surrounding states since the mid-1980s. Offi-cial estimates certainly underestimate the magnitude of clandestine migration. The government recently admitted that it has no idea how many foreigners are in the country. The apartheid state, despite draconian measures such as border electrification, was unable to control the influx.

Formal and informal cross-border migration to South Africa have always been closely linked. When opportunities in the mines dry up (as they did for northern workers between 1913 and 1932, and Malawians and Zimbabweans in the 1970s and 1980s) clandestine migration inevitably increases (Jeeves, 1986). The Nige-rian option would inevitably lead to a dramatic surge in informal migration to South Africa. One problem would be replaced by another. The ANC might then be forced to use the same draconian border control measures as its predecessor. It is doubtful they would be any more successful.

THE SOUTH AFRICANISATION OPTION
Under this scenario, the ANC would actually adopt the strategy mistakenly at-tributed by the International Labour Organisation (ILO) to the South African government and the mining industry in the 1980s. The basic premise is the *gradual* (partial or complete) withdrawal of foreign miners from South Africa. South Africanisation might be planned over a period of years with a final target date and a series of intermediate target dates set by the state. Alternatively, it might occur by a process of attrition where foreign miners were simply replaced by South Africans as they retired from mine employment. The government might also treat foreign suppliers individually or as a group. Earlier target dates might be set for countries less dependent on migrancy (such as Botswana and Swaziland) with a greater capacity to reabsorb repatriated workers into the local economy.

Some researchers have recently argued that Lesotho should be treated as a "special case" (Cobbe, 1992; Matlosa, 1992; Coplan, 1993) on the following grounds: first, Lesotho is the largest foreign supplier of mine labour and mine migrancy and employment in South Africa are deeply entrenched throughout the country. It is hard to conceive of alternative opportunities for repatriated migrants and their communities. Second, the Nigerian or South Africanisation options would produce massive rural hardships with resultant mass clandestine in-migration to South Africa exacerbating rather than stemming cross-border movement between the two countries. Third, Lesotho is completely dependent geographically and economically on South Africa and is highly integrated into the South African economy. The repatriated earnings of Basotho miners leak quickly back into South Africa and circulate within the South African economy. Fourth, Basotho miners possess an unmatched reservoir of skills and experience that the mines would find hard to do without (Guy and Thabane, 1988). Finally, since miners from Lesotho played a pivotal role in the struggle for miners' rights in the 1980s, and have consistently shown higher levels of union membership and participation than workers from other countries, they should not be rewarded by the ANC with expulsion and unemployment (Crush, 1989).

These are powerful arguments but, for reasons which are not altogether apparent, the Lesotho government seems struck with a strange kind of paralysis. Rather than approaching the ANC to present its case, the Lesotho government seems to be relying instead on the COM to pull it through. Basotho miners are accordingly bitter that their government is doing nothing to fight for their right to work in South Africa.

THE ECONOMIC COMMUNITY OPTION

In contrast to the others, this scenario would give the highest priority to South Africa's historical and future relations with its neighbours by situating the foreign labour question within broader considerations of post-apartheid regional and economic integration and the fostering of positive relations with other states in the region. Formal labour migration across international borders in southern Africa is one of the most important, though unrecognised, forms of economic linkage and integration in southern Africa. The termination of such links (in the short or longer term) would impact negatively on all the partners, raising political tensions and compromising economic co-operation. Its continuation provides direct and indirect benefits to South Africa as well as easing the severe economic difficulties of the supplier states. The economic community option could be operationalised in one of two ways:

◆ As a continuation of the status quo but governed by inter-government agreements which guaranteed certain rights, freedoms and conditions of employment to foreign miners in South Africa. It seems unconscionable that a post-apartheid government would want to see foreign miners subjected to the indignities and systematic abuses that characterised the migrant labour system under apartheid, and government-to-government agreements and guarantees might be one way to ensure a break with the past (De Vletter, 1985);

◆ Through the unshackling of all constraints on freedom of movement in the region comparable to the changes introduced within South Africa with the abolition of influx controls and internationally with the European Community model (King, 1993). However much this option might be desired by foreign miners, it seems very unlikely given prevailing unemployment rates in the region and the likelihood of a regional rush to the cities of South Africa.

THE NORMALISATION OPTION

This scenario is the one developed by the IDRC Migrant Labour Project and forms the basis of policy advice recently given to the ANC by the project. It takes what the project regards as the best features of some of the other scenarios and combines them into one fundamental principle: that it is no longer acceptable to treat migrant mineworkers as a category apart, subject to "special status" which, in practice, restricts basic rights and freedoms and facilitates victimisation by an exploitative, state-endorsed system. If there is agreement on this point, then it follows that the status of all miners should be normalised. South African miners should be entitled to the same rights and freedoms as all other workers in the country. Foreign miners should be entitled to the same rights, freedoms and guarantees as all other immigrants to the country. To normalise the situation in this way is the fundamental policy goal of the option.

What would be the implications for regional labour migration to South Africa? The mining companies (like all other employers) could continue to hire workers from wherever they chose, including all the countries of the region. The Employment Bureau of Africa (Teba) could continue to act as an employment agency in the surrounding states, though its existing monopoly over hiring procedures and practices would need close scrutiny to ensure that these are consistent with the principle of normalisation. The mines should be allowed to hire miners on exactly the same terms and conditions as they hire other workers with a range of agreement types and lengths. Workers would not have to return home to renegotiate their employment contracts but could do so *in situ*. They would also no longer be compelled to return home on leave.

All of the other institutional props of the migrant labour system would disappear (as they already have within South Africa). This would include compulsory deferred pay which constitutes a fundamental violation of employees' rights to receive and spend their earnings where they choose. The only reason for its existence is the pecuniary benefits it brings to the sending governments of Lesotho and Mozambique at the expense of miners. Workers do not want it, neither do employers. Arrangements for voluntary deferment through the commercial or mining industry banks could continue. Laws governing the taxation of earnings by temporary residents of South Africa would also be applied to miners.

The other central question concerns the conditions of entry and residence in South Africa by foreign miners from the region. Here we would argue that foreign miners should be treated exactly the same as all other potential immigrants or temporary residents of the country. The mining companies would have to be accountable to government for their hiring decisions and observe the protocols of immigration law. Employment of any worker from a neighbouring state would have to be justified in the normal way. Under existing law, for example, when an employer wants to hire someone from outside the country they have to assure the immigration authorities that no South African can do the job and explain why it is necessary to hire a foreigner.

Once hired, foreign miners would be entitled to the rights and benefits that pertain to the particular category under which they are hired. In the case of temporary residents, for example, they would have the right to bring accompanying dependants. In the case of permanent residents, they would also have access to all the rights, privileges and protections of other immigrants. Foreign miners who have already worked and lived in South Africa for an extended period (and who were eligible to vote in the April election) could apply for permanent residence status.

The implications of normalisation, for all its moral force, are surprisingly revolutionary and destabilising of entrenched interests and mechanisms of exploitation. Certainly the procedures for implementation would have to be carefully thought through to ensure minimum disruption during the changeover. Implementation would also have to fly in the face of the arguments of employers and the neighbouring states, both of whom might prefer to retain the exceptional status of the foreign mineworker. It is unlikely, once the system is explained, that it would be opposed by foreign miners who would welcome the end of the old system with its deep insecurities and abuses of basic rights.

CONCLUSION

In this paper, we presented several scenarios which, in highly abbreviated form, try to capture the main policy options confronting a democratic government on the question of the perpetuation of international labour migration to the South African mines. All are implementable but the constraints on and consequences of each would be very different. This paper suggests that the formulation of an appropriate alternative policy should be developed from first principles, the most fundamental one of which is to normalise the status of workers who have always been regarded as exceptional by the mines and the state. With normalisation should come a set of new rights and freedoms long denied to workers in a brutal industry which has killed 60 000 and maimed over a million miners during the course of the 20th century. ◆

REFERENCES

Aluko, O. 1985. "The expulsion of illegal aliens from Nigeria: a study of Nigeria's decision-making," in African Affairs, Vol 84: 539-60.

Brydon, L. 1985. "Ghanaian responses to the Nigerian expulsions of 1983," in African Affairs Vol 84: 561-86.

CEA 1987. "Mozambican migrant workers in South Africa: the impact of the expulsion order," Migration for Employment Project, Working Paper No 37. Geneva: International Labour Office.

Cobbe, J. 1992. "Lesotho and the new South Africa," paper presented at African Studies Association meeting, Seattle.

Coplan, D. 1993. "Damned if we know: public policy, labour law and the future of the migrant labour system," paper presented to Conference of Labour Law, Durban.

Crush, J. 1989. "Migrancy and militance: the case of the National Union of Mineworkers of South Africa," in African Affairs, Vol 88: 5-24.

Crush, J and W James. 1991. "Depopulating the compounds: migrant labour and mine housing in South Africa", in World Development, Vol 19, No 9: 301-16;.

Crush, J. 1992. "Power and surveillance on the South African gold mines," in Journal of Southern African Studies, Vol 18.

Crush, J and W James. 1994. "Mine migrancy in a democratic South Africa," consultancy report for the ANC Department of Economic Planning, University of Cape Town.

De Vletter, F. 1985. "The rights and welfare of migrant workers: scope and limits of joint action by southern African migrant-sending countries," ILO Working Paper No 23, Geneva.

Gravil, R. 1985. "The Nigerian aliens expulsion order of 1983," in African Affairs, Vol 84: 523-38.

Guy, J and M Thabane. 1988. "Technology, ethnicity and ideology: Basotho miners and shaft sinking on the South African gold mines," in Journal of Southern African Studies, Vol 14: 257-78.

Jeeves, A. 1986. "Migrant labour and South African expansion, 1920-1950," in South African Historical Journal, Vol 18: 73-92.

King, R. (ed,) 1993. Mass Migrations in Europe: The Legacy and the Future. London: Belhave Press.

Leger, J. 1987. "Mozambican miners' reprieve," in South African Labour Bulletin, Vol 12, No 2: 29-32.

Matlosa, K. 1992. "The future of international labour migration: focus on Lesotho," in International African Bulletin, Vol 16, No 9: 32-51.

Moodie, TD with V Ndatshe. 1992. "Town women and country wives: migrant labour, family politics and housing preferences at Vaal Reefs mine," in Labour, Capital and Society, Vol 25, No 1: 116-32.

RESPONSE

DR PAUL JOURDAN
*Department of Mineral and Energy Affairs,
ANC, Johannesburg,
South Africa*

Two points are raised by these presentations, both relevant to the ANC's Reconstruction and Development Programme. The first concerns the issue of regional integration and the ANC's commitment to a movement from a free trade area to a customs union, a common market, economic integration and, finally, political integration.

The second raises the issue of workers' rights. ANC policy, drawn up in collaboration with the Congress of South African Trade Unions, states that all workers shall have the right to reside at or near their place of work; shall have full control over their after-tax salaries; and shall not be subjected to any form of discrimination. This has enormous ramifications for the migrant labour system.

Concerning the first point, there has been a lot of discussion on restructuring the South African Customs Union (Sacu) to make it more equitable. Proposals include, for instance, that the Board of Trade and Tariffs become a Sacu body and not a South African body and that in future South Africa be prevented from unilaterally setting tariffs that affect other countries without consulting them.

Also relevant to this point is the debate within the ANC of a different system for Lesotho, whose relationship to South Africa is already something of a *de facto* common market. A future agreement that allows the free movement of Basotho labour should be considered. Obviously at this time not all countries of the region can be included in a common market, but that certainly is a long-term objective. Whatever changes will be introduced will affect the region and will therefore have to be negotiated with the governments involved. After all these countries suffered alongside us in our struggle against racism and apartheid. ◆

INDEX